IMAGES
of America

GLENDALE

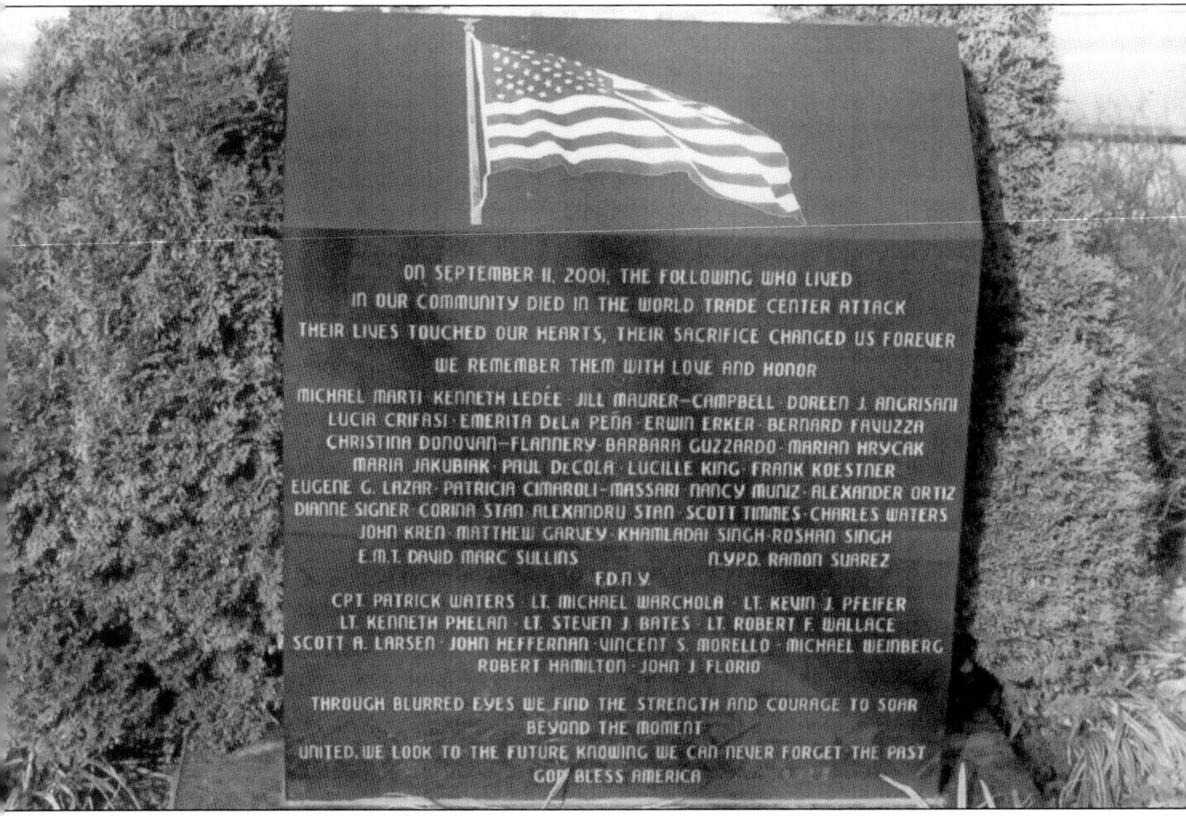

In memory of the members of the Glendale community who lost their lives in the World Trade Center attacks of September 11, 2001, this monument was erected at the Dry Harbor playground, along Myrtle Avenue near Eightieth Street. (Courtesy of the author.)

ON THE COVER: This 1915 photograph shows one of the many sporting clubs and community organizations that used the meeting rooms of local saloons as their headquarters. The Lafayette Fishing Club met at Julius Moog's saloon, located on Lafayette Street. The street was later renamed Seventy-ninth Avenue when the numbering system for Glendale Streets was begun. (Courtesy of GRHS.)

IMAGES
of America

GLENDALE

Ralph F. Brady

ARCADIA
PUBLISHING

ISBN 978-1-4671-2230-6

Published by Arcadia Publishing
Charleston, South Carolina

Printed in the United States of America

Library of Congress Control Number: 2014932585

For all general information, please contact Arcadia Publishing:
Telephone 843-853-2070
Fax 843-853-0044
E-mail sales@arcadiapublishing.com
For customer service and orders:
Toll-Free 1-888-313-2665

Visit us on the Internet at www.arcadiapublishing.com

To my parents, Frank R. Brady, volunteer Civil Defense Fireman at Engine Company No. 286, and Agnes Reis Brady, who played her trumpet at the veterans' monuments during Memorial Day parades

Contents

ACKNOWLEDGMENTS

This book would not have been possible without the tireless efforts of George Miller of the Greater Ridgewood Historical Society. As I said to George during the many hours that we spent together going through the photographs in the society's archives, "You are far more qualified to write this book than I am." George has been a vital part of the Glendale community for most of his life, while, even though I was born there, I moved out to Long Island many years ago. Nevertheless, the task fell to me, and this project has given me a unique opportunity to get back to my own roots and rekindle memories of the wonderful years that I spent growing up in Glendale. The majority of the images appearing in this book were graciously provided by George Miller and the Greater Ridgewood Historical Society (GRHS).

George is a dedicated historian and meticulous manager of the historical society's archives. He never ceased to amaze me with the amount of information that he could produce when I posed a question to him about a particular photograph or bit of local history. If this book can measure up to his standards and make him happy that he put as much time into it as he did, then I will have to regard it as a success.

In the course of my research, I was also privileged to work with Richard Hourahan of the Queens Historical Society in Flushing and Ian Lewis of the Queens Borough Central Library. They are both dedicated historians providing a valuable service to the community.

I also wish to thank my editor at Arcadia Publishing, Sharon McAllister, who was always supportive and guided me through the logistical challenges of organizing this work, and my wife, Madeline, and her sister Helen Henneberger, who assisted me throughout the process that made this book a reality.

INTRODUCTION

To the early Native American people in the area, it would not have held any great significance. It was more an area to go through to engage in commerce with neighboring tribes or to hunt the deer and other animals that were plentiful in the woods, drawn there by the nearby freshwater ponds. That was the land that became the village of Glendale, a study in contrasts; a playground for early residents of New York City even though it was surrounded by cemeteries.

There is no record of any Native American settlements on the land that actually became Glendale, while the surrounding towns of Ridgewood and Maspeth have produced evidence of settlements by the Rockaway tribe. The many artifacts discovered from that period indicate that there was a large village in an area that was referred to as the Ridgewood Plateau, where it slopes down into nearby Maspeth. A major requirement of those early people would have been a source of freshwater, and the section later known as Fresh Ponds provided this because of the number of freshwater ponds near the village. Other water sources nearby such as Newtown Creek were brackish, and the name *Maspeth* actually derives from the Indian word for "bad water place." The informal dividing line between Glendale and Ridgewood is Fresh Pond Road, which takes its name from one of the old Indian trails that crisscrossed the area.

With the arrival of the Dutch settlers in the early 1600s, Europeans began their development of the New York area, and the first settlement was built in 1623. By 1642, the Dutch presence was well established, and a 74,000-acre plot that included Glendale was named Newtown and chartered to the Reverend Francis Doughty by the Dutch West India Company. The colony of New Netherland, which Newtown was part of, remained under Dutch control until the signing of the Treaty of Westminster in 1674. That treaty ended years of hostilities between the Dutch and English and effectively turned over Newtown and the rest of the early colony to England.

Under British rule, the area remained mostly unchanged from the days of Dutch control. Many of the Dutch settlers remained on their land, and the entire Newtown area continued to develop as a rural farming community. Even during periods of conflict in New York between early settlers and local Indian tribes, Newtown was hardly touched and remained a sparsely settled town outside of the main part of New York City. In the early days of the Revolutionary War, except for troop movements through the area, farmers in the area saw little of the war until the Battle of Long Island in 1776. Following that defeat of the Colonial forces, the British occupied Newtown and the surrounding communities to solidify their hold on all of New York City. It was not until 1783, when the new nation won its independence, that the British forces left and life for the Newtown farmers returned to normal.

In the years following the war, there was in influx of German farmers to what would become the Glendale/Ridgewood area, and as in many other parts of the new country, the practice of slavery was prevalent. As the early farms began to change hands and be subdivided, communities began to develop their own identities, and the name *Newtown* fell out of favor, to be replaced by Greater Ridgewood. Making up this one large community were five individual sections: Ridgewood,

Middle Village, Maspeth, Liberty Park, and Fresh Ponds. It was this last section that would later come to be known as Glendale.

As part of a business transaction in 1860, a developer named George C. Schott was given a large amount of land in Fresh Ponds, supposedly as payment for a debt. He renamed it Glendale after his hometown in Ohio, and the name seems to have been widely accepted. Nine years later, a real estate agent named John C. Schooley purchased land adjacent to Schott's property and named it Glendale as well. Schooley mapped out the land, laid out streets, divided his property into 469 plots measuring 25 feet by 100 feet, and began offering them for sale at $300 each. Glendale always lagged behind the surrounding towns as far as development went. Even as late as 1908, it was known more as a rural farming community than adjacent areas like Ridgewood and Maspeth, which had begun to build more homes and attract industry to bolster their economy.

Much of the land near Glendale remained undeveloped until a law passed by the New York State legislature in 1847 put it in high demand. Under the State Rural Cemeteries Act, cemetery owners were no longer able to establish any new cemeteries in Manhattan. That left large parcels of vacant land in the vicinity of Glendale as an obvious choice, and as they began to purchase and develop large tracts of it, they almost completely surrounded Glendale with the cemeteries that are still seen today. In contrast to the somber note that was struck by all of this cemetery development, much of the remaining undeveloped land in Glendale was turned into parks, picnic areas, and other recreational venues that drew people from Brooklyn and all over New York City. Throughout the end of the 19th century and the early years of the 20th century, Glendale had a reputation as a playground for residents from all of the city's five boroughs.

Following World War I, the economic base of the area shifted from farming to a variety of industries, which resulted in the construction of a huge industrial complex known as Atlas Terminal. Most of this was demolished in 2004 to make way for an equally massive shopping center called The Shops at Atlas Park. Today, Glendale remains a thriving community of about 80,000 people from many different nationalities besides the German, Irish, and Italian people that figured so prominently in its development. It is approximately six miles from Manhattan, which can mean a 30-minute drive on a good day or a 40-minute subway ride. The golf course at Forest Park, along with outdoor concerts and a more-than-100-year-old carousel, continue to attract visitors to this unusual town that offers the appeal of a rural community along with the convenience of easy access to New York City.

One

Glendale Is Born

With Dutch influence dating back to the beginning of the 17th century, land ownership, rights of the early settlers, and all other legal matters in the colony were governed by Dutch law. This was administered by their governor-general, Peter Stuyvesant, the ruling authority of the New Amsterdam colony. When an English fleet entered the harbor in 1664, their representatives went ashore and demanded that Stuyvesant surrender the colony. He eventually did, but he sought guarantees that land transactions made under Dutch law would remain valid, legal decisions made by Dutch courts would not be overturned, and the remaining Dutch settlers would continue to enjoy religious freedom.

Under English rule, much of the Dutch population remained and coexisted with English settlers as they began to move into the area. Life for the early settlers, who were mostly farmers, remained unchanged until the outbreak of the Revolutionary War. Some went to join with the Colonial forces, but for the most part, the early town of Newtown was spared some of the horrors of the war, even during the Battle of Long Island, which was won by the British. There were some incidents in surrounding areas during the British occupation, when Hessian troops employed by the British stole cattle and damaged property owned by the colonists, but the farmers who worked the land that would eventually become Glendale remained mostly unscathed by the war.

Prior to the adoption of the name Glendale, the early settlement went by Dry Harbour, which was later Americanized to Dry Harbor. During this period, it was identified on maps and legal documents as a hamlet within the Town of Newtown until January 1, 1898, when it came under the jurisdiction of the new City of New York. Even as part of the Town of Newtown, it was already recognized as a Queens County postal village named Glendale Station as far back as 1874. Dry Harbor Road and some of the other old street names help to preserve elements of the community's early history.

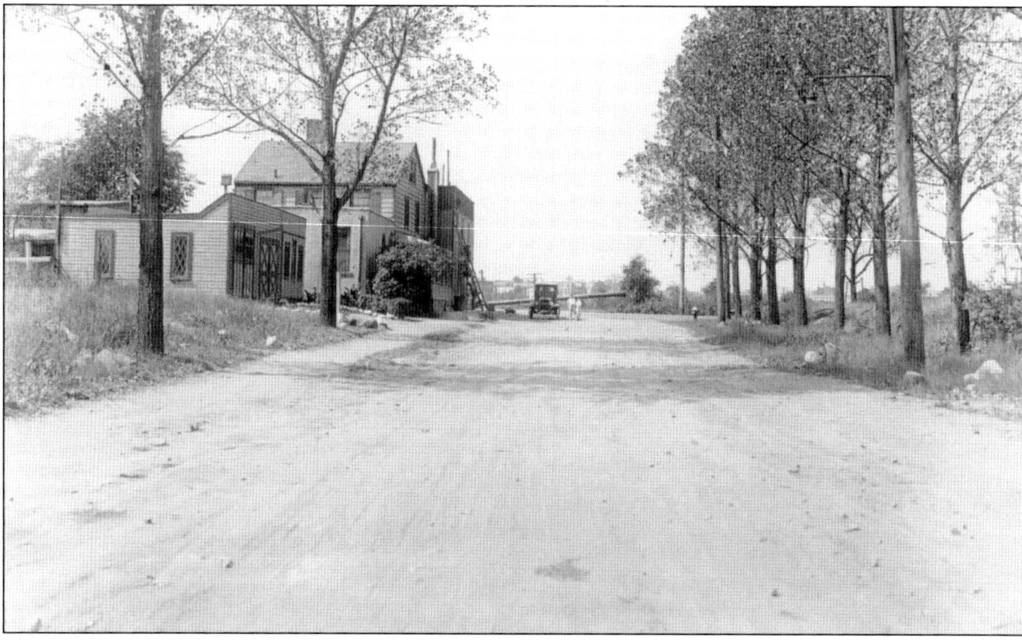

This undated photograph shows a farmhouse typical of what the early settlers in Glendale would have called home. It was built in 1860 on land that would later become Seventy-fifth Avenue in the vicinity of Eighty-eighth Street. The scene appears to be from the 1920s based on the appearance of the automobile on the road. (Courtesy of GRHS.)

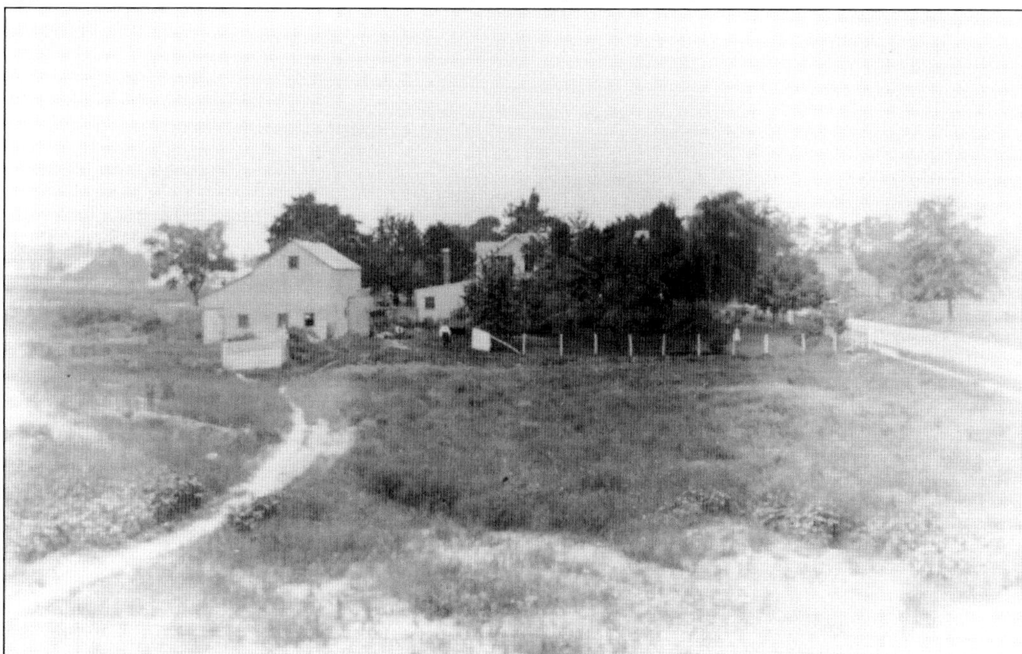

Another good example of the early farming period before Glendale's development, this image shows the William Denton farm and homestead, which stood at 6222 Cooper Avenue from 1845 until it was demolished in 1913. The distance to the next home in the background gives a good idea of the size of the early farm properties. (Courtesy of GRHS.)

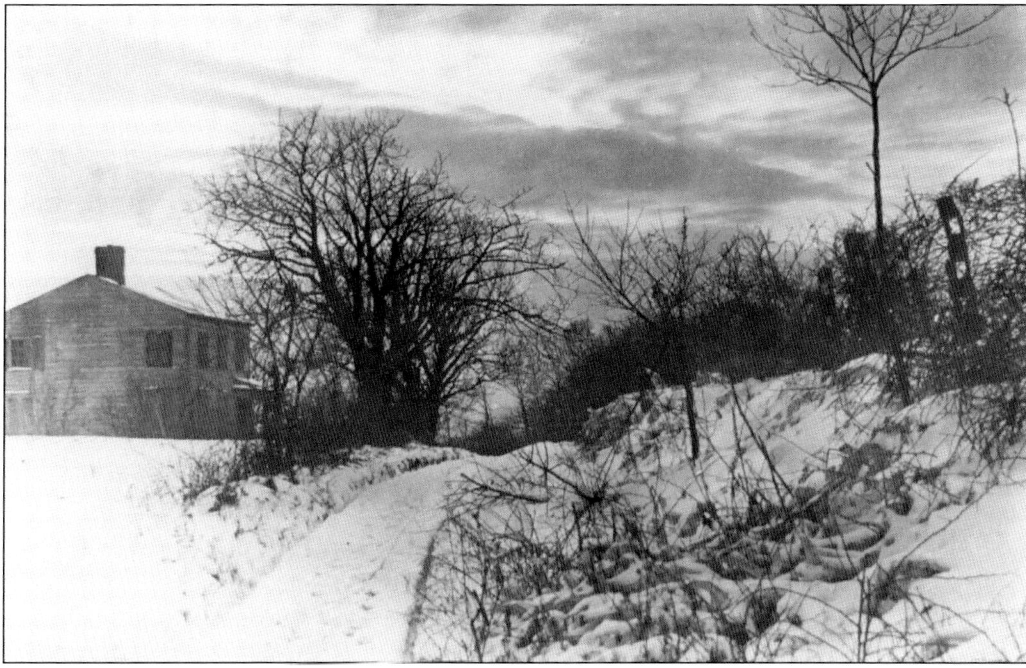

This 1900 photograph shows the rural nature of 19th century Glendale and features the William March house, built on Seventy-seventh Avenue. The construction is all wooden clapboard, and the remote location of the property would have meant a long period of isolation during heavy snows. (Courtesy of GRHS.)

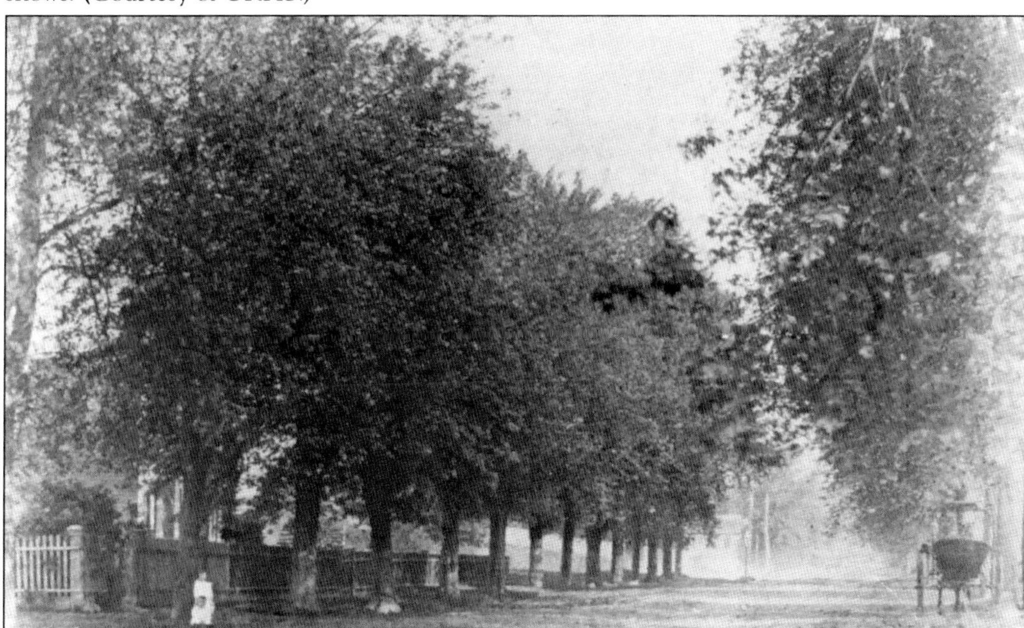

The photographer pointed his camera up Seventy-third Place looking north from Central Avenue in this photograph from 1900. The fenced house on the left dates back to 1870, and the early Long Island Railroad station is barely visible up the street. The aging of the photograph makes it appear almost like an oil painting. (Courtesy of GRHS.)

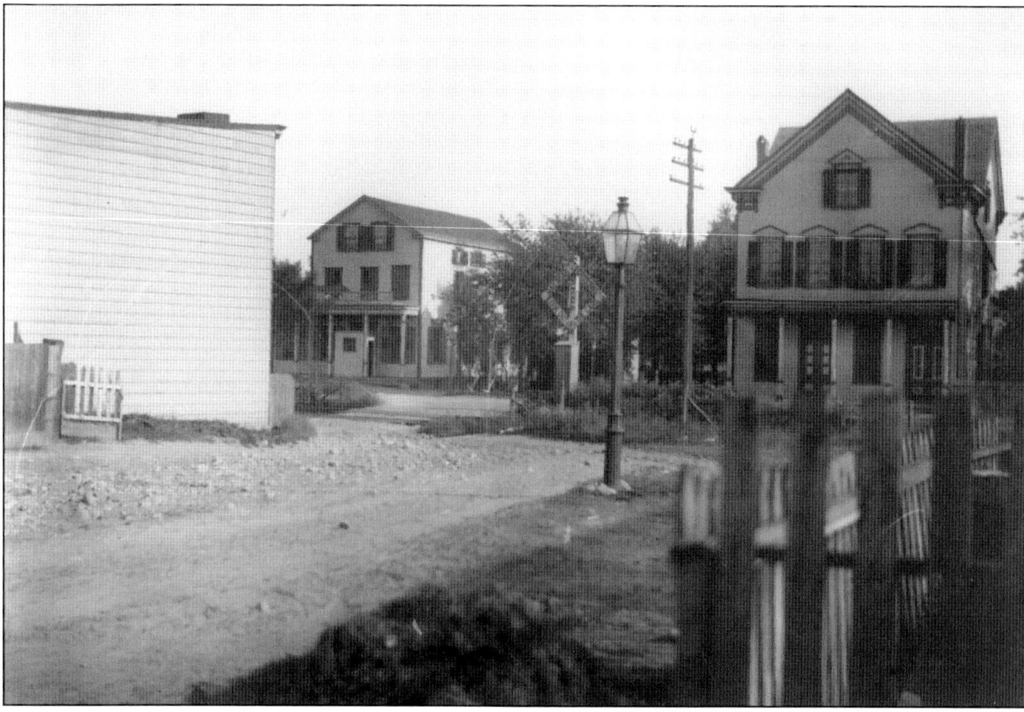

Showing a little more development in the area, this 1906 photograph shows Seventy-third Street near the site of the Lutheran Cemetery. On the left is a side view of Philip Knack's florist shop, and the other two businesses are saloons. George Gundolph's is in the center, and Christian Kirschmann's is on the right. (Courtesy of GRHS.)

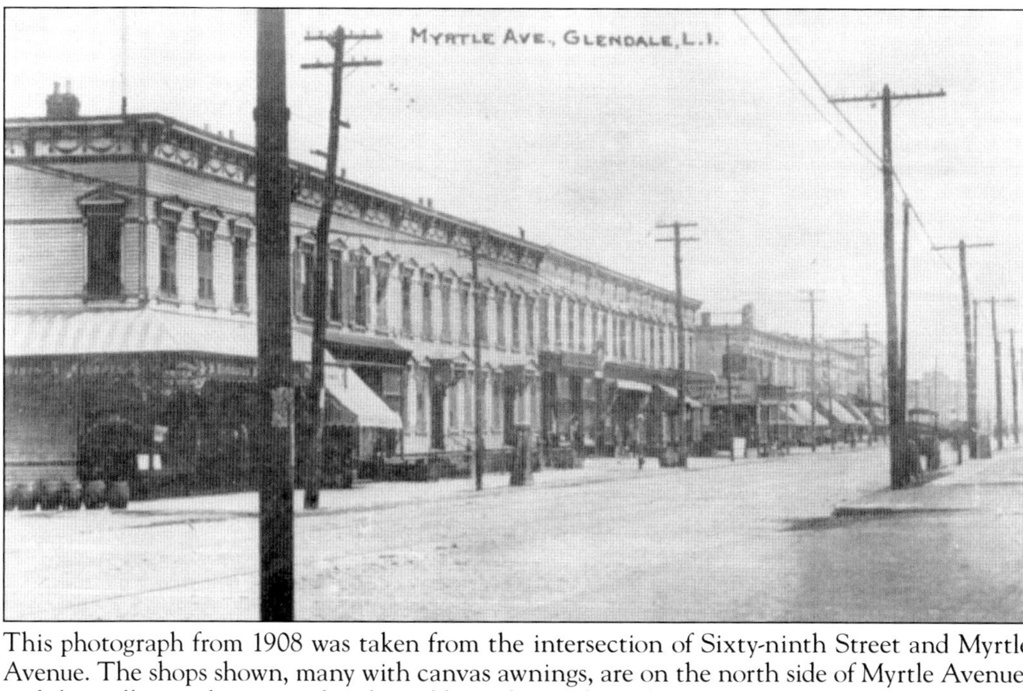

This photograph from 1908 was taken from the intersection of Sixty-ninth Street and Myrtle Avenue. The shops shown, many with canvas awnings, are on the north side of Myrtle Avenue, and the trolley tracks are just barely visible in the roadway. (Courtesy of GRHS.)

As seen in this 1911 photograph, the influx of new residents prompted developers to build this type of row house, many of which are still standing more than 100 years later. The four shown here were constructed by builder John A. Fisher, who lived in one of his own homes for many years. (Courtesy of GRHS.)

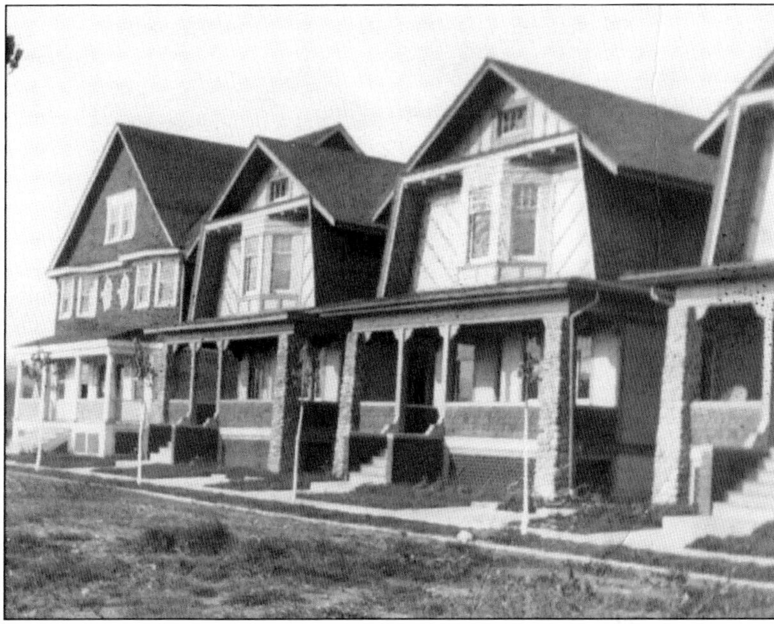

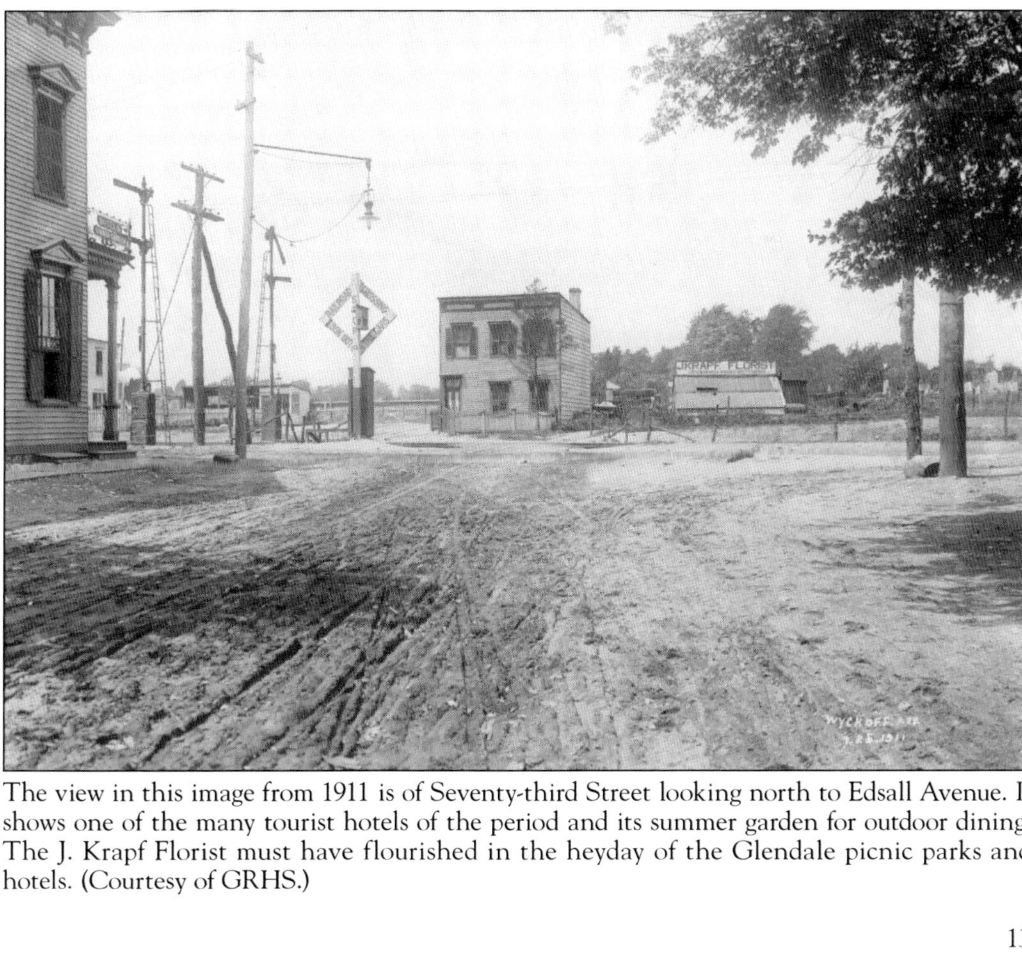

The view in this image from 1911 is of Seventy-third Street looking north to Edsall Avenue. It shows one of the many tourist hotels of the period and its summer garden for outdoor dining. The J. Krapf Florist must have flourished in the heyday of the Glendale picnic parks and hotels. (Courtesy of GRHS.)

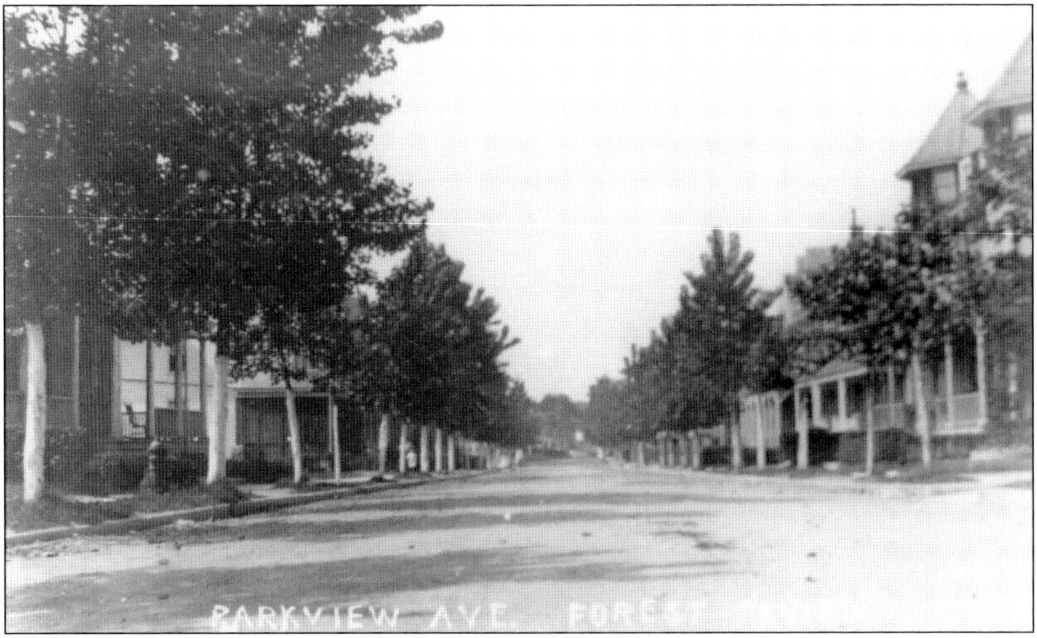

Around 1912, Eightieth Street was known as Parkview Avenue in this view, looking north from Myrtle Avenue. The tree-lined streets and front porches on most of the homes give a sense of the quiet rural atmosphere and prosperity of upper Glendale. (Courtesy of GRHS.)

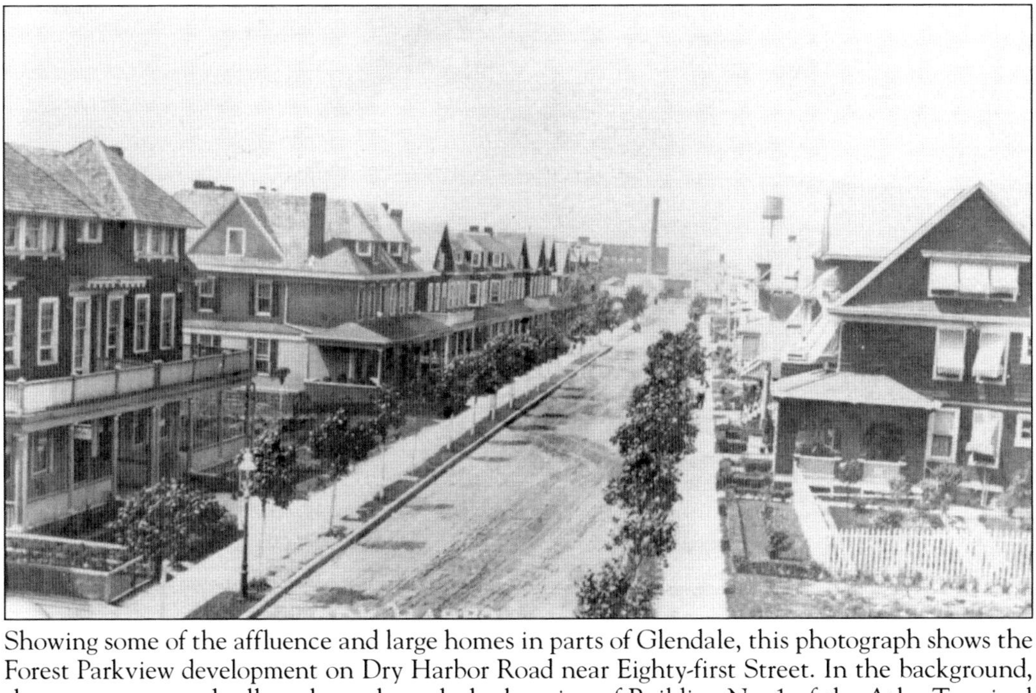

Showing some of the affluence and large homes in parts of Glendale, this photograph shows the Forest Parkview development on Dry Harbor Road near Eighty-first Street. In the background, the water tower and tall smokestack mark the location of Building No. 1 of the Atlas Terminal industrial park as it appeared in 1912. (Courtesy of GRHS.)

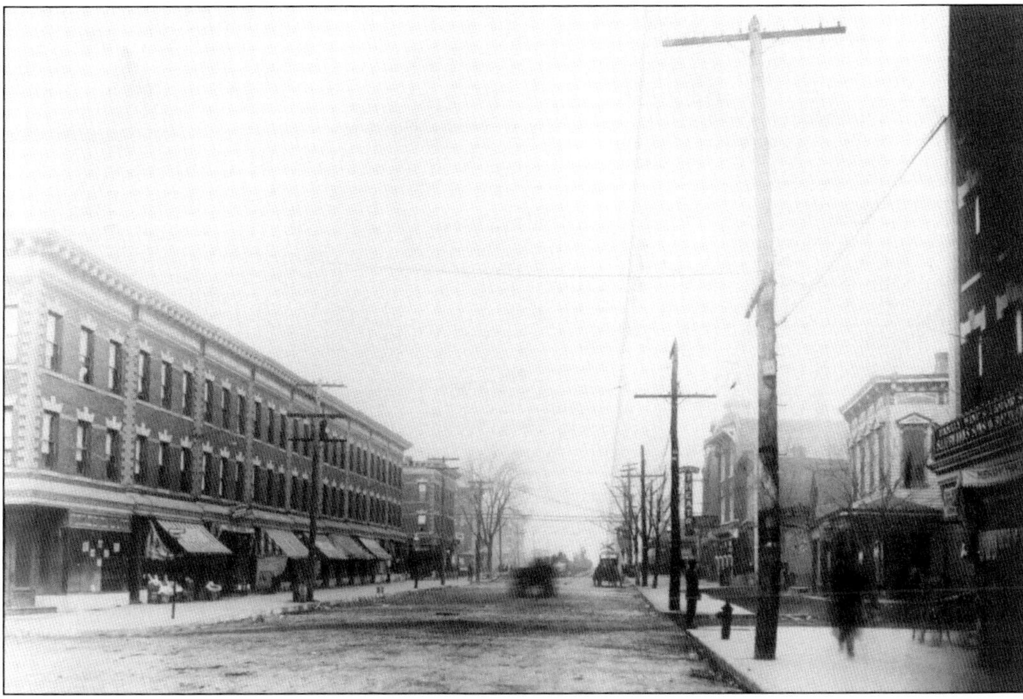

Looking north from Myrtle Avenue up Fresh Pond Road, this 1910 image shows the Whitney Theater, with its small marquee and tall sign, on the right side toward the end of the block. There seems to be a mixture of horse-drawn and automobile traffic, which is difficult to see because of some blurring in the photograph. (Courtesy of Queens Historical Society.)

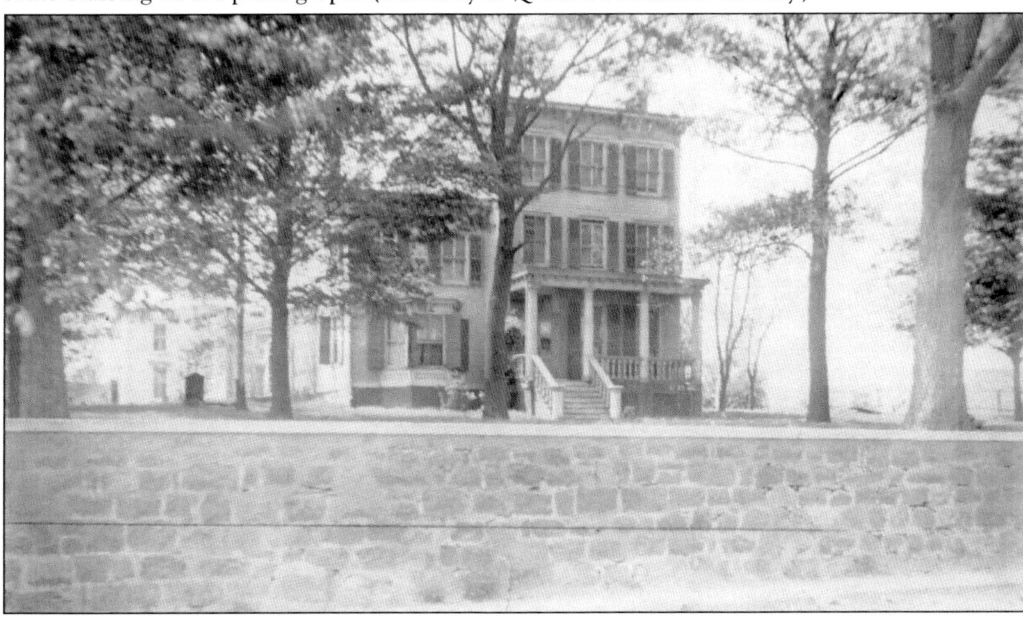

This prestigious home was owned by John Holzhauer, a successful contractor during the height of the Glendale building boom. He also owned horse stables in the vicinity of Forest Park. The house, which was located on the north side of Cooper Avenue near Seventy-sixth Street, has since been torn down. (Courtesy of Queens Historical Society.)

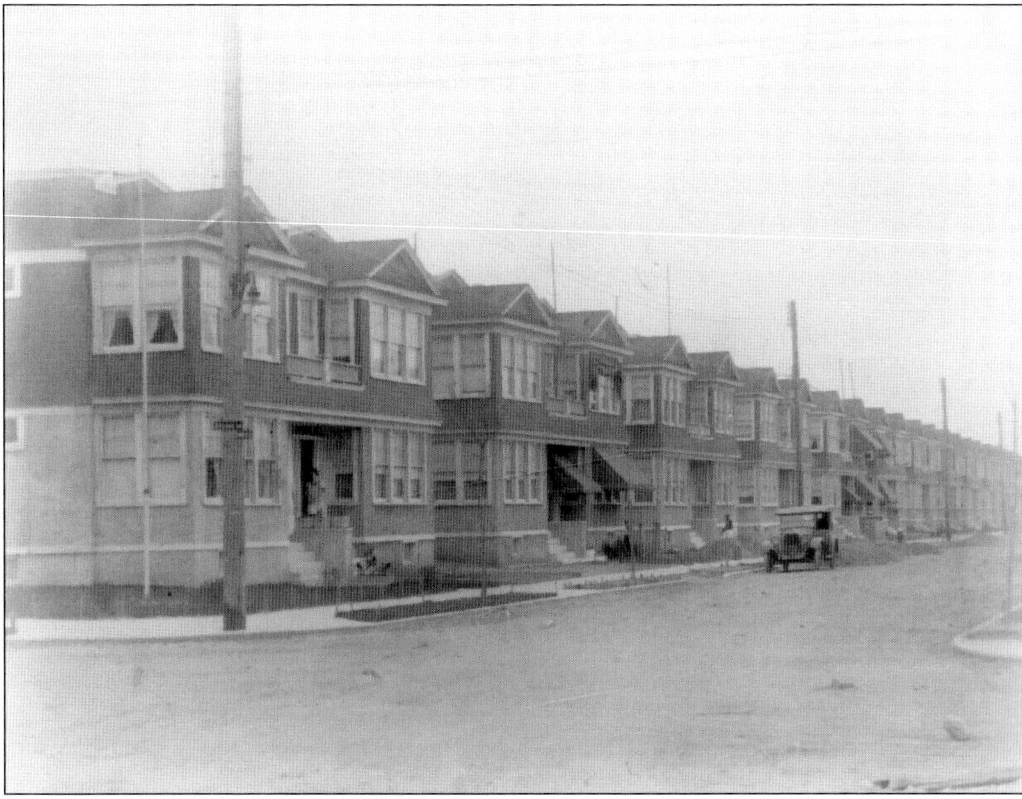

In the 1920s, many of the Glendale streets that were later numbered still carried names. This photograph shows Seventy-eighth Street (when it was Lambert Avenue) looking north from Seventy-eighth Avenue (Copeland Avenue). (Courtesy of Queens Historical Society.)

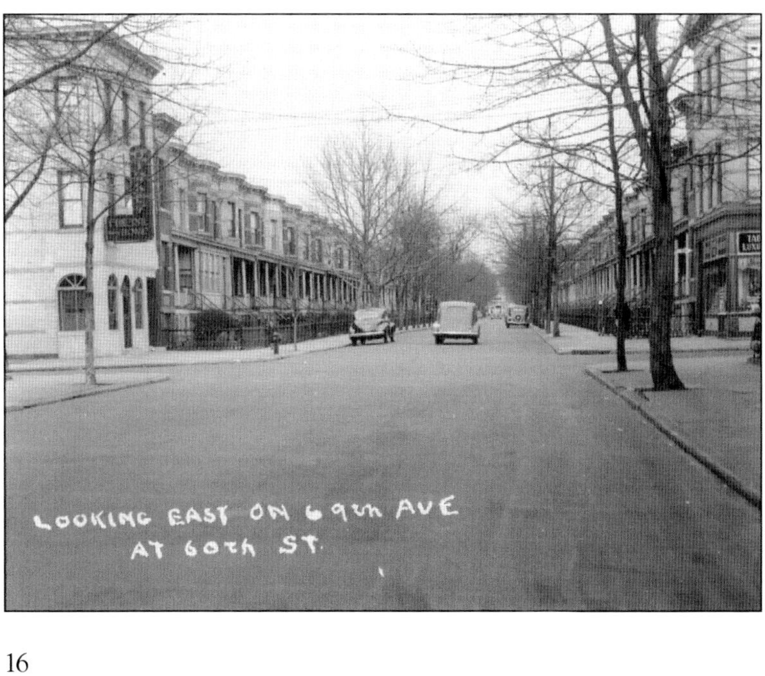

Except for the automobiles, this 1930s photograph of Sixty-ninth Avenue looks pretty much as it would today, but there is no longer a funeral home on the corner. Like so many of the old corner businesses, it was converted to additional ground-floor apartment space in later years. (Courtesy of Queens Historical Society.)

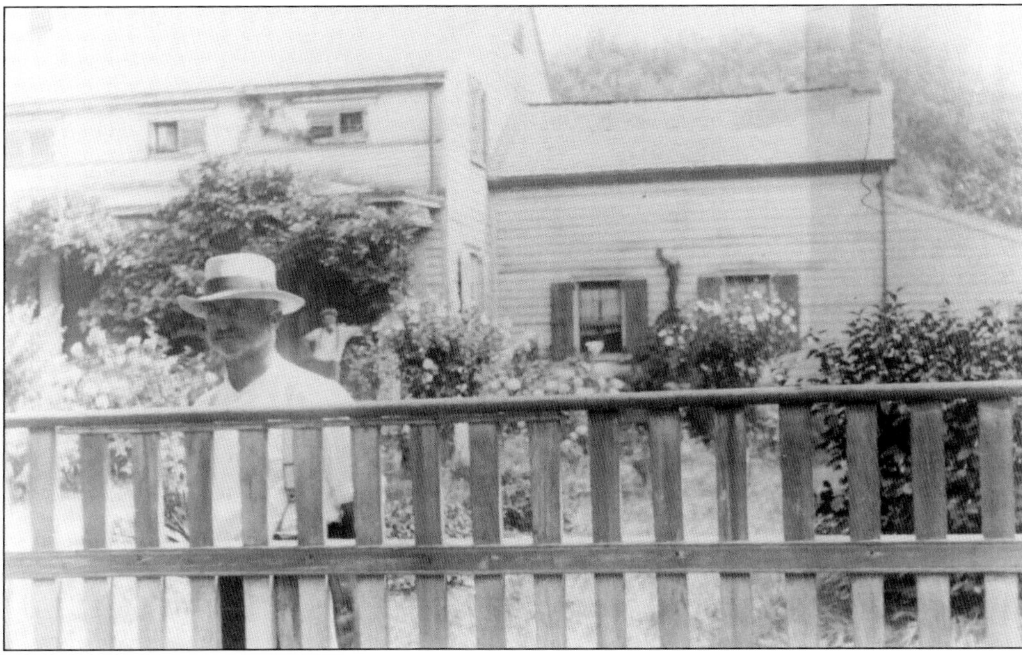

In the 1600s, when the land was still known as Fresh Ponds, this home, located at Fresh Pond Road and Sixty-eighth Street, belonged to an early family of farmers by the name of Edsall. It was later owned by the Wagner-Lahr family after they sold their farm in Bushwick, Brooklyn, and moved out to Glendale. Contractor Henry W. Wagner is shown in the foreground. (Courtesy of GRHS.)

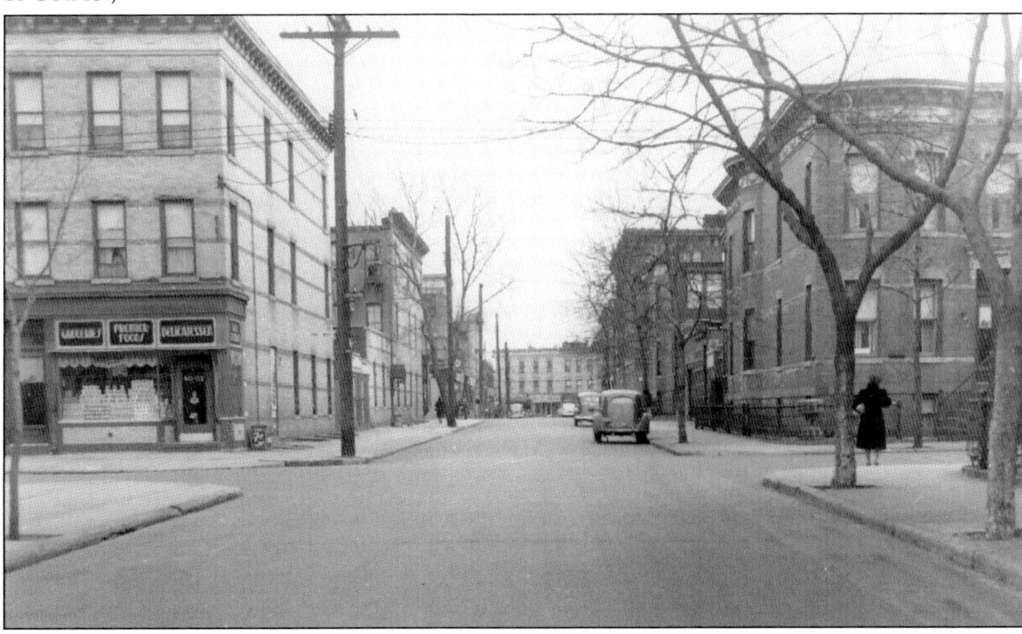

Again using the automobiles to date this photograph as being from the late 1930s, this view is looking south on Sixtieth Street. The corner store was always a characteristic of Glendale residential blocks, but in later years, many were converted to additional residential apartments. (Courtesy of Queens Historical Society.)

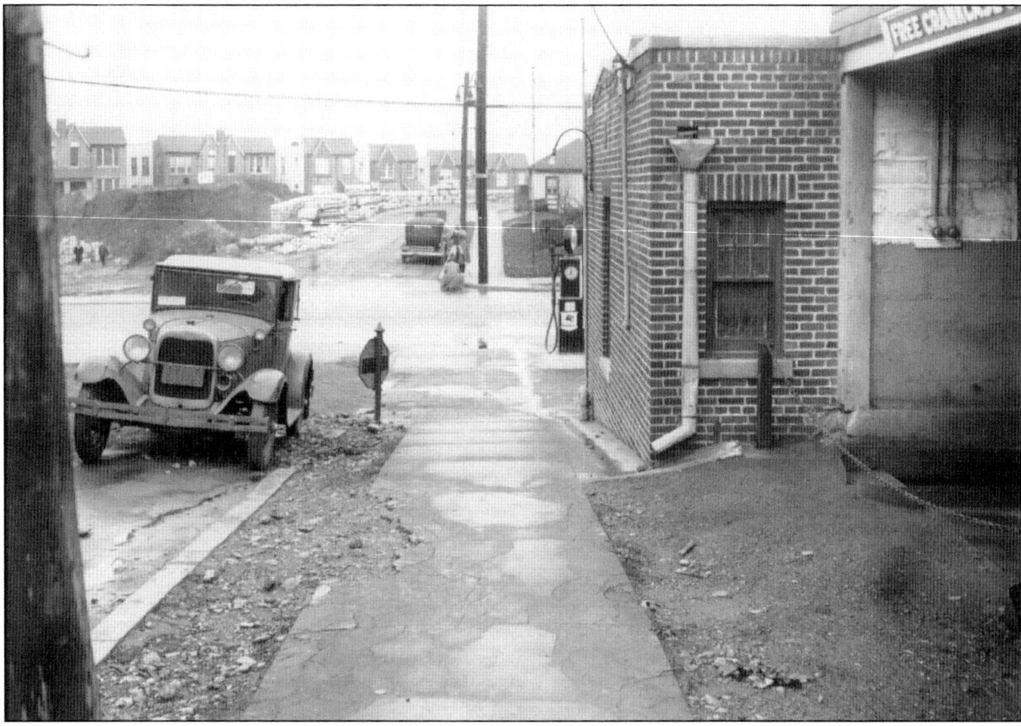

Development continued, as shown in this 1934 photograph on Eighty-second Lane looking down toward Myrtle Avenue. Note that the Texaco service station felt that "Free Crankcase Service" would bring in customers. From the looks of the roads, it seems safe to assume that crankcase breakdowns were a common problem. (Courtesy of Queens Historical Society.)

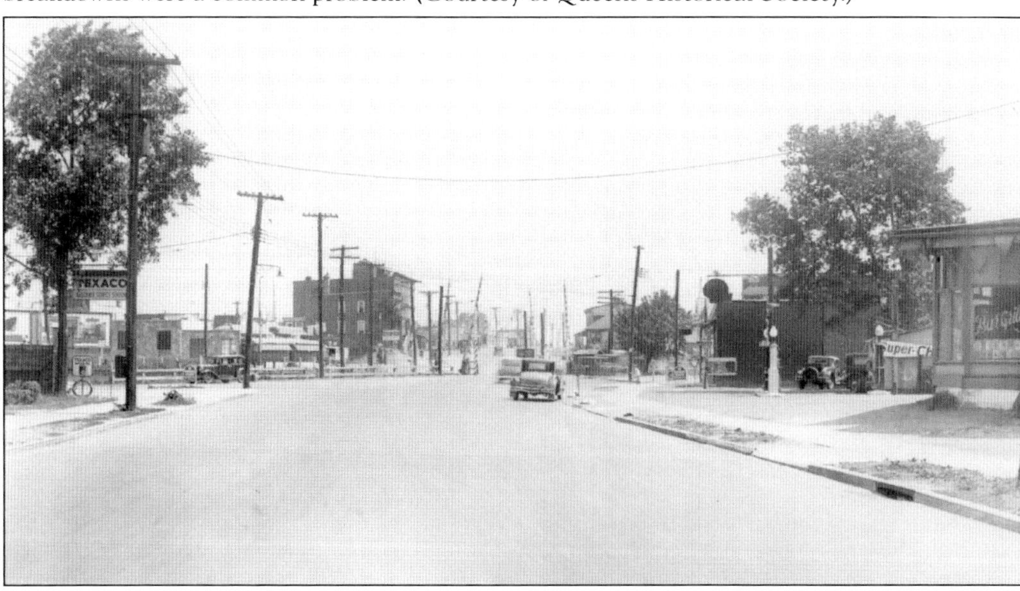

The absence of automobiles parked alongside the curb up and down every block always makes the streets in these old photographs look wider than they really are. This 1934 photograph looking along Cooper Avenue shows another Texaco station ready to service the growing number of automobiles in the Glendale community. (Courtesy of GRHS.)

This 1930 builder's advertisement, taken from the *Ridgewood Times* newspaper, helped accelerate the boom in home sales in Glendale. Though it still lagged behind Ridgewood and Maspeth in development, Glendale offered the amusements and shopping that the builder thought would attract people to the area. (Courtesy of GRHS.)

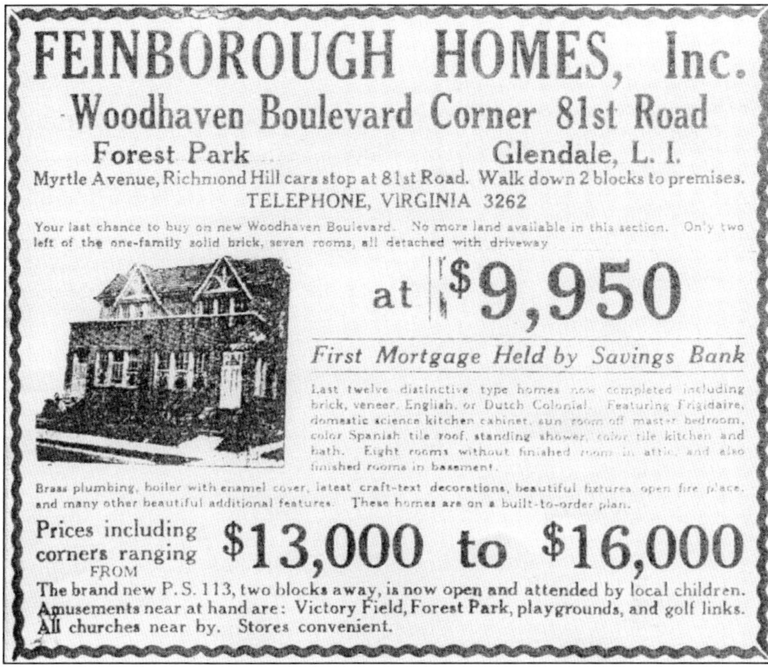

FEINBOROUGH HOMES, Inc.

Woodhaven Boulevard Corner 81st Road

Forest Park Glendale, L. I.

Myrtle Avenue, Richmond Hill cars stop at 81st Road. Walk down 2 blocks to premises.

TELEPHONE, VIRGINIA 3262

Your last chance to buy on new Woodhaven Boulevard. No more land available in this section. Only two left of the one-family solid brick, seven rooms, all detached with driveway

at $9,950

First Mortgage Held by Savings Bank

Last twelve distinctive type homes now completed including brick, veneer, English, or Dutch Colonial. Featuring Frigidaire, domestic science kitchen cabinet, sun room off master bedroom, color Spanish tile roof, standing shower, color tile kitchen and bath. Eight rooms without finished room in attic, and also finished rooms in basement.

Brass plumbing, boiler with enamel cover, latest craft-text decorations, beautiful fixtures, open fire place, and many other beautiful additional features. These homes are on a built-to-order plan.

Prices including corners ranging FROM $13,000 to $16,000

The brand new P. S. 113, two blocks away, is now open and attended by local children. Amusements near at hand are: Victory Field, Forest Park, playgrounds, and golf links. All churches near by. Stores convenient.

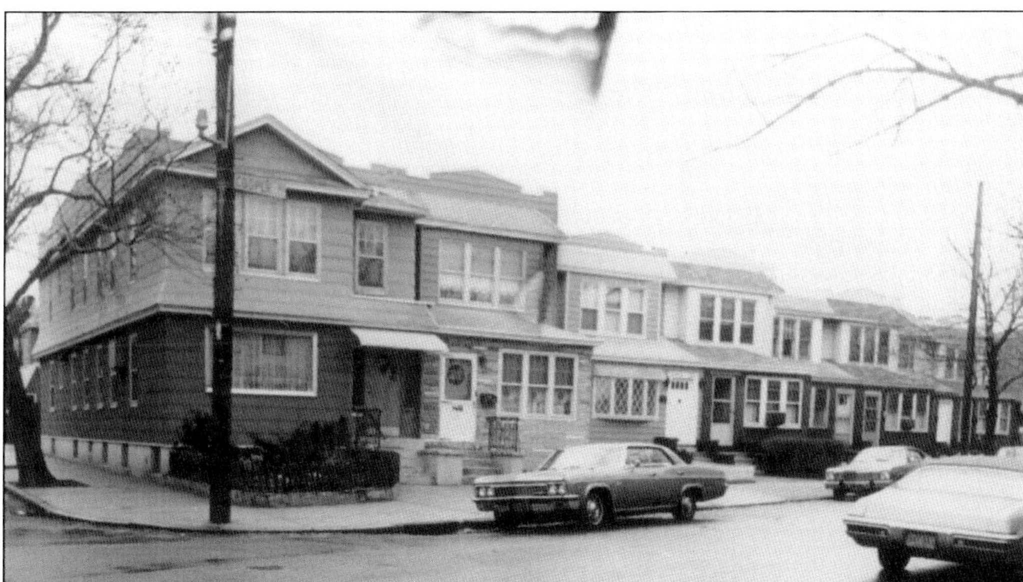

It would be hard to find a better street than Seventy-second Place near Cooper Avenue to typify what 1970s life was like in Glendale. This 1976 photograph shows homes that predate the picture by more than 40 years. An image taken today would show many more automobiles, but almost nothing else has changed. (Courtesy of GRHS.)

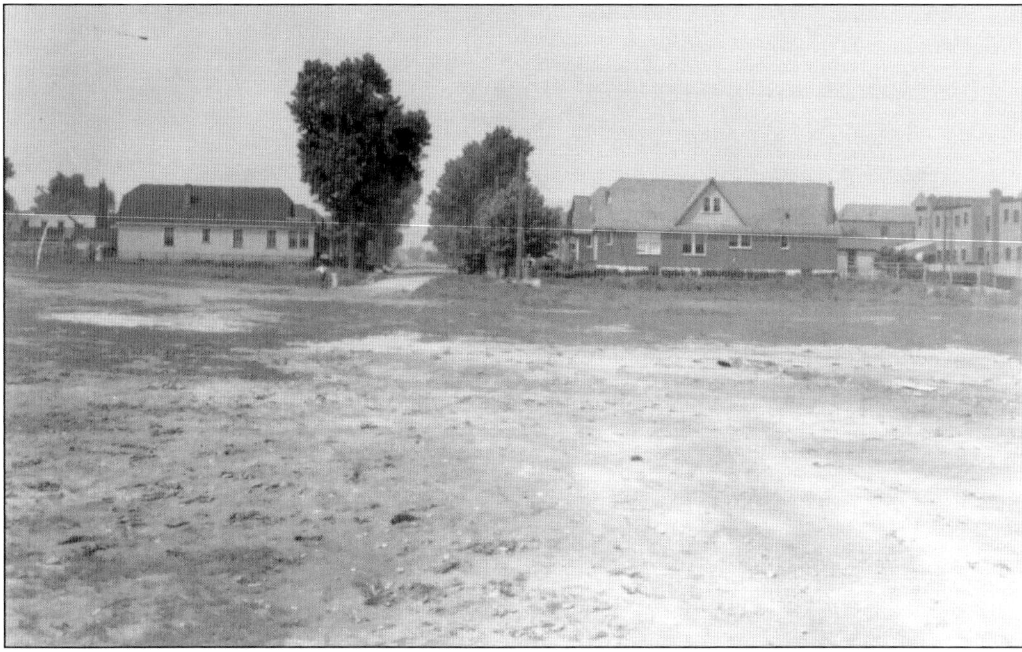

As late as 1935, in spite of all of the homes shown in the background, there was still plenty of land available in Glendale for additional development. This photograph from that time is of Seventy-sixth Street near Woodhaven Boulevard before ground was broken for the next round of building. (Courtesy of GRHS.)

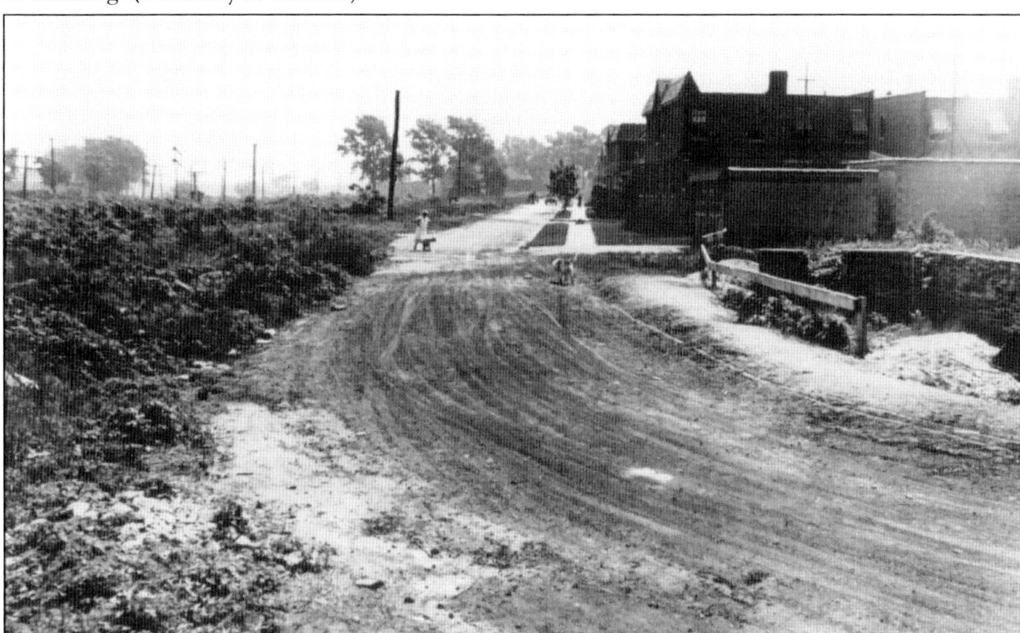

There were also many multifamily homes being built during Glendale's early development. In this image of Seventy-seventh Avenue east of Eighty-fifth Street, the undeveloped land to the left borders the railroad tracks, and residents took advantage of this to stake out small home garden plots in 1935. (Courtesy of GRHS.)

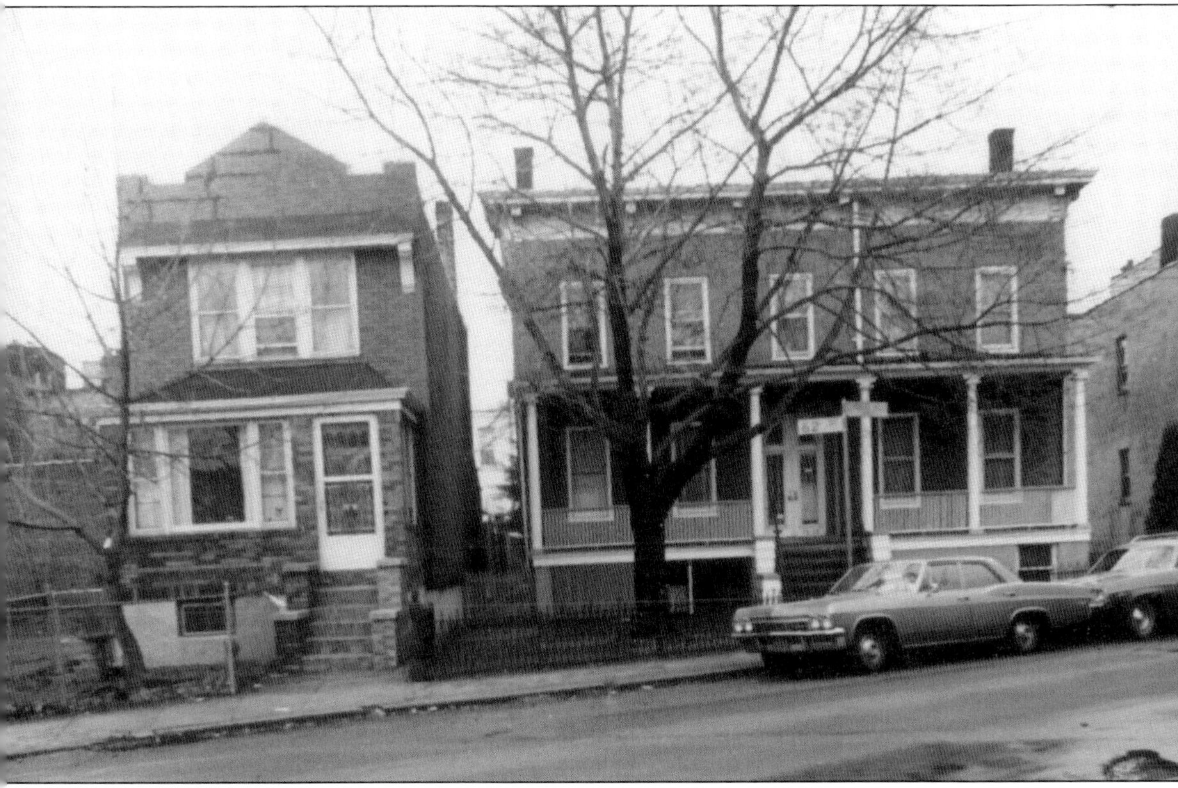

The Frederick Ring Jr. family were farmers and members of the early Fresh Ponds community. The farmhouse shown here dates to 1860 but was originally built at a different location. It was moved from Fresh Pond Road to Cypress Hills Street near Seventy-first Avenue around 1911 and remained a residence up until 1927. At that time, it was taken over by the Van & Schenck Club, which was founded by a group of vaudeville performers. They used it as a meeting place and staged vaudeville shows there, many of which raised money for charitable institutions. The club occupied the old farm homestead until the 1950s, which is a surprise because the age of vaudeville had passed long before the 1950s. By the time this 1976 photograph was taken, it had reverted to private ownership again and was a family residence. (Courtesy of GRHS.)

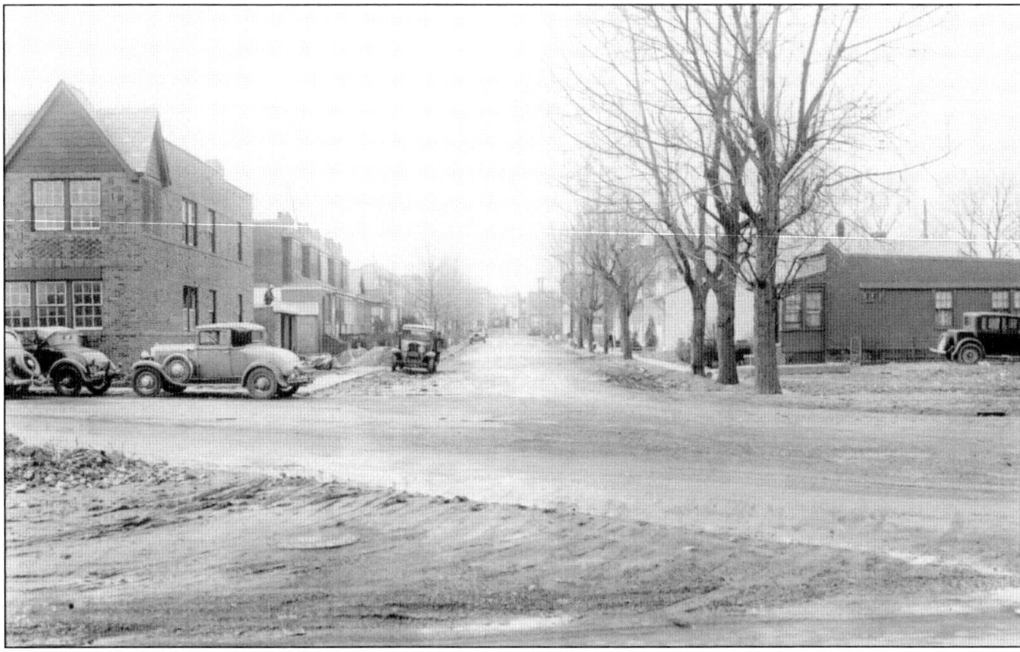

A number of small businesses had started to move into the Dry Harbor Road area near Seventy-seventh Avenue by the time this 1936 photograph was taken. This typified the usual mix of residential homes and small shops in the days before large shopping centers took business away from neighborhood stores. (Courtesy of GRHS.)

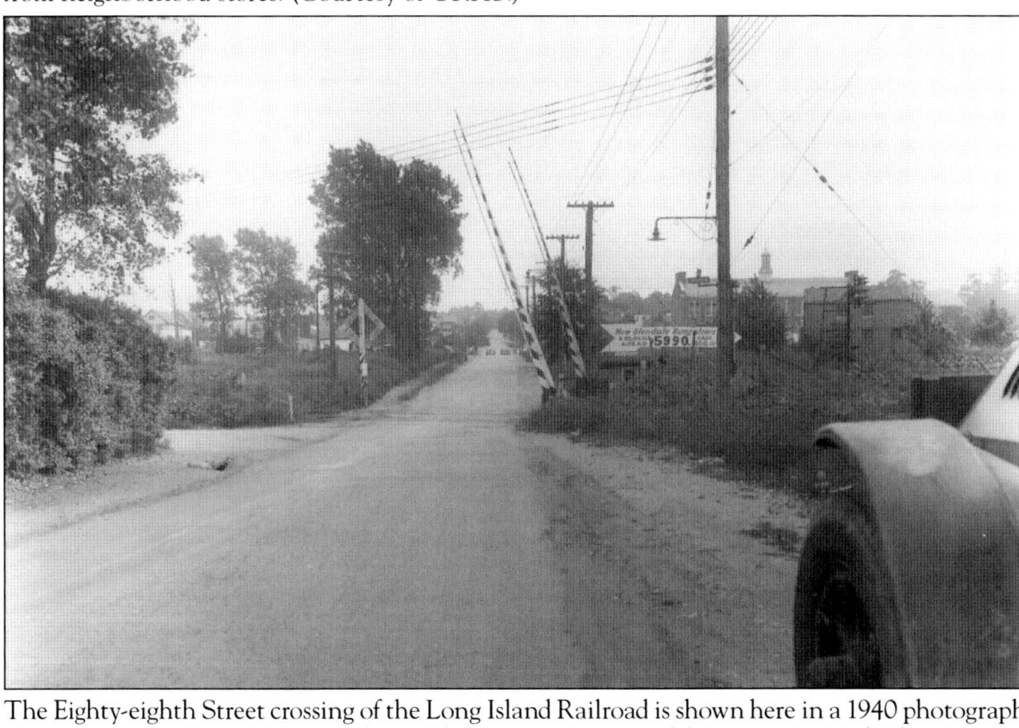

The Eighty-eighth Street crossing of the Long Island Railroad is shown here in a 1940 photograph. The railroad surveyed the area and started eliminating many of these crossings, which sometimes posed a hazard to automobile traffic. (Courtesy of GRHS.)

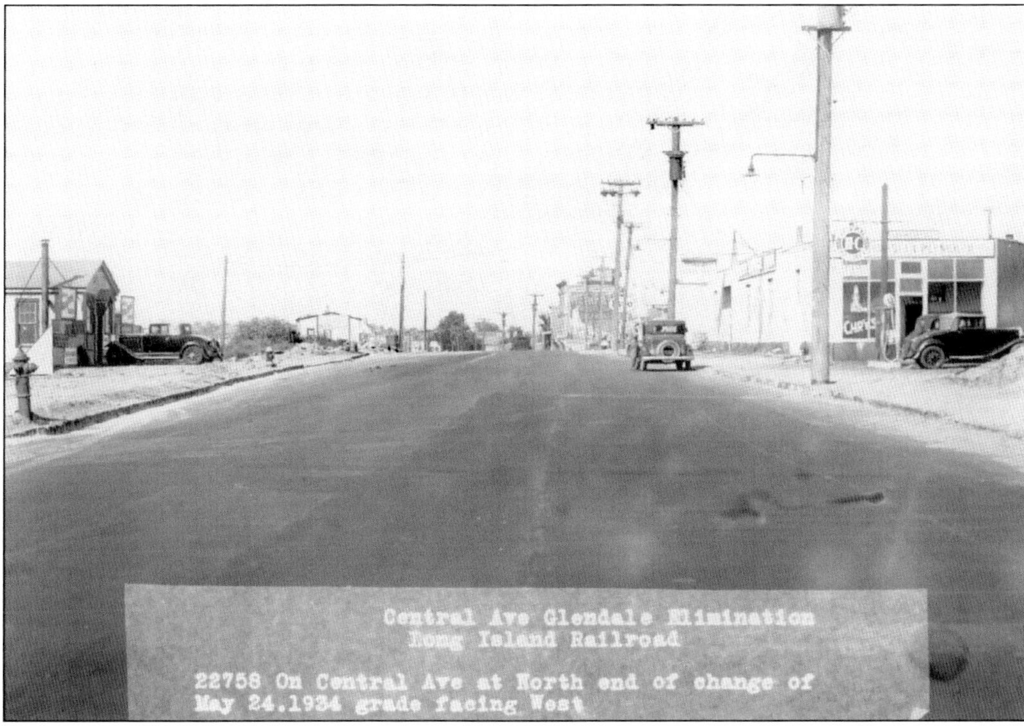

This is one of the railroad's official photographs, taken at Cooper Avenue and Sixty-ninth Road in 1934. It was taken after the crossing was removed, allowing Central Avenue to run parallel to the railroad right-of-way. (Courtesy of GRHS.)

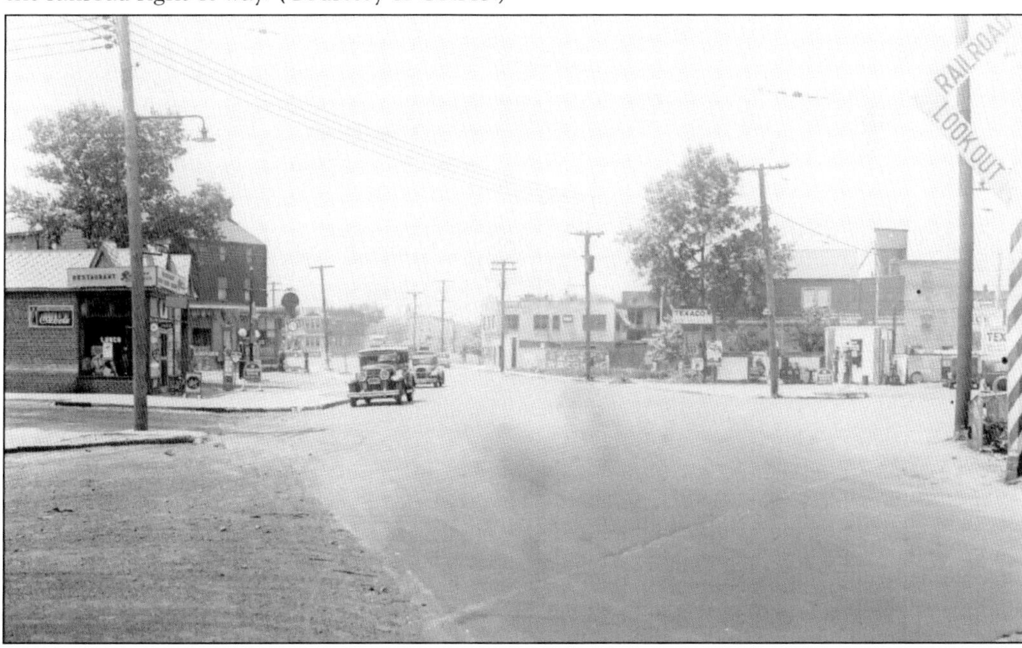

In this additional railroad photograph from 1934, the railroad crossing intrudes on what was certainly a busy intersection at Cooper Avenue and Seventy-fifth Street. Later maps of the area show an overpass created to bypass the tracks and eliminate the crossing gate. (Courtesy of GRHS.)

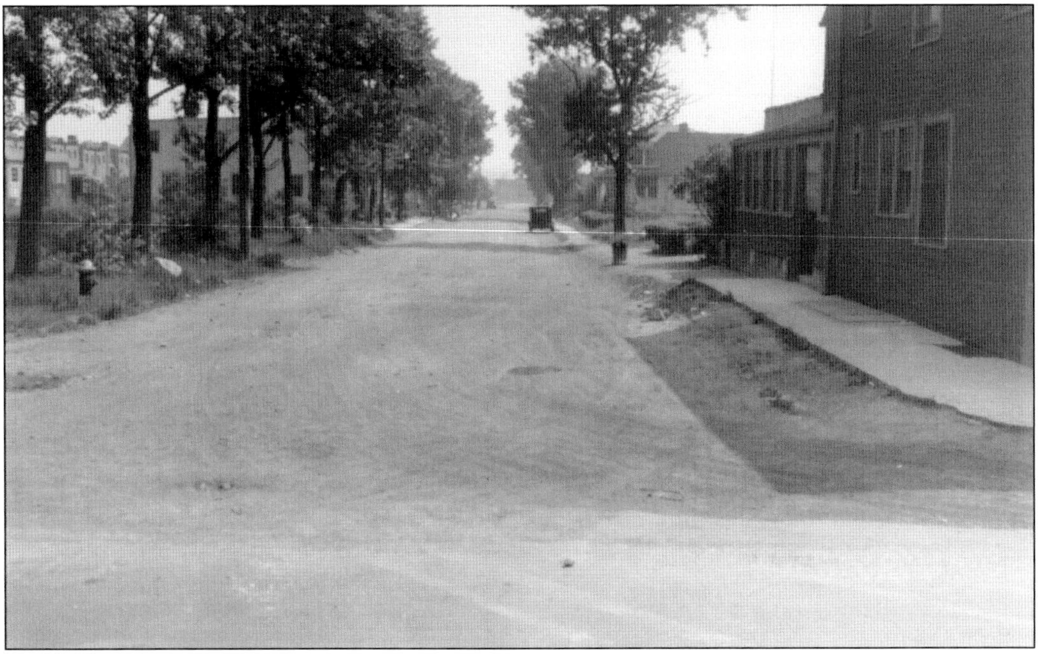

This view of Seventy-sixth Avenue looking east from Eighty-eighth Street in 1935 shows further development well underway. Fire hydrants now featured prominently in street construction, but sidewalks were not always part of the plan, and the road surfaces still left a lot to be desired. (Courtesy of GRHS.)

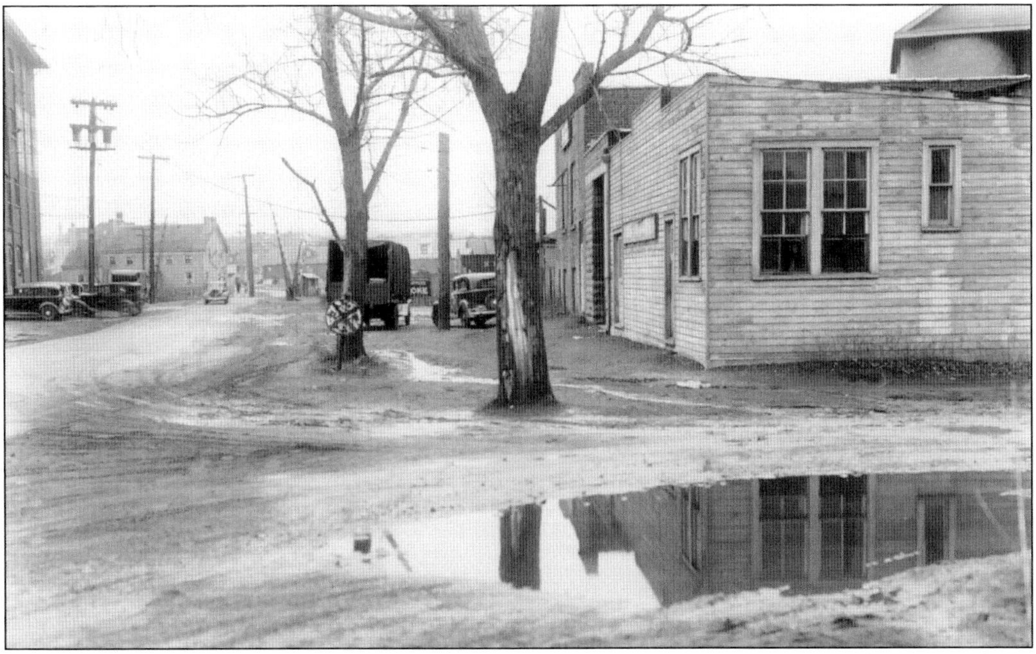

Industry began moving to the Dry Harbor Road area, but New York City lagged behind in making the streets more suitable for commercial traffic. Employees who did not think to bring a pair of boots with them following a rainy day would not have been in a good frame of mind by the time they got to work. (Courtesy of GRHS.)

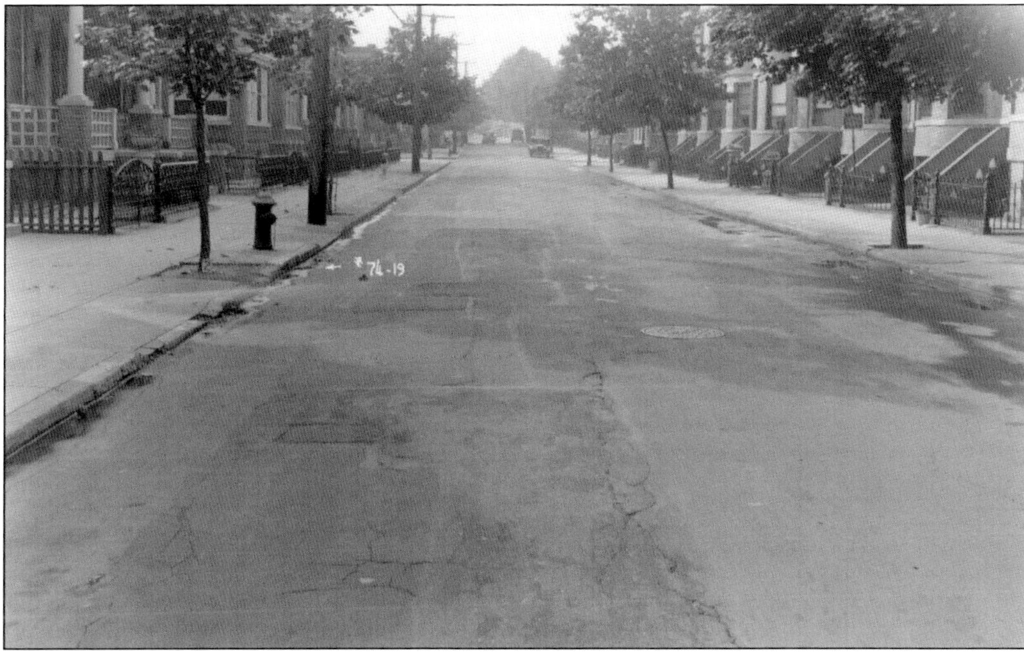

In 1938, standing on Sixty-second Street at the intersection with Seventy-fourth Avenue, this is what one would have seen. Behind the photographer and to the left was Otto Voight's delicatessen, and to the right rear, there was a candy store just a few steps up from Myrtle Avenue. This street looks pretty much the same today, more than 75 years later. (Courtesy of GRHS.)

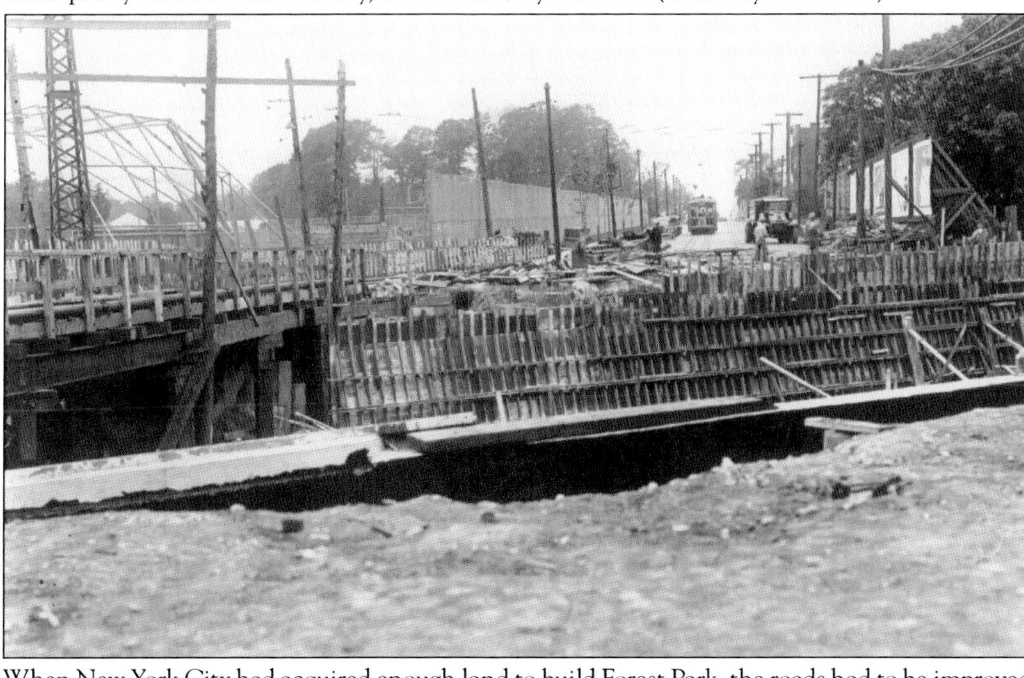

When New York City had acquired enough land to build Forest Park, the roads had to be improved to handle the additional traffic. This photograph from 1936 shows Victory Field on the left and construction on Myrtle Avenue and Woodhaven Boulevard that would have interfered with the trolley service. (Courtesy of GRHS.)

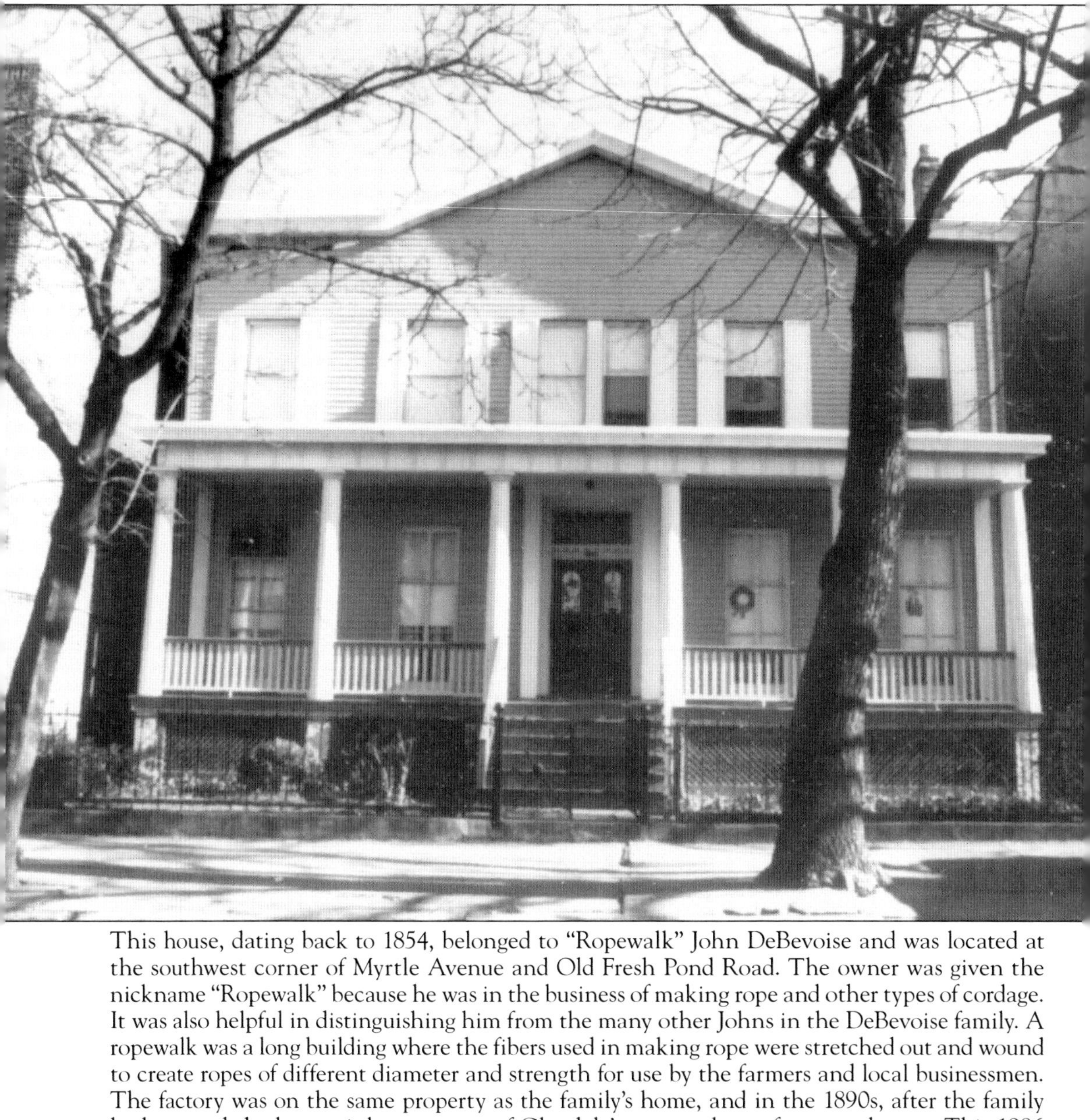

This house, dating back to 1854, belonged to "Ropewalk" John DeBevoise and was located at the southwest corner of Myrtle Avenue and Old Fresh Pond Road. The owner was given the nickname "Ropewalk" because he was in the business of making rope and other types of cordage. It was also helpful in distinguishing him from the many other Johns in the DeBevoise family. A ropewalk was a long building where the fibers used in making rope were stretched out and wound to create ropes of different diameter and strength for use by the farmers and local businessmen. The factory was on the same property as the family's home, and in the 1890s, after the family had vacated the house, it became one of Glendale's many saloons for several years. This 1986 photograph shows the house remarkably preserved more than 130 years later, but it has since been torn down. (Courtesy of GRHS.)

Two

From Farming to Industry

As the development of Glendale continued, more and more of the original farms were sold off and the land subdivided to accommodate additional home building. Open land was becoming harder to find in the surrounding communities, so Glendale experienced its own building boom in the early part of the 20th century. Along with the new home building came commercial growth, as many different types of businesses opened up to service the growing population. Myrtle Avenue, which was the main thoroughfare in the town, drew most of the retail stores, and before long, both sides of the street running from Fresh Pond Road out to Woodhaven Boulevard were lined with the usual array of small shops and service businesses.

Around 1904, the area of Cooper Avenue near Eightieth Street began to see other types of industry move in as well. Developers started building factories and warehouses in an area adjacent to the Long Island Railroad, and this came to be known as Atlas Terminal. In 1922, one of the earliest tenants, a man named Henry Hemmerdinger, began expanding the site until there were a total of 16 industrial buildings. The industries that chose Glendale for their operations included everything from a safety match company and an oil distributor to one that made fine china known throughout the world and another that manufactured small aircraft. In its peak years, Atlas Terminal accounted for 60 railcar loads of materials moving in and out each day.

While some of those early tenants are still in business at other locations, the site itself has become one of the most popular shopping centers in the Queens County section of New York City. It is now known as The Shops at Atlas Mall.

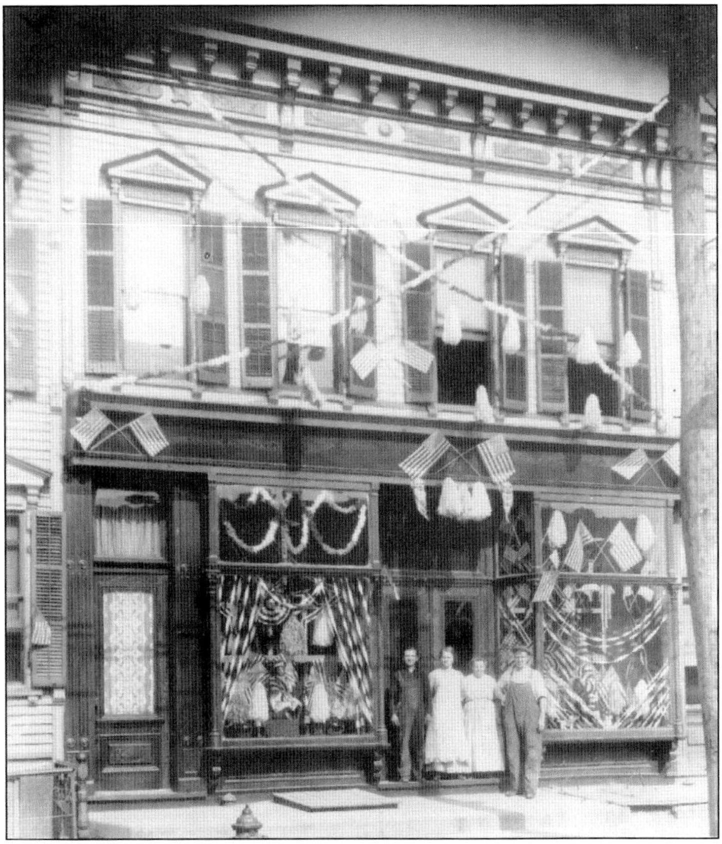

In this 1912 photograph, proprietor George Mader and some of his employees are standing outside of the George Mader Home Furnishings & Hardware Store, located at Sixty-ninth Place and Myrtle Avenue. The flag decorations indicate that this photograph was taken during a holiday celebration. (Courtesy of GRHS.)

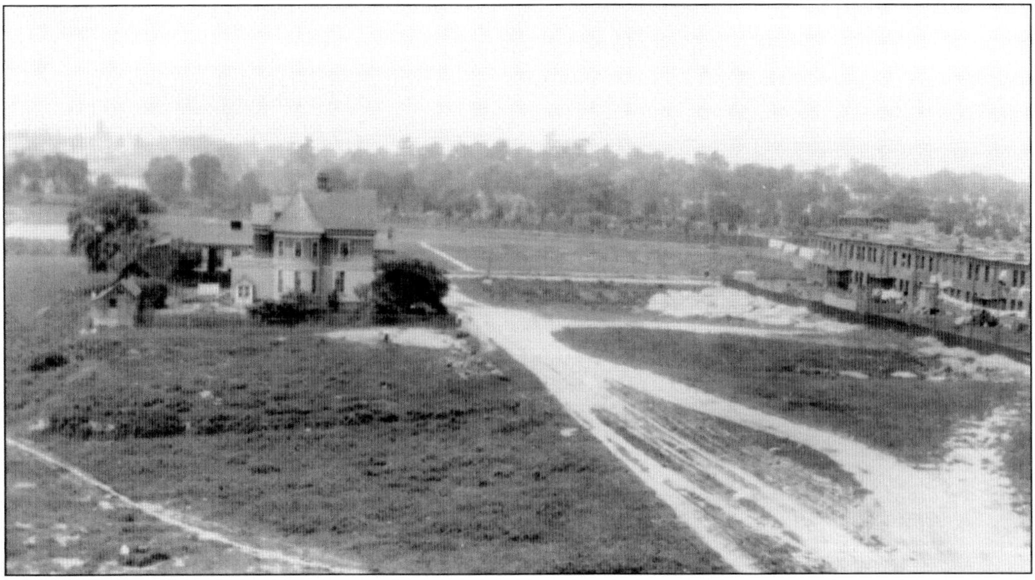

This 1917 photograph shows the Finley farm, which dates back to 1889 on a plot that would be in the area of Sixty-ninth Street and Seventy-second Avenue. In addition to farming, the family operated manufacturing plants that built furniture and lighting fixtures. To the right in the image, barely visible in the background, is the Trinity Lutheran Church. (Courtesy of GRHS.)

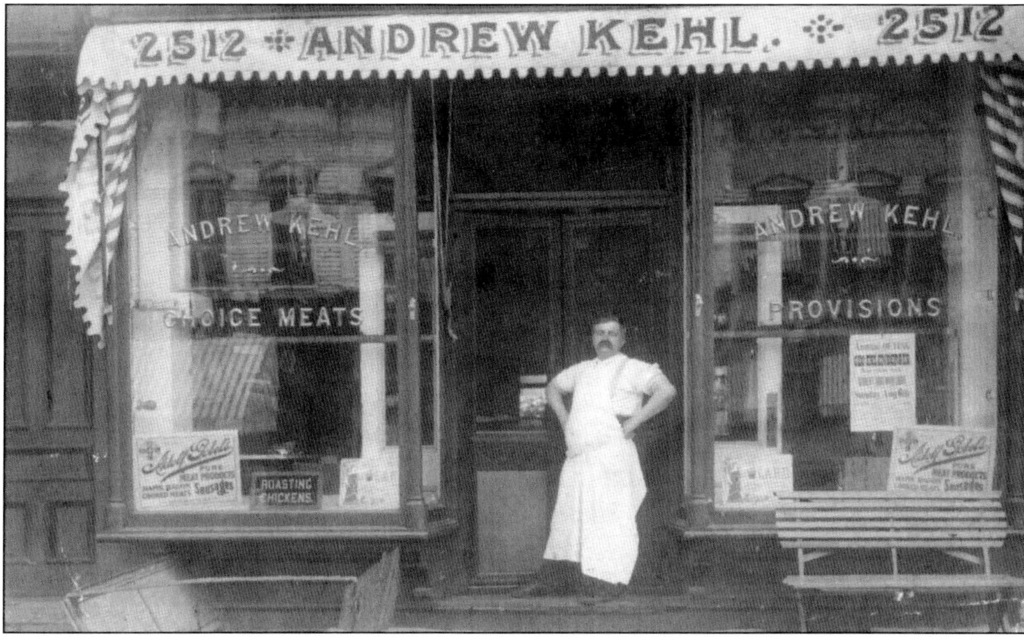

Proud store owner Andrew Kehl posed for this picture in 1910 in front of his butcher shop on Myrtle Avenue. The old address shown on the awning, 2512, later became 6910 Myrtle Avenue when the street numbering system was changed. (Courtesy of GRHS.)

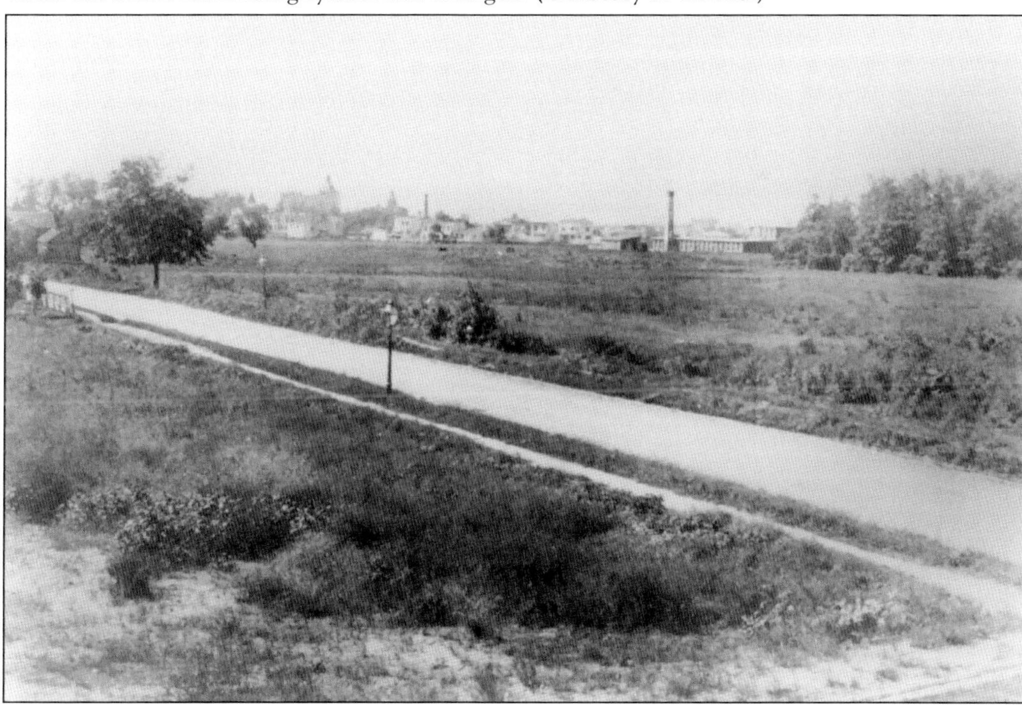

Still waiting in 1904 for someone to snatch it up, this open field was located at Cooper Avenue and Sixty-fourth Street. Toward the left rear portion of the photograph is the Frank Brewery, situated on Cypress Avenue, and the last building on the right, with the large smokestack, is the Darling Match Company. (Courtesy of GRHS.)

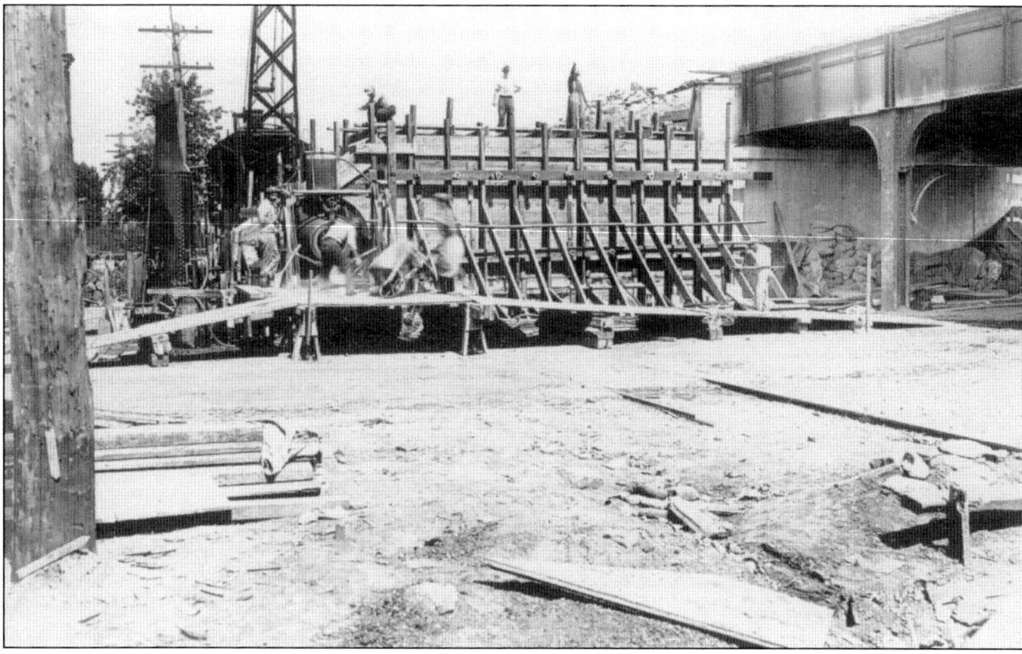

Railroad construction continued in Glendale in 1913, as seen in this photograph showing an embankment and trestle being built along Cypress Hills Street. Based on similar photographs from another angle, the Dietz Coal Company yard would be just on the other side of the trestle. (Courtesy of GRHS.)

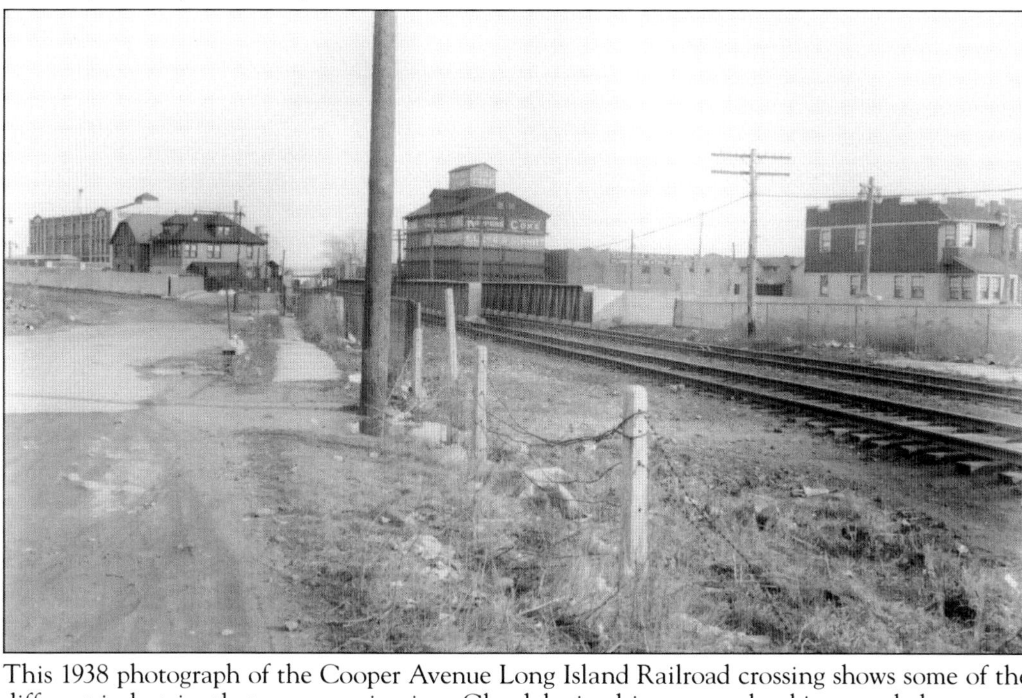

This 1938 photograph of the Cooper Avenue Long Island Railroad crossing shows some of the different industries that were moving into Glendale; in this case, a plumbing supply house and a coal and coke distributor. Neighbors on the residential street to the right would have had to contend with the coal dust as well as the noise of passing trains. (Courtesy of GRHS.)

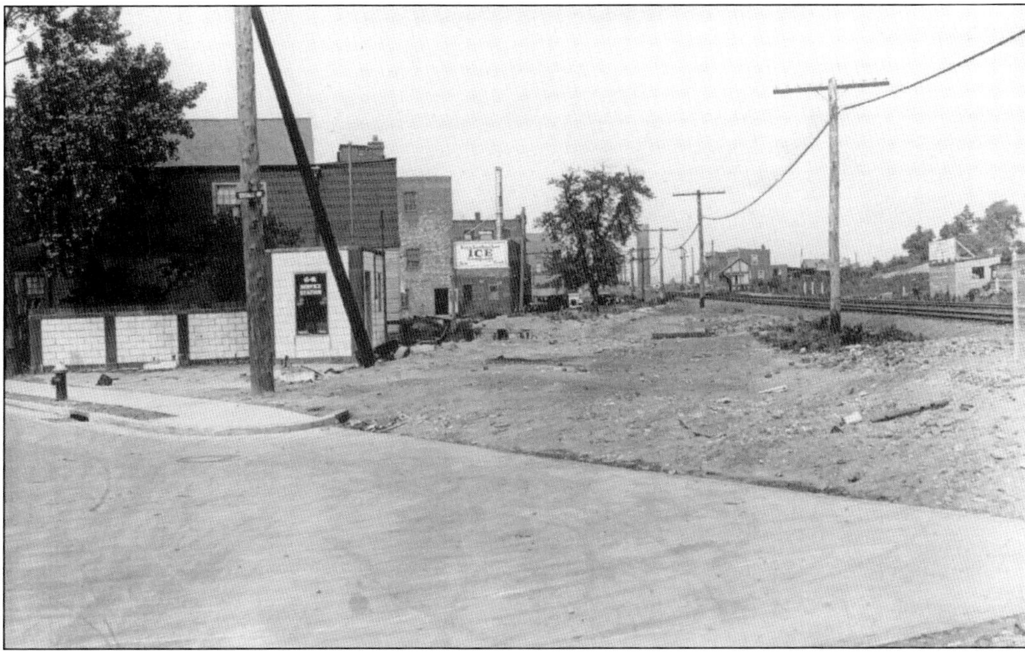

Even as late as 1935, there were still a number of unpaved streets in Glendale. This photograph was taken on Edsall Avenue near Cooper Avenue, showing a local ice distributor and a service station right next to the railroad tracks. Before electric refrigerators were widely used, everyone used blocks of ice at home to keep their food fresh. (Courtesy of GRHS.)

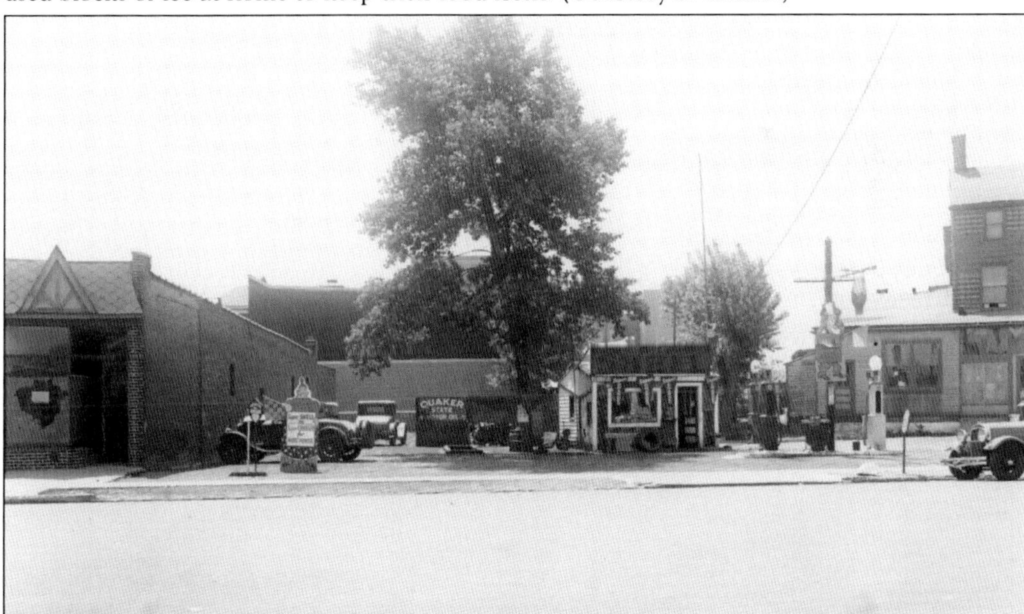

The owner of this gas station made the unusual decision to not completely clear the property when he opened his business. This photograph, taken in 1934, shows the south side of Cooper Avenue near Seventy-fourth Street, and the large tree in the middle of the property gives the scene a nice rural feel and conveys some of the small-town atmosphere that made Glendale so appealing. (Courtesy of GRHS.)

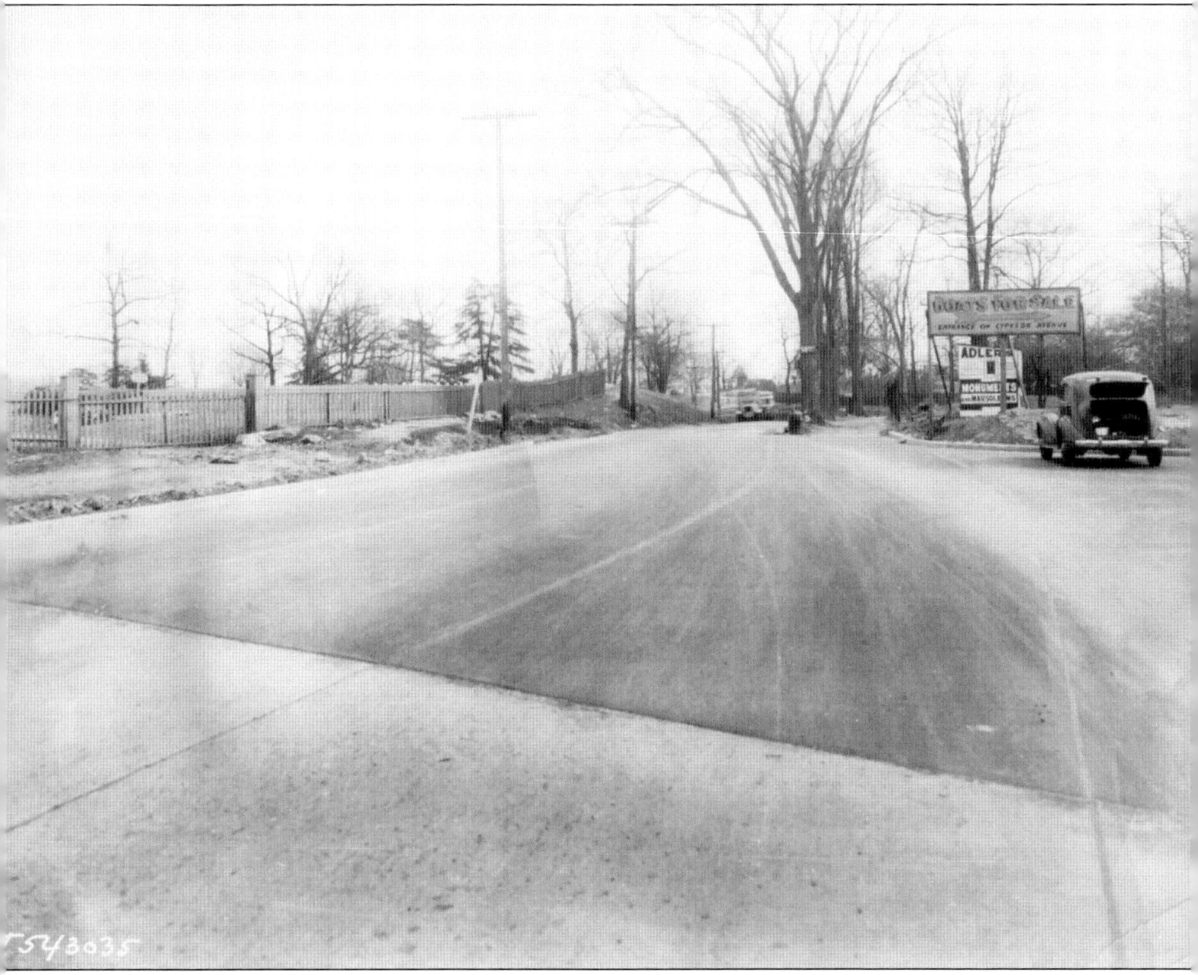

Considering the location of this 1935 photograph, taken on Cypress Hills Street near Cypress Avenue, it would have been an unusual place to have boats for sale. The lakes in the early picnic parks were long gone, and the Interboro Parkway was scheduled to be opened in June of that year. Construction of the parkway changed the entire nature of this part of Glendale. It had been proposed in 1901, and it required a change in the New York State Cemetery Act to move many of the graves along the proposed route when construction finally began in 1933. Ironically, in spite of efforts to minimize the impact to the cemeteries and local parks, the resulting 4.7-mile parkway, with all of its sharp curves, was ranked as one of the most dangerous roads in New York State as recently as 2007. (Courtesy of GRHS.)

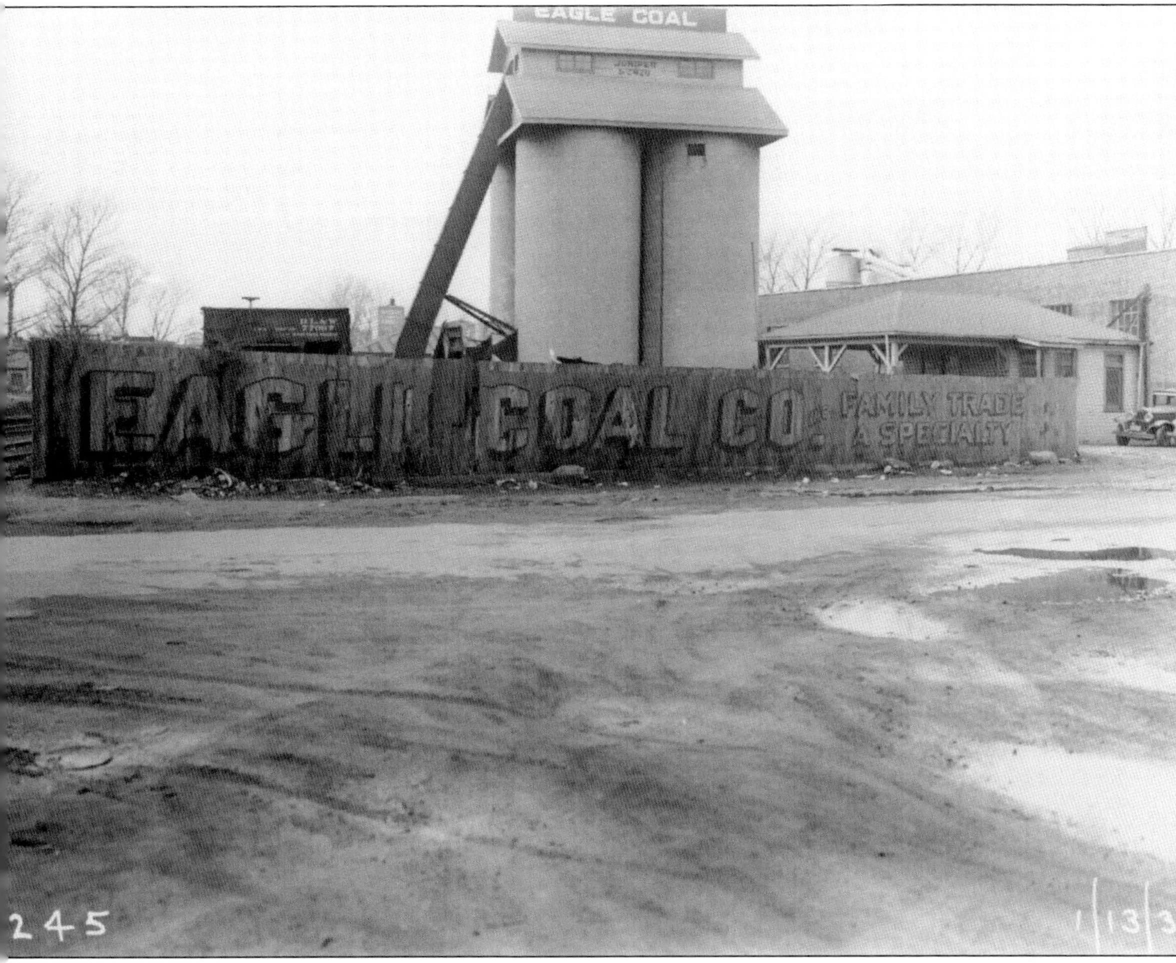

The local coal yards were probably not the best neighbors to have in 1936, when this photograph was taken. Eagle Coal Company, located on Dry Harbor Road near Seventy-first Avenue and the railroad tracks, must have had a steady stream of railcars and trucks coming into its yard to transport coal. The property shown was at the edge of a piece of farmland that had been owned by Henri Wulfurst. In 1902, he sold 18.72 acres of his land to American Grass Products, and the company began construction of a 40,000-square-foot, multistory brick factory building that became one of the first buildings in the Atlas Terminal industrial complex. Several years later, that building was sold to a Rhode Island company that operated part of it as a knitting mill and the remainder as a power plant to provide steam and electricity to the industrial park's tenants. Eagle Coal could not have been at a better location to satisfy their energy needs. (Courtesy of GRHS.)

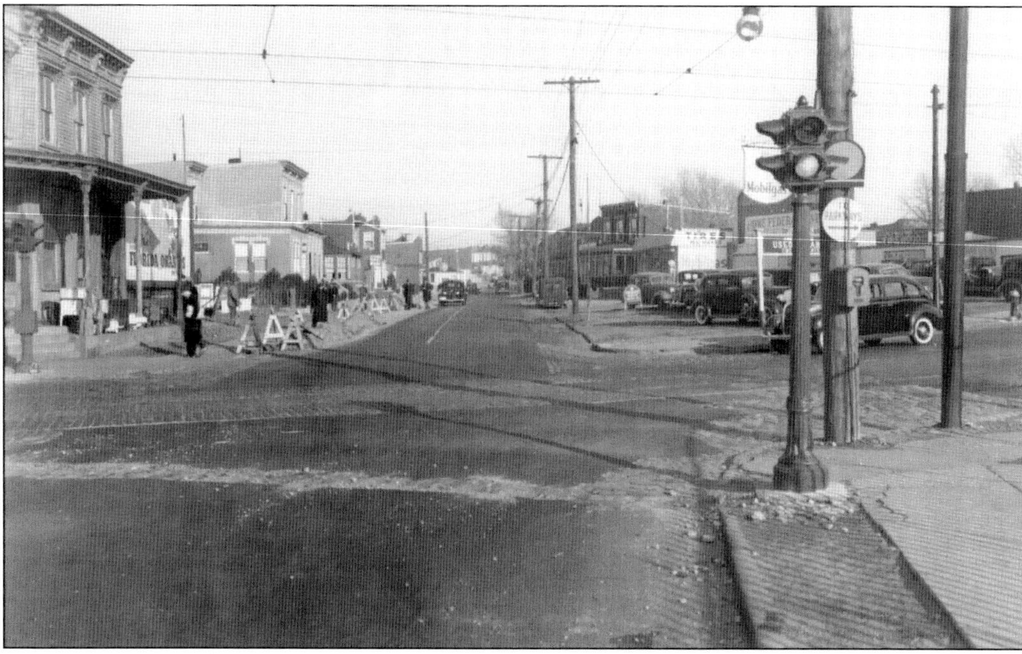

By 1939, America's love affair with the automobile was in full swing, as this view looking east on Cooper Avenue from Cypress Avenue shows. Most commercial areas had a multitude of businesses to service the rapidly growing automotive market. The small box with the handle on the utility pole to the right is a fire department call box. (Courtesy of GRHS.)

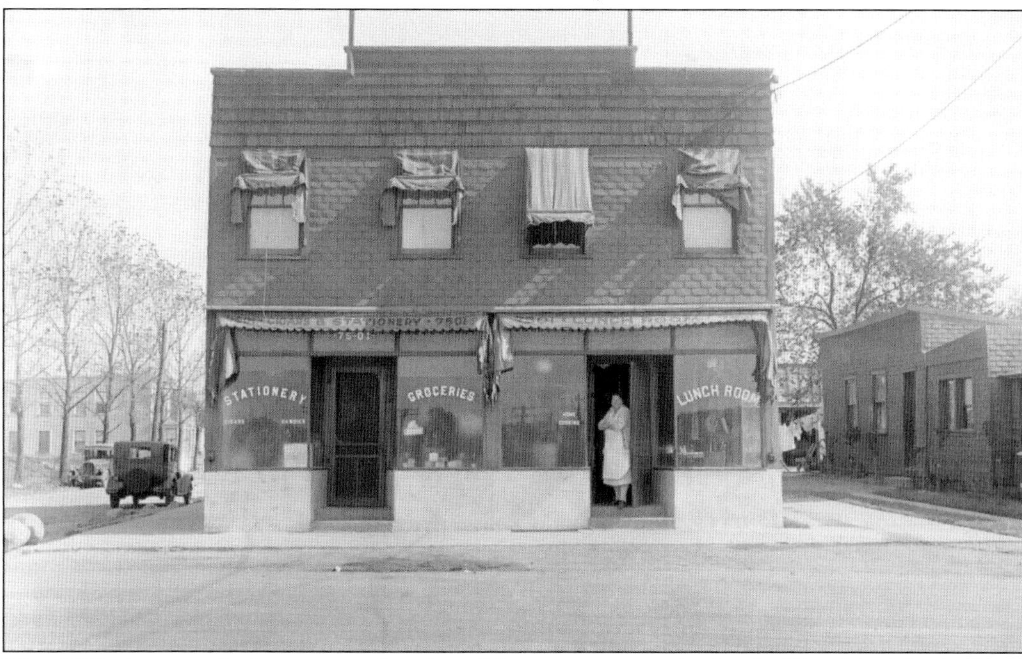

This 1929 photograph shows a couple of small businesses typical of early Glendale. The building located on Seventy-fifth Avenue near Eighty-eighth Street is unusual in that it is not attached on either side. In many cases, store owners lived in apartments right above their place of business. (Courtesy of GRHS.)

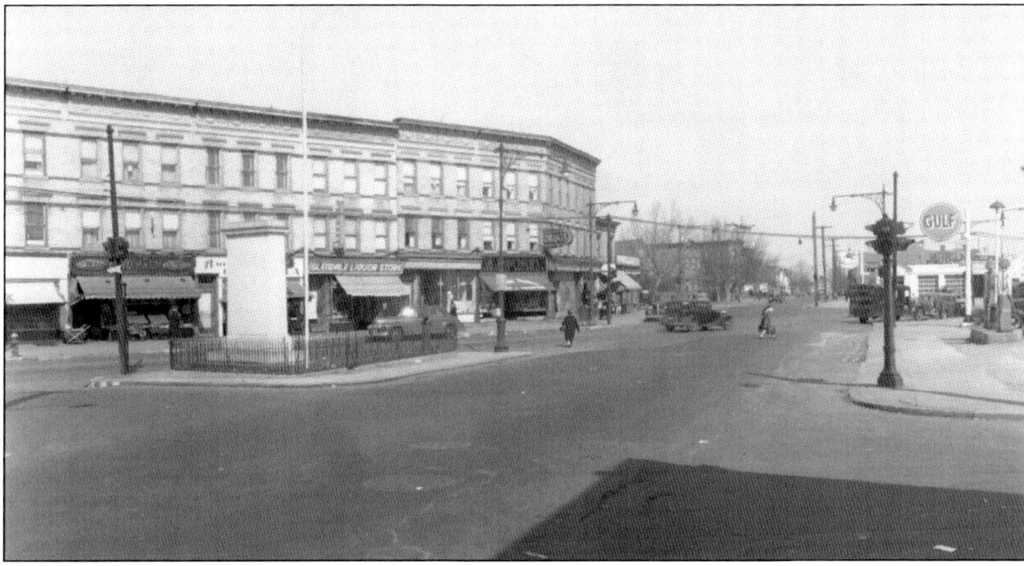

The intersection of Cooper and Myrtle Avenues looked like this in 1945. It is probably the most photographed part of Glendale, since it is in the center of the town. The monument in the center is still there, but in earlier years, it included a small cannon in the grass. The Gulf station was replaced by a McDonald's in later years. (Courtesy of GRHS.)

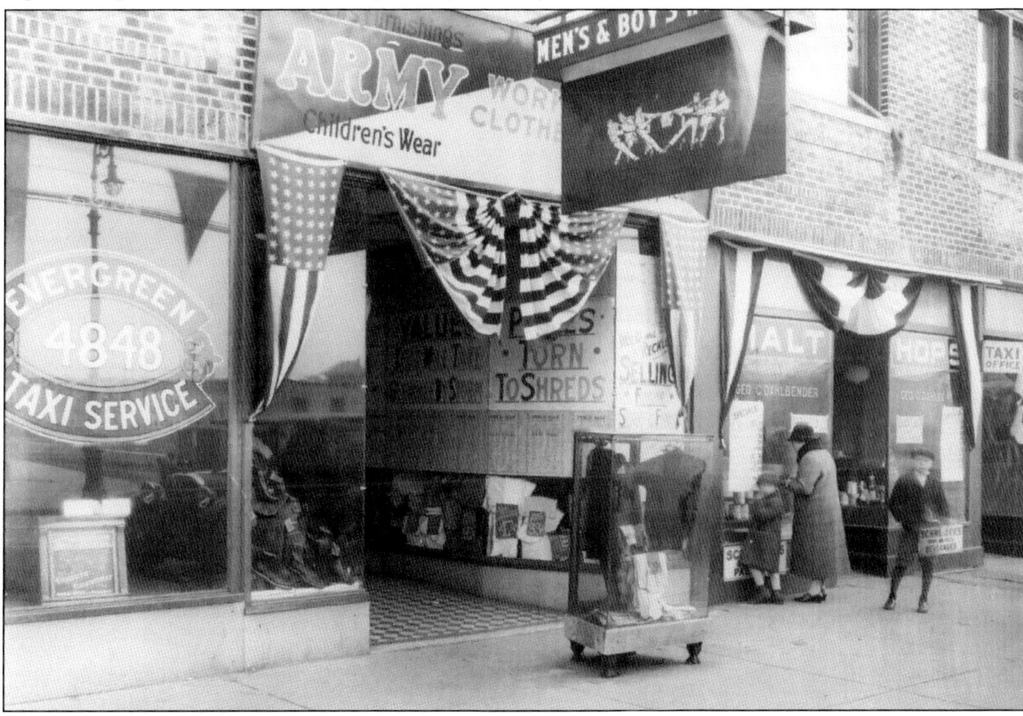

The diversity of local business is apparent in this 1928 image taken along Myrtle Avenue. It features a men's and children's clothing store with a flair for advertising. Note their claims of "Wild & Reckless Selling" and "Prices Torn to Shreds" to highlight the bargains that they offered. The old Evergreen telephone exchange shown (EV 4848) pays tribute to an earlier name for part of Glendale. (Courtesy of GRHS.)

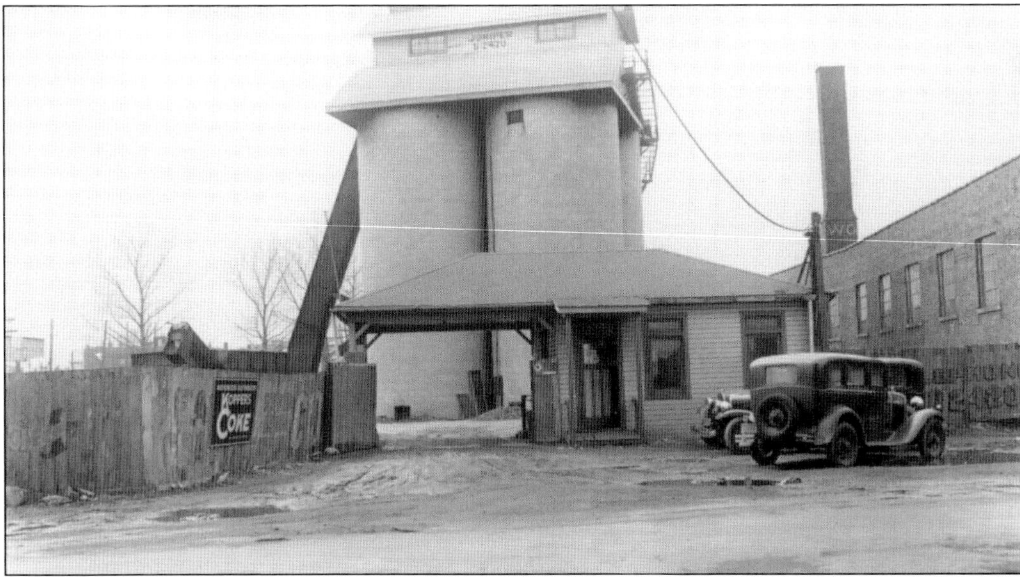

Coke, which is a refined form of coal after processing, was one of the main heating materials for residents of Glendale in the 1930s. This view of the Eagle Coal Company yard identifies Kopper's Coke as one of the many companies that supplied their products to local distributors to meet the energy needs of the growing Glendale community. (Courtesy of GRHS.)

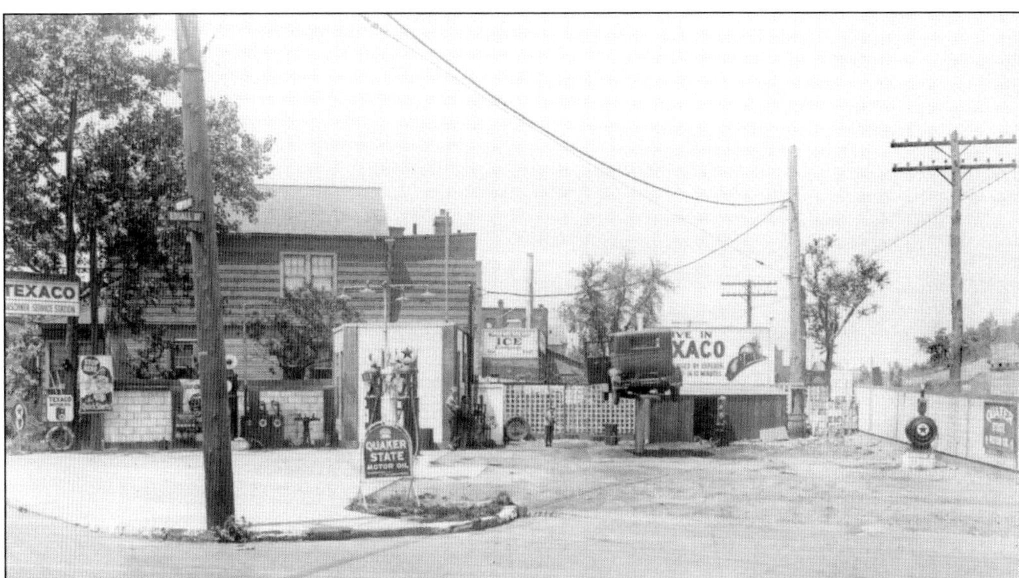

Pictured is another local service station in 1934 at the intersection of Edsall and Cooper Avenues. It is not clear whether the raised car on the right is an advertising gimmick or the way a mechanic could get underneath an automobile to check out its exhaust system. (Courtesy of GRHS.)

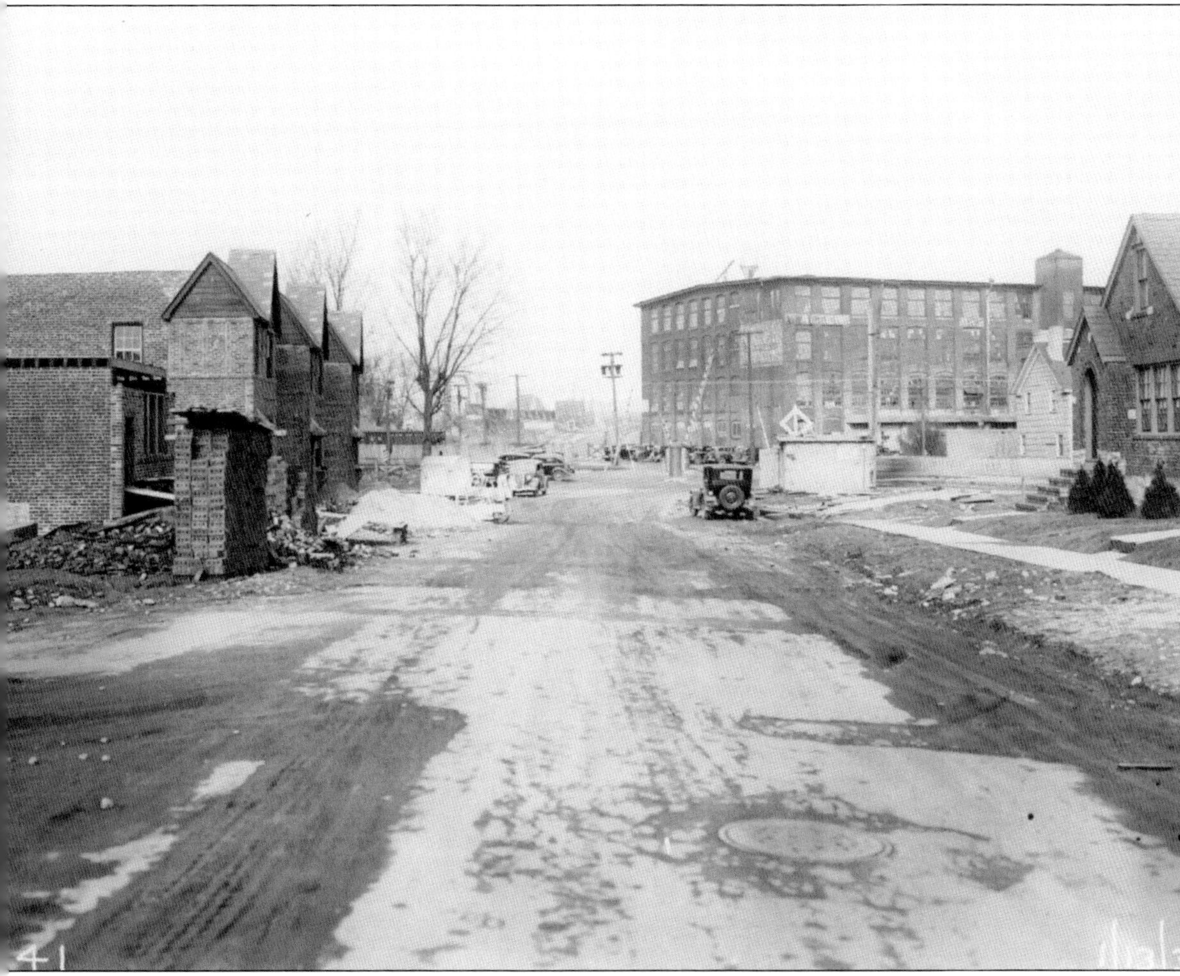

This 1936 photograph of Eightieth Street near Seventy-seventh Road shows some of the large buildings marking one entrance to the Atlas Terminal industrial park. It was begun in 1922 when Henry Hemmerdinger purchased a tract of land in the area of Cooper Avenue and Dry Harbor Road, which would later become Eightieth Street. His father was what used to be described as a "rag merchant," who made his living buying and reselling fabric strips that could be used in a number of different industries. That business evolved into a company named Atlas Waste Manufacturing, which Henry later moved into the Glendale site. The few industrial buildings that were already on the land at one time manufactured underwater telephone cables for transatlantic transmission. Building space not required by Atlas Waste Manufacturing was rented out to other tenants, and the complex eventually grew to include 31 buildings. Many of the early homes in the area were later torn down as the industrial park expanded. (Courtesy of GRHS.)

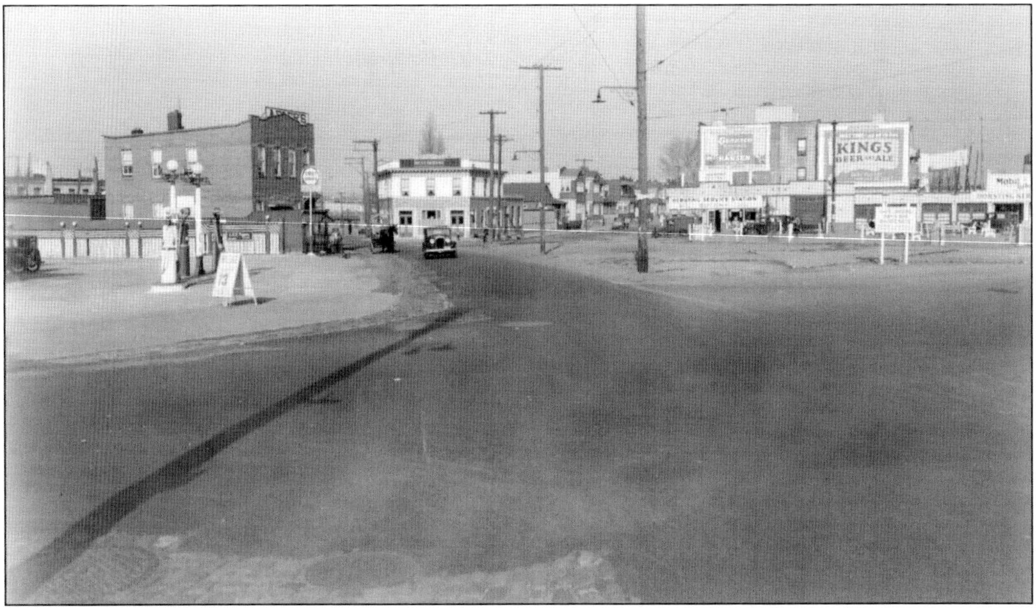

In this 1935 view of Cypress Hills Street looking north from Cooper Avenue, the gas station on the left was one of many that would occupy that same location over the years. The brand of gas sold has changed many times, but the corner is still the site of a gas station in the present day. (Courtesy of Queens Historical Society.)

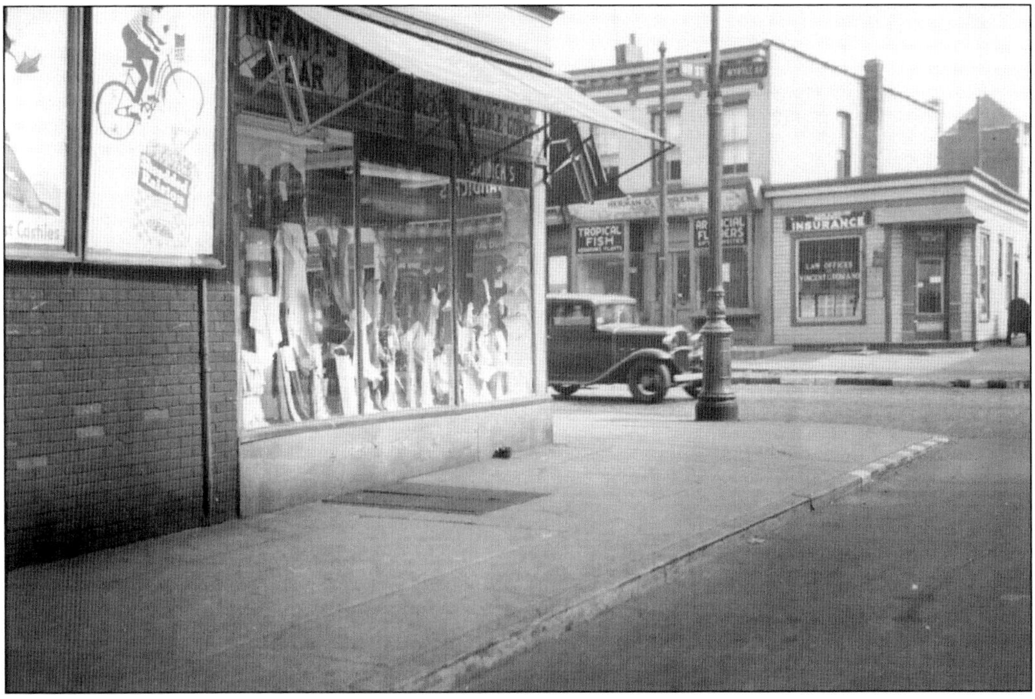

Right in the heart of the Glendale shopping district, this 1938 photograph of Sixty-ninth Street at Myrtle Avenue shows some of the types of businesses that moved into the community. The tropical fish store is a bit of a surprise, since one does not think of that as being a popular hobby in the 1930s. (Courtesy of Queens Historical Society.)

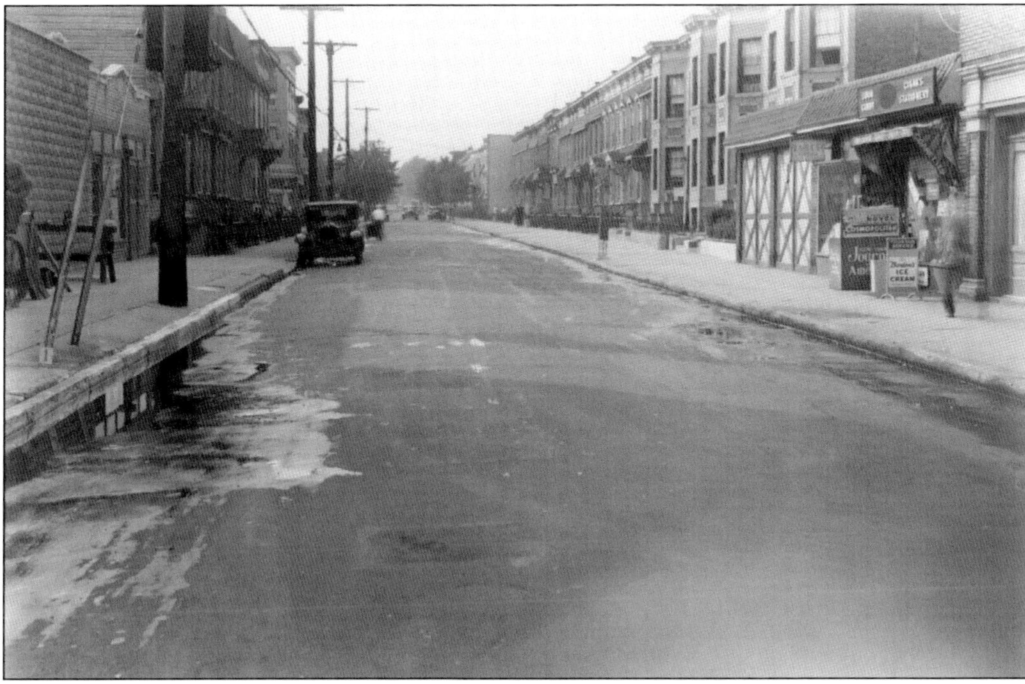

This 1938 photograph of Sixty-second Street looking up from Myrtle Avenue shows a lonely candy store at the end of a residential block. It was owned at one time by George Eck and, later, by a man named Larry, who also owned an Italian ice delivery route. (Courtesy of GRHS.)

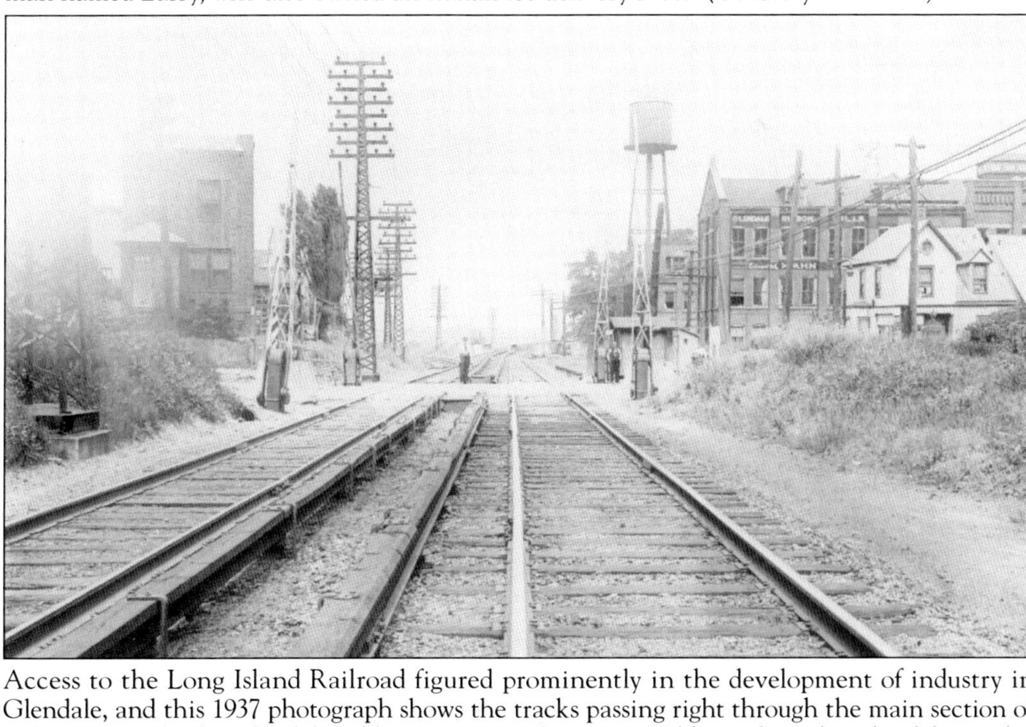

Access to the Long Island Railroad figured prominently in the development of industry in Glendale, and this 1937 photograph shows the tracks passing right through the main section of Atlas Terminal. The Glendale Ribbon Company factory is visible on the right side of the tracks. (Courtesy of www.trainweb.com.)

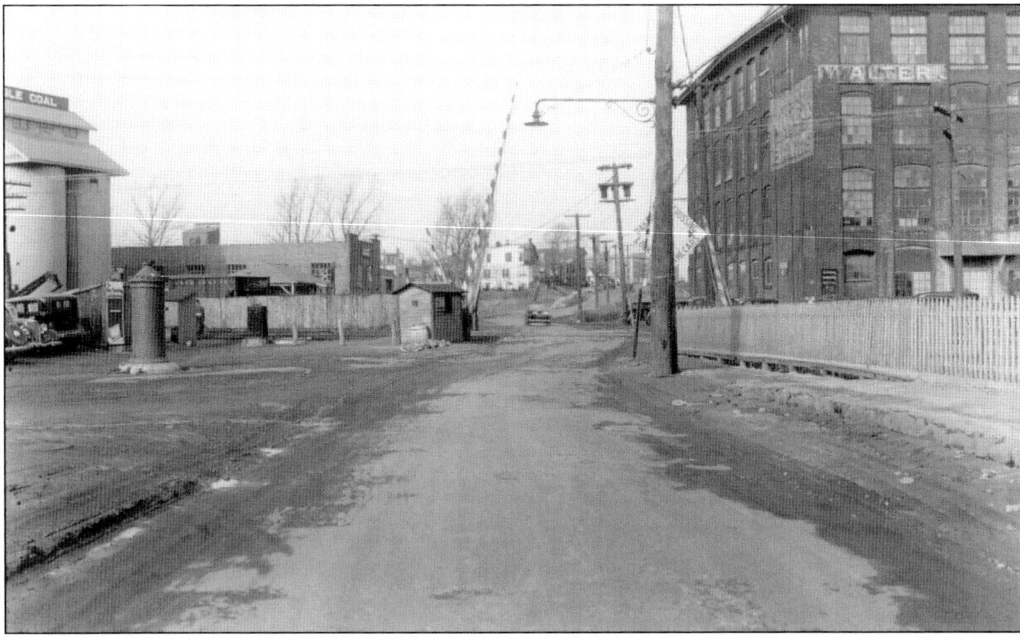

Even with all of the industrial development, there were still unpaved streets leading into Atlas Terminal in 1936, as seen in this photograph of Eighty-first Street near Dry Harbor Road. The area shown is now part of the new shopping mall named after Atlas Terminal. (Courtesy of GRHS.)

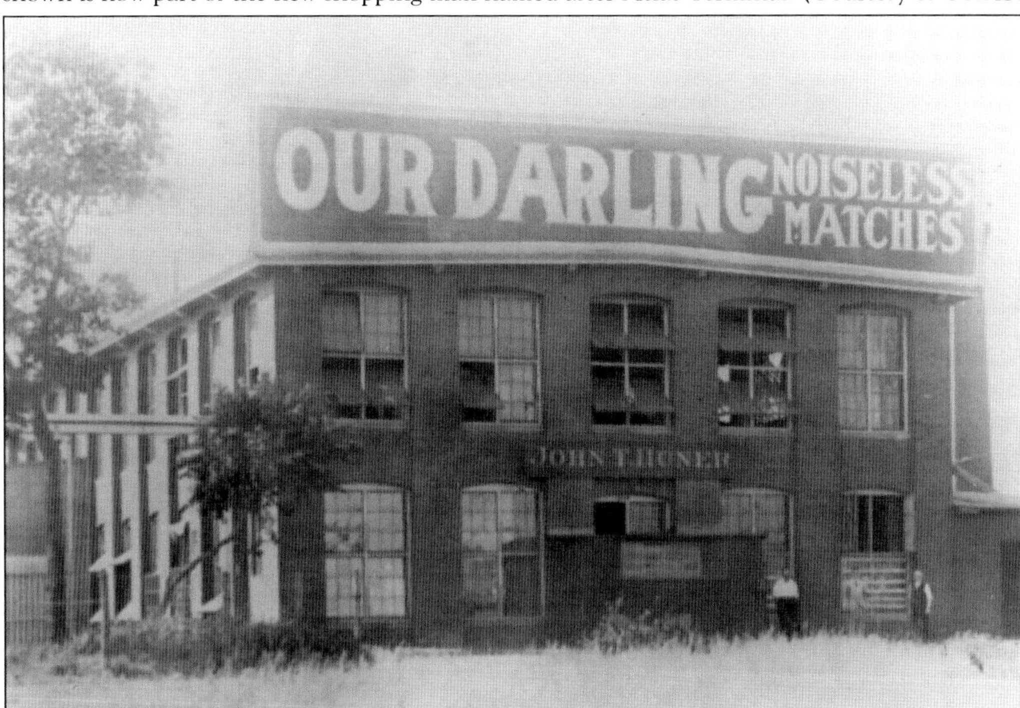

The Our Darling Match Company, whose claim was that its matches were noiseless, was on Sixtieth Lane south of Myrtle Avenue. Seen in this 1910 photograph, the company began in 1904 and burned down in 1912. (Courtesy of GRHS.)

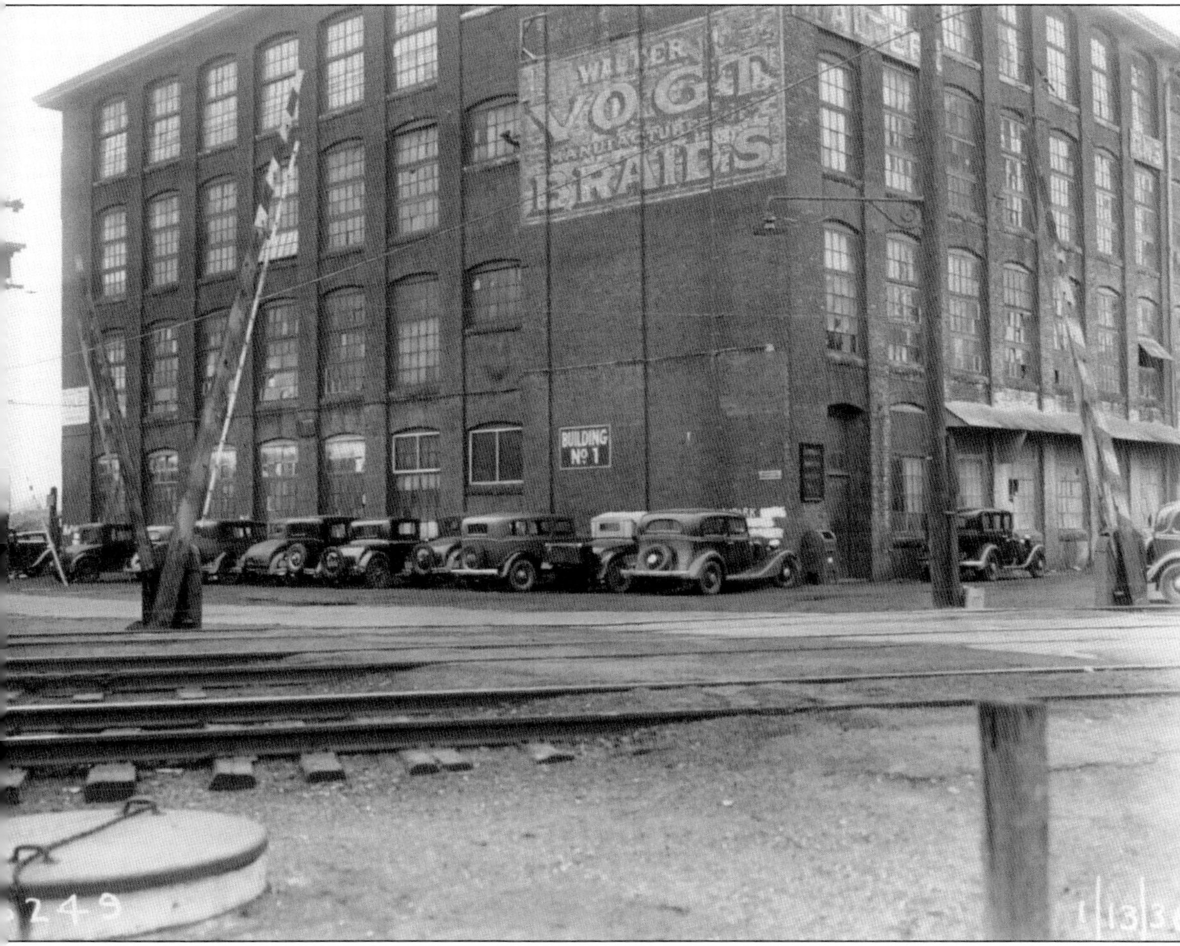

Building No. 1 in Atlas Terminal was the home of the Walter Vogt Braid Company at the time of this 1936 photograph. It was one of several tenants in the industrial park that served the textile industry, but the company does not appear to have survived into modern times. Beginning with Henry Hemmerdinger's Atlas Waste Manufacturing Company, the textile industry always figured prominently in this part of Glendale. Atlas Waste alone occupied a total of 300,000 square feet of industrial space and employed 200 people, processing more than 100 tons of textile products each day. Companies like Walter Vogt Braid would have provided some of this raw material and may also have used some of the stuffing and related materials produced by Atlas Waste. (Courtesy of GRHS.)

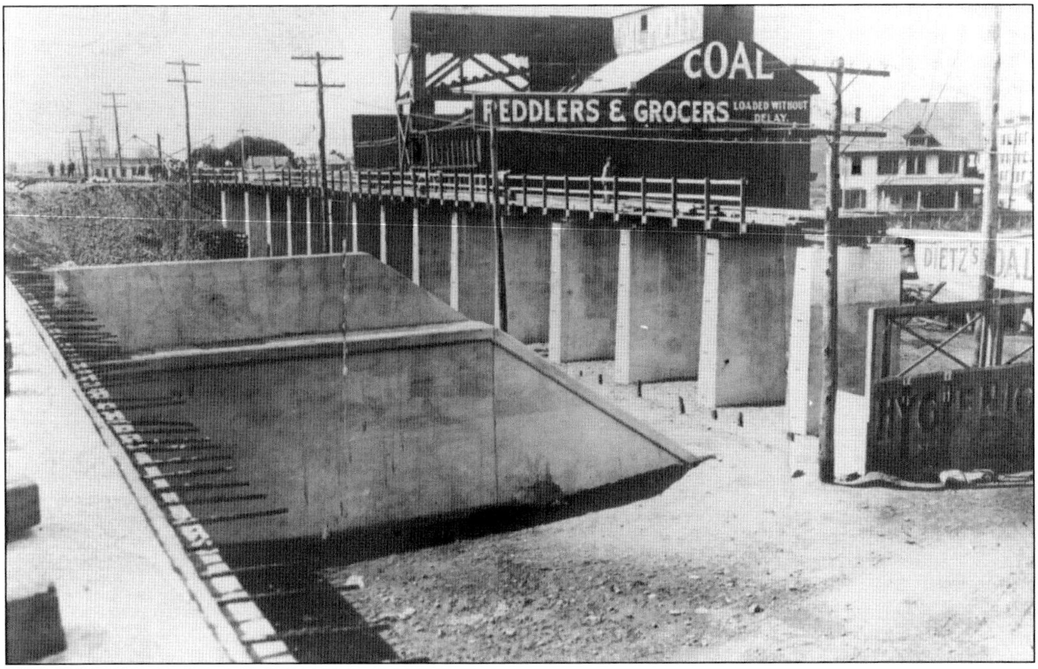

The Philip Dietz Coal Company, located at Seventy-first Avenue and Cypress Hills Street, was one of the largest distributors of coal in Glendale and the rest of the Greater Ridgewood community. In the photograph above, the Long Island Railroad overpass is still under construction in 1913, and a house owned by a family named Pflug is to the right. Dietz advertises that in addition to supplying industrial needs, they also valued coal peddlers and small grocers who would then resell to the general public. In the more modern view below, automobiles pass under the completed overpass in 1976, and the Dietz buildings are on the right. (Both, courtesy of GRHS.)

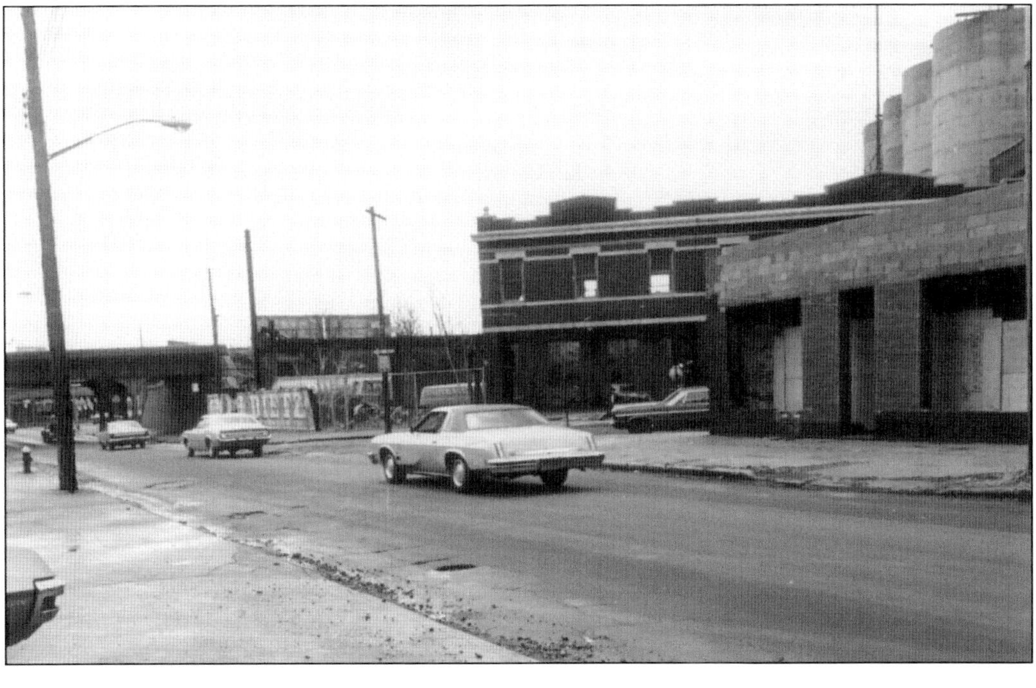

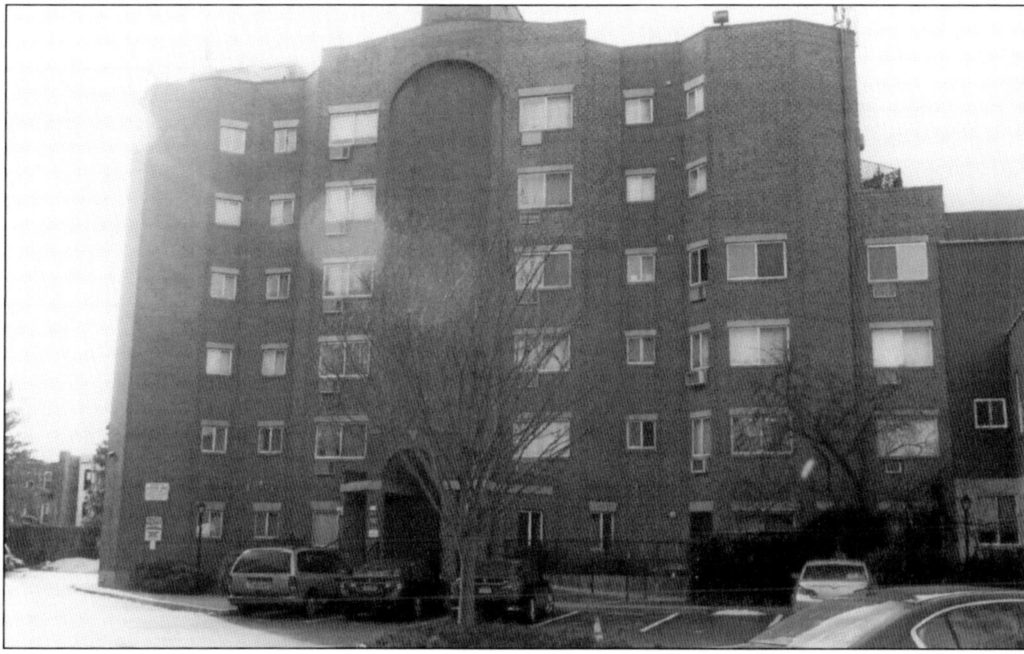

As communities throughout New York switched their energy needs away from coal, the Dietz Company was forced to close its doors, but it still retained a valuable piece of property in Glendale. Developers retained about half of the original buildings and created a 65-condominium complex on the site, which they named Glenridge Mews because it sits on the unofficial Glendale-Ridgewood border. One of the original buildings shown below still retains the original Philip Dietz Coal Company name over the entrance to the management office. (Both, courtesy of the author.)

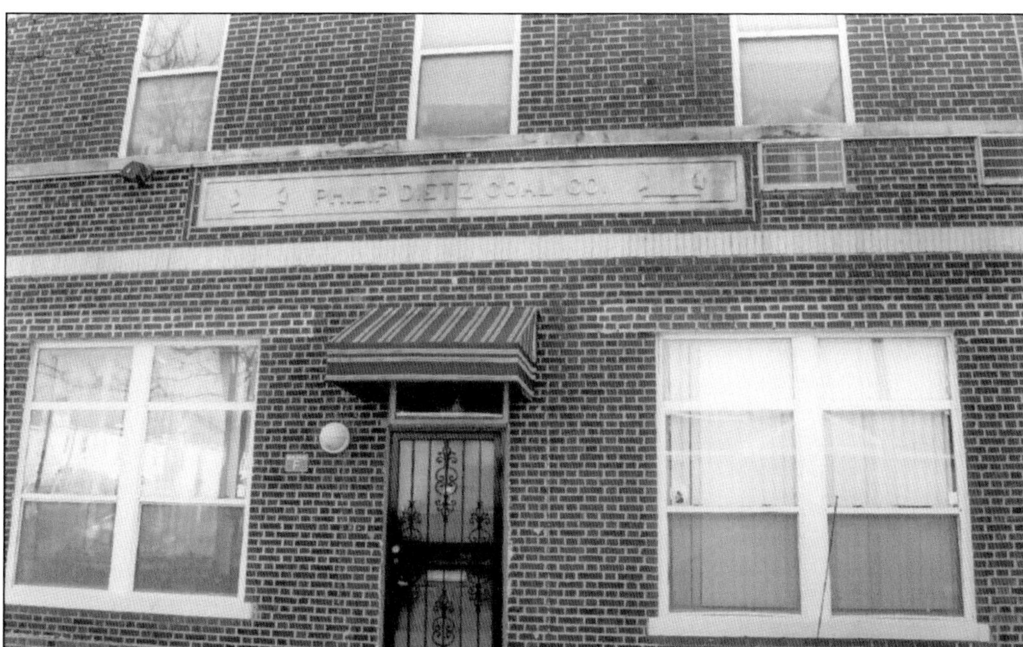

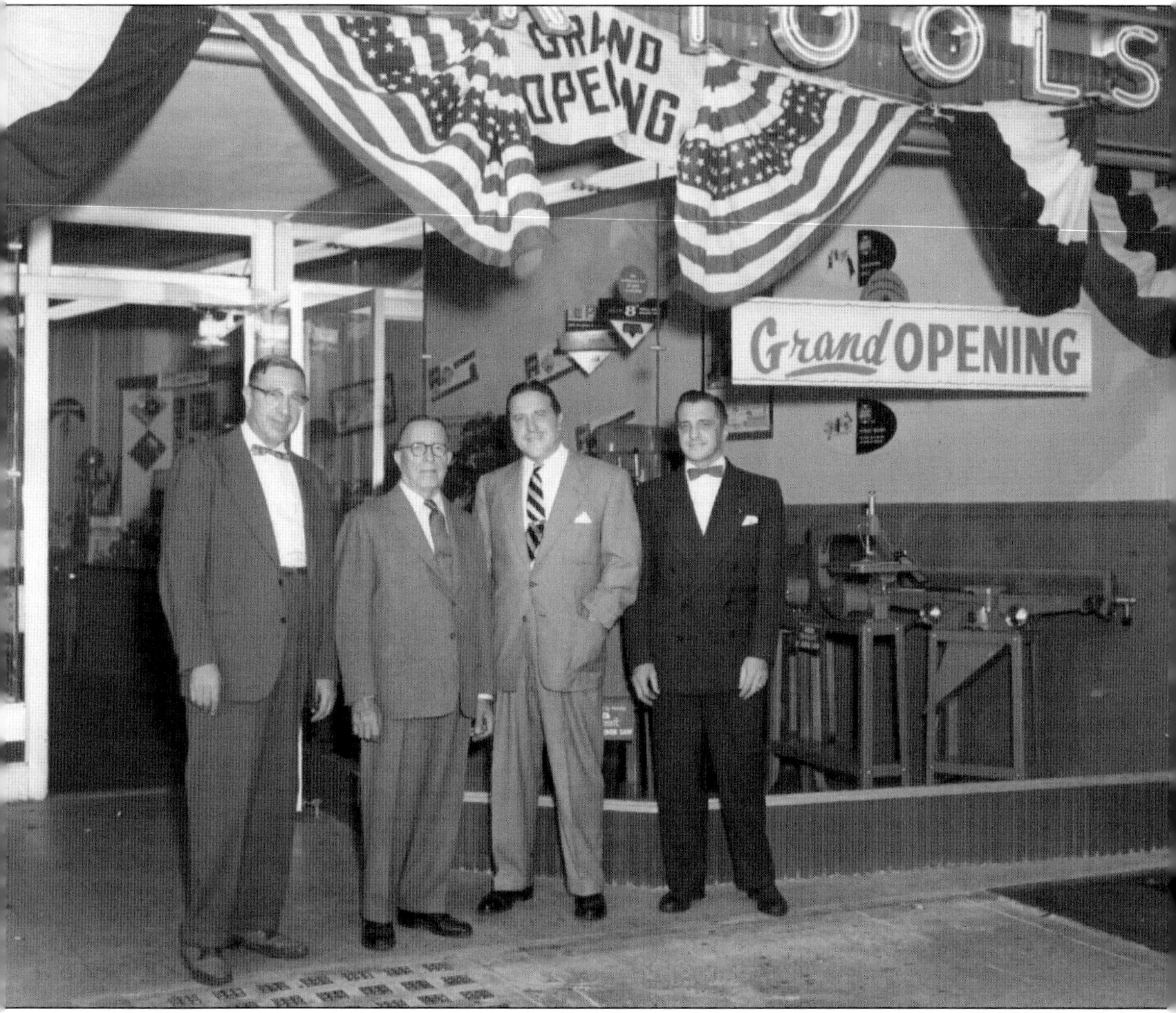

Otto Herrmann, Inc., has been a fixture in the Glendale community since it was first opened in 1921 on Myrtle Avenue at the corner of Sixty-seventh Place. It is reportedly the oldest continually operating retail establishment in Glendale, and it continues to adjust its business plan to meet the changing times. This photograph was taken in 1955, during a renovation and expansion of the business. From left to right are Otto Jr., Otto Sr., and two employees identified as Neil and Gus. (Courtesy of GRHS.)

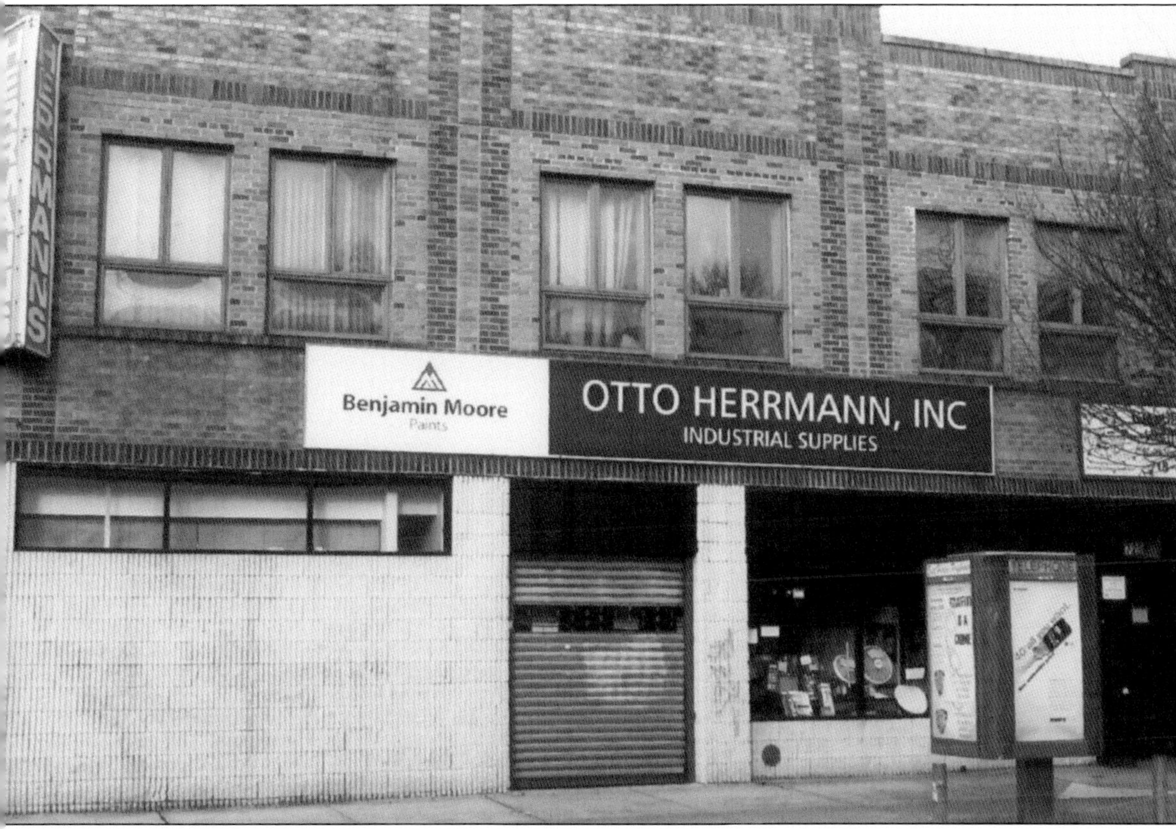

From its humble origins as a paint store in a one-story building, Otto Herrmann, Inc. grew to sell automotive accessories, assorted hardware, power tools, and household appliances, in addition to its original offerings of paint and related materials. Boys growing up in Glendale in the 1950s would look forward to a trip to the store with their parents, so that they could rummage through the drawers of the wooden cabinets lining the ground floor and handle every imaginable type of screw, nail, hinge, bolt, and hardware item in the store's inventory. A trip upstairs to the appliance department might then include a donut or other sweet treat from Fred Schilling and the other salesmen on duty that day. The present-day Otto Hermann, Inc. appears to cater more to wholesale and building trade customers, but the retail store continues to operate on a part-time basis to service home owners through Glendale and the surrounding communities. (Courtesy of the author.)

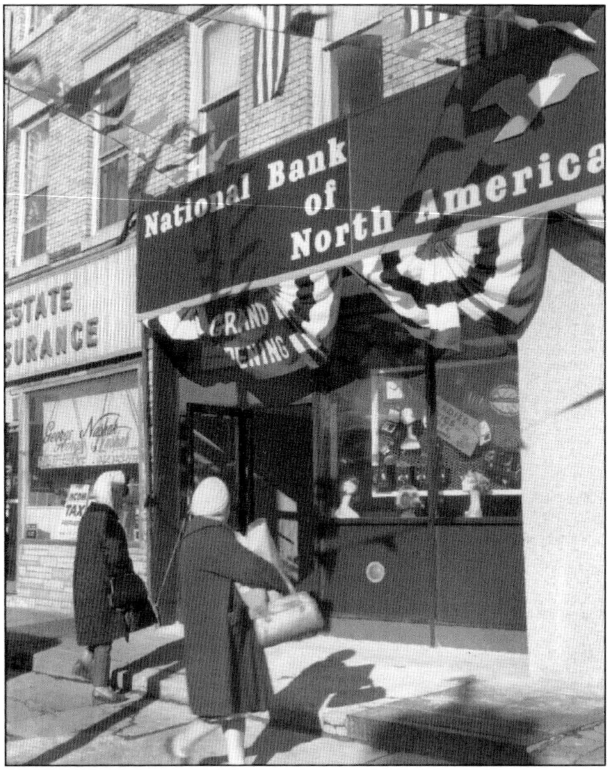

When the National Bank of North America opened its branch at 70-11 Myrtle Avenue in 1971, it attempted to lure in new female customers with an irresistible giveaway. No toasters or irons for these ladies—the bank was going to give them free wigs for opening a new account. (Courtesy of GRHS.)

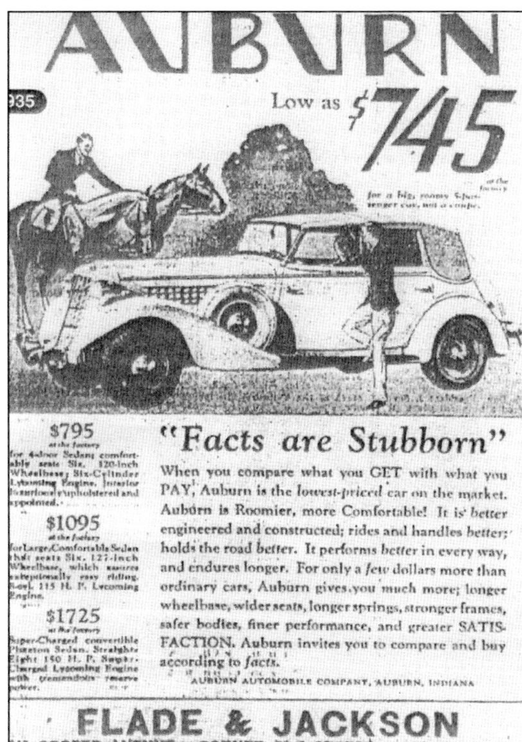

Glendale followed America's love affair with the automobile, and by the 1930s, numerous car dealerships had sprung up throughout the town. This 1935 advertisement highlights the Auburn, which was a bargain at $745 for its basic model. Interestingly, the company's demise was due to its vehicles being perceived as luxury cars that were priced too low to attract the more sophisticated buyers. (Courtesy of GRHS.)

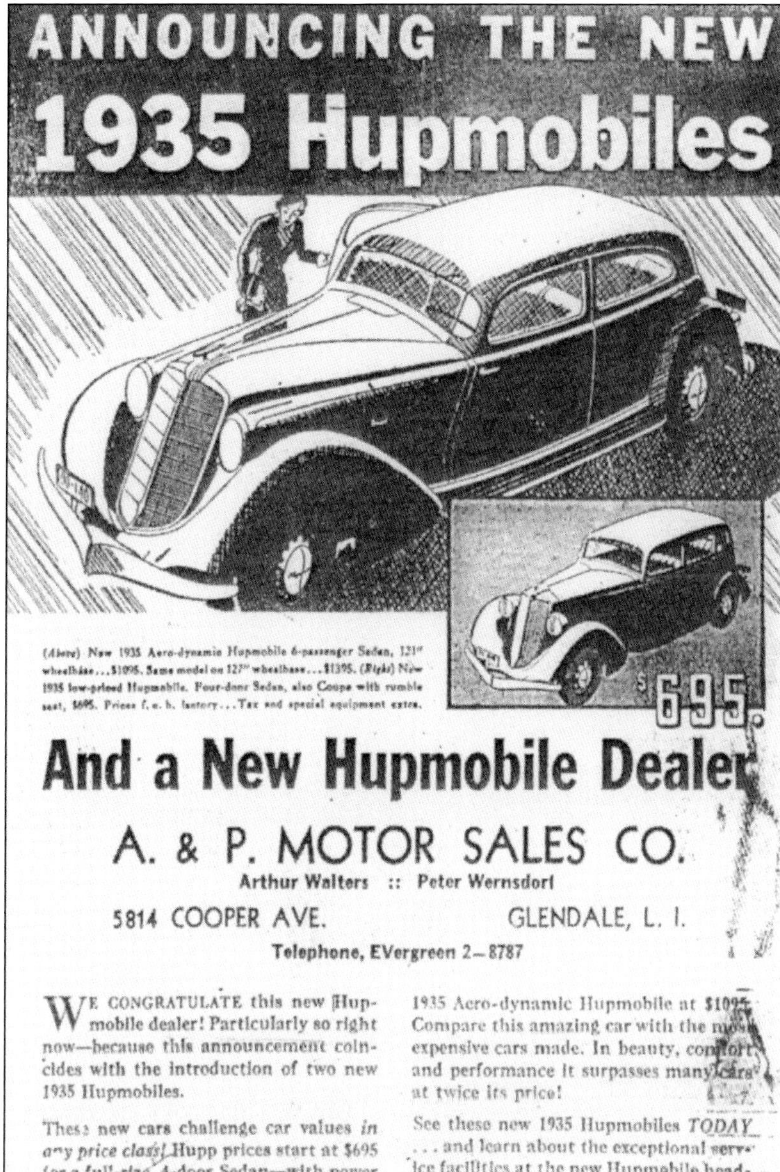

By the time that this 1935 advertisement appeared in local newspapers, the Hupp Motor Corporation was already nearing its end. The early Huppmobiles were among the first mass-produced automobiles in America, and approximately 38,000 vehicles were sold each year during the 1920s. They were known for their streamlined styling and affordable prices, which created a strong market for them in Europe and Great Britain. The extensive use of aluminum wheels and parts kept the vehicle weights low and provided better gas mileage than many of their competitors. This made them even more attractive to drivers paying high gas prices on the European continent. Unfortunately, the Great Depression marked the end of many independent automobile manufacturers, but the Hupp Corporation went on to manufacture automotive parts, kitchen equipment, and electronics. (Courtesy of GRHS.)

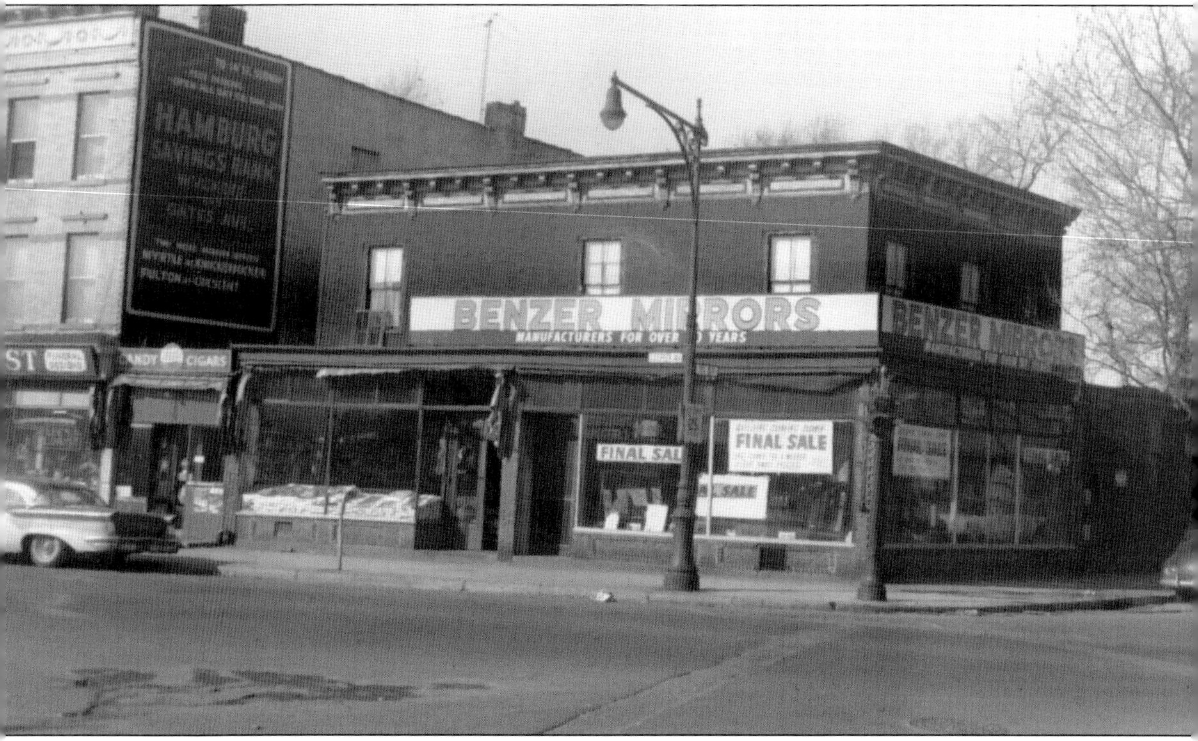

Beneath the facade of this corner building, located at Cooper Avenue and Seventy-first Street, lies an old building with its own history as part of early Glendale. From 1880 to 1885, it housed the Old Homestead Hotel & Beer Garden, one of the many popular diversions that Glendale offered to the hardworking residents of nearby Brooklyn. The building has since been torn down to make way for another funeral home, but this photograph from 1960 shows it in one of its many incarnations as a glass business. Benzer Mirrors is fondly remembered by Glendale residents for the quality of its products. The small candy and cigar store to its left was typical of those found on most of the commercial streets of Glendale for many years, and the building on the left side of the picture still houses a florist. (Courtesy of GRHS.)

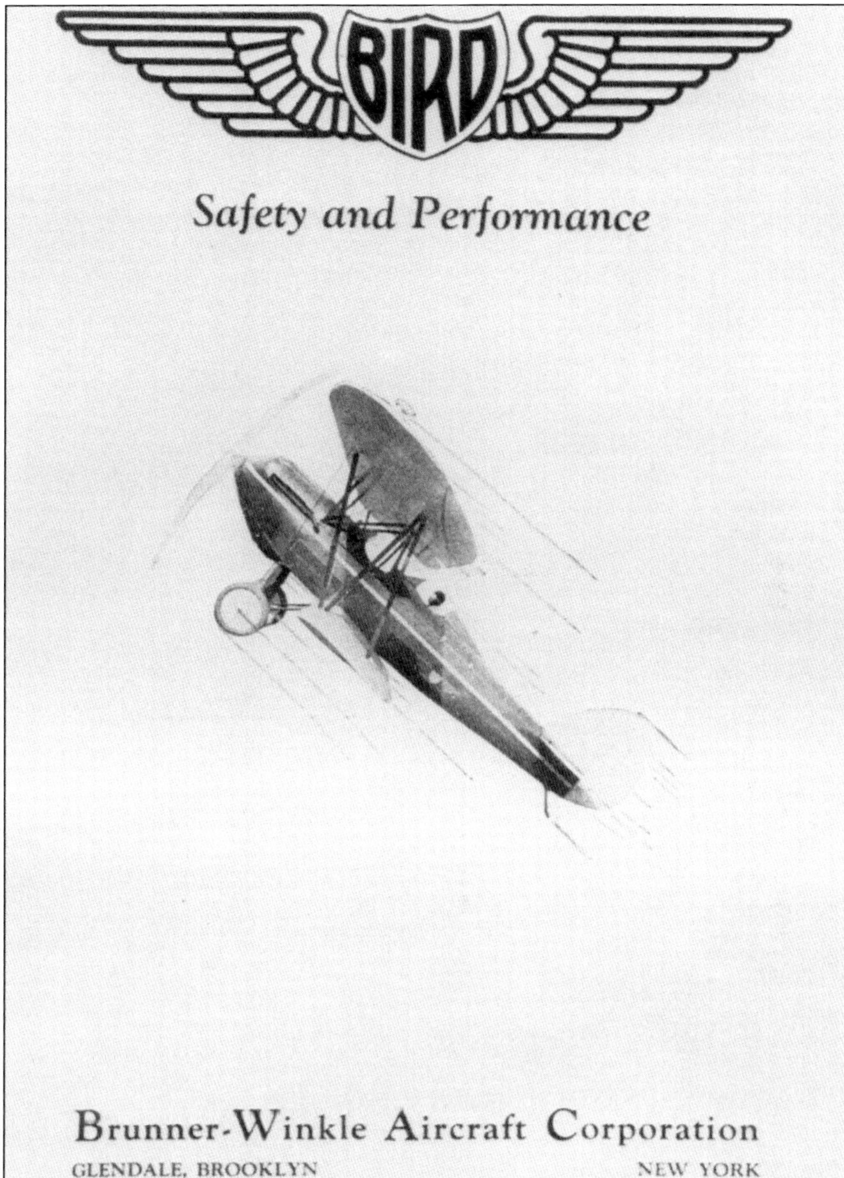

Certain to surprise most people is the fact that airplanes were actually manufactured in Glendale. The Brunner-Winkle Company, formed in 1926 as the Royal Aircraft Company, was located at Roosevelt Field on Long Island. A. Brunner and William Winkle renamed the company and moved its headquarters to 17 Haverkamp Street, near the Eightieth Street industrial area in Glendale, in 1928. A later reorganization saw the company's name changed to Bird Aircraft Company after its most popular model, the Bird. The plane was known for its ability to take off on a short runway and quickly gain altitude. It could become airborne in a distance of only 100 feet and leave the ground going only 40 miles per hour. Charles Lindbergh was so impressed with the Bird aircraft that he bought one for his wife, Anne Morrow Lindbergh. The factory price in those days was $4,095. Of the 220 aircraft made at that time, 70 are known to still be in existence. Pictured here on the cover of the company's catalogue is the Bird, demonstrating its impressive rate of climb. (Courtesy of GRHS.)

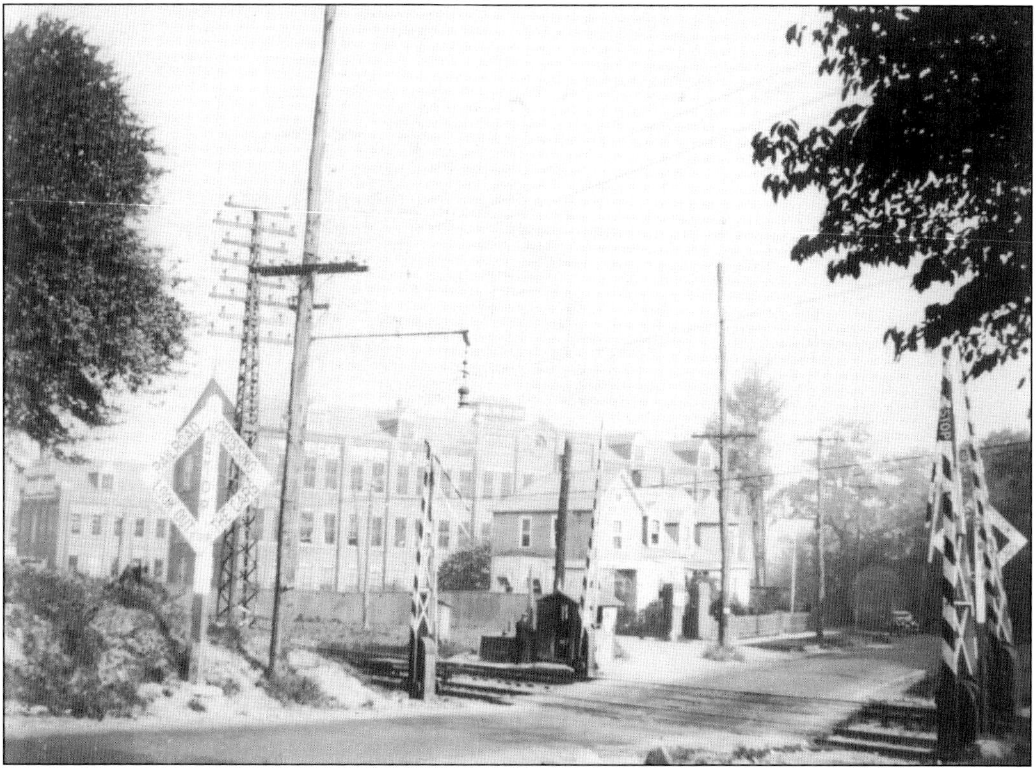

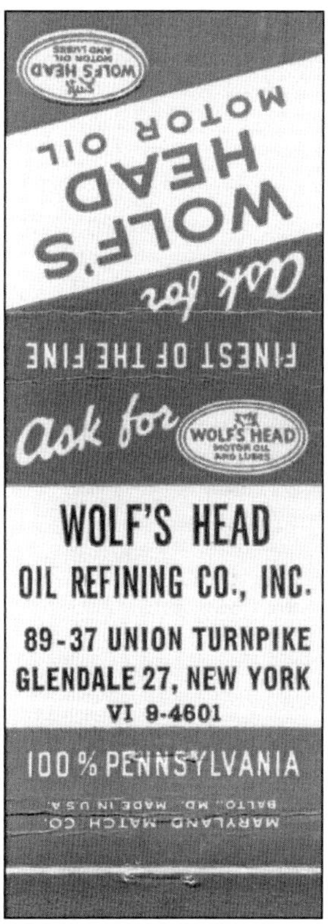

Another lost chapter of the Atlas Terminal story is Wickes Ribbon Company, which was located near the railroad crossing at Trotting Course Lane, as seen in this 1922 photograph. Companies like Wickes supplied the rapidly growing garment industry of New York City in the early 20th century, but there is no further mention of the company in the records of later years. (Courtesy of Queens Borough Public Library.)

The world-famous Wolf's Head Motor Oil Company, founded in 1879 in Pennsylvania, maintained a refining facility and distribution center in Glendale during the 1950s. They followed a popular trend of the day and gave out promotional matchbooks to advertise their products and promote their company slogan, "Finest of the Fine." (Courtesy of the author.)

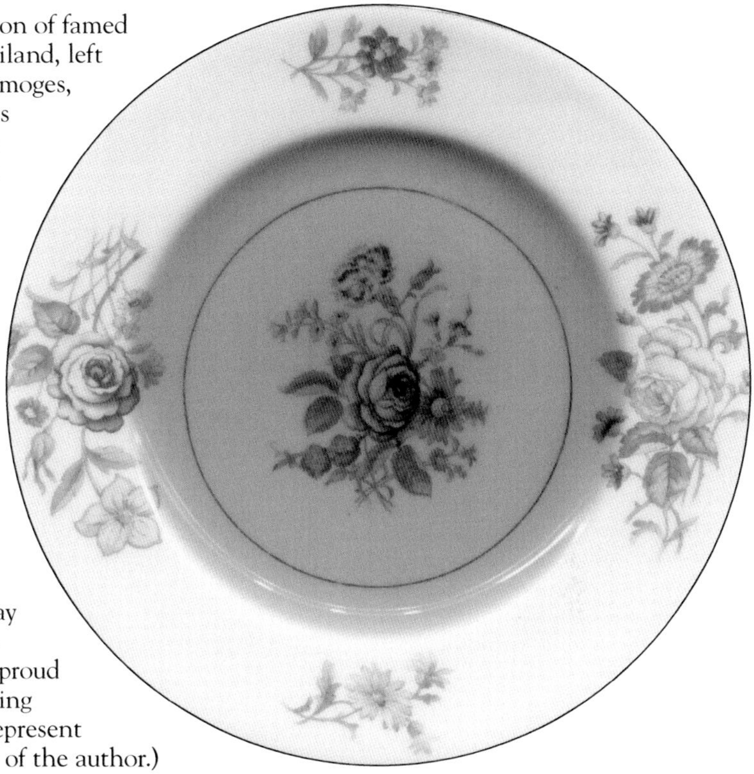

Theodore Haviland, the son of famed china maker Charles Haviland, left his father's company in Limoges, France, in 1893 to start his own business. He was one of several family members to become known for producing fine china, and he moved his company from France to the United States in 1936. That move made the company part of the growing Glendale industrial community until the manufacturing operation closed down in 1957. Haviland china continues to be known throughout the world today for its quality and delicate floral patterns, and it is a proud symbol of the manufacturing excellence that came to represent Glendale. (Both, courtesy of the author.)

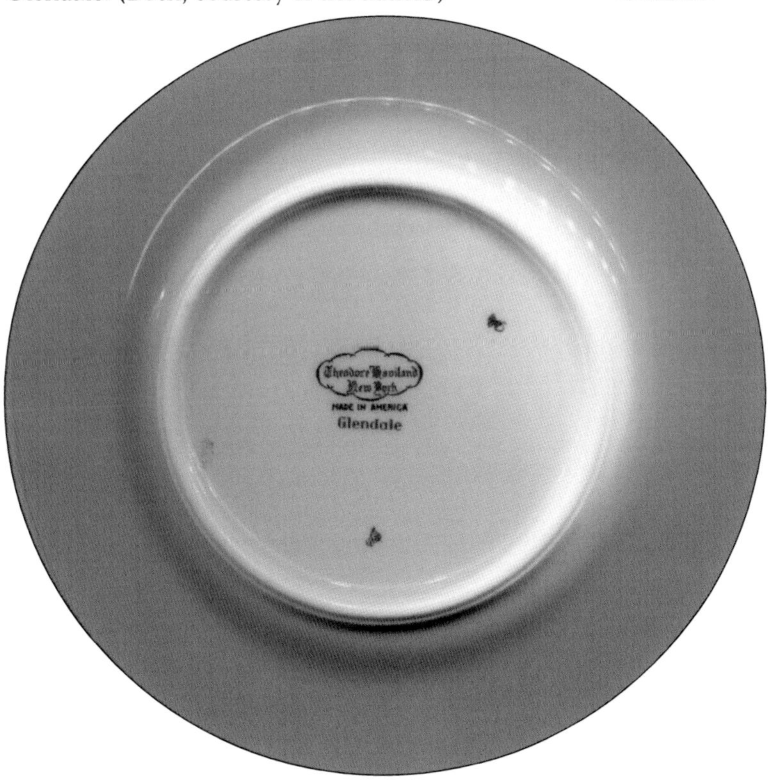

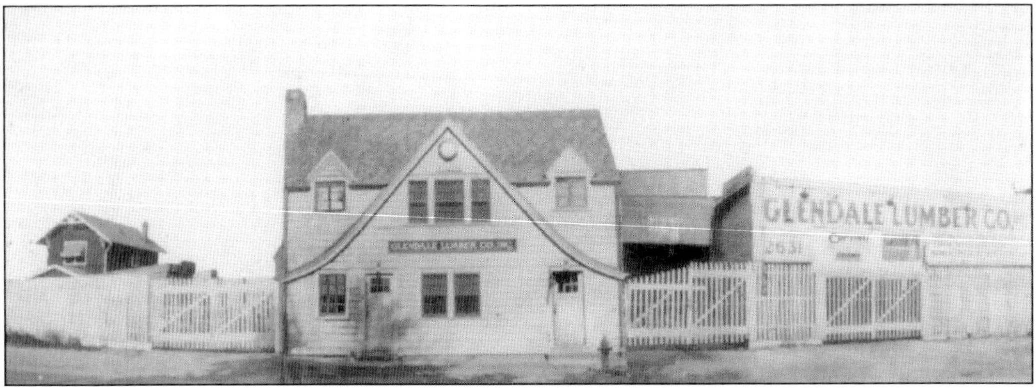

Glendale Lumber Company was founded in 1920 by Edward Wagner and conducted business on Procter Street, which later became Seventy-third Place. Amazingly, members of the Wagner family continue to operate the business and will be celebrating their 100th anniversary in 2020. In addition to being a vital part of the Glendale community, members of the Wagner family served with pride in the armed forces from World War II through the Vietnam era. Edward's grandson Jack was a decorated soldier with two Purple Hearts earned during World War II. Seen here are the original building from the company's early days and an equally vintage delivery truck. (Both, courtesy of Lance Wagner.)

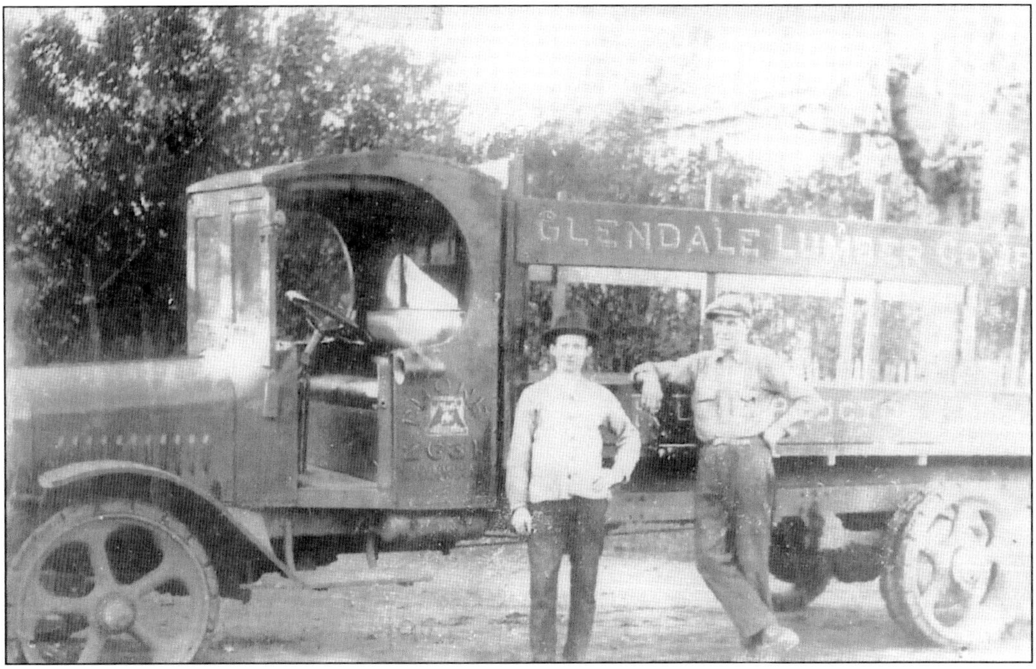

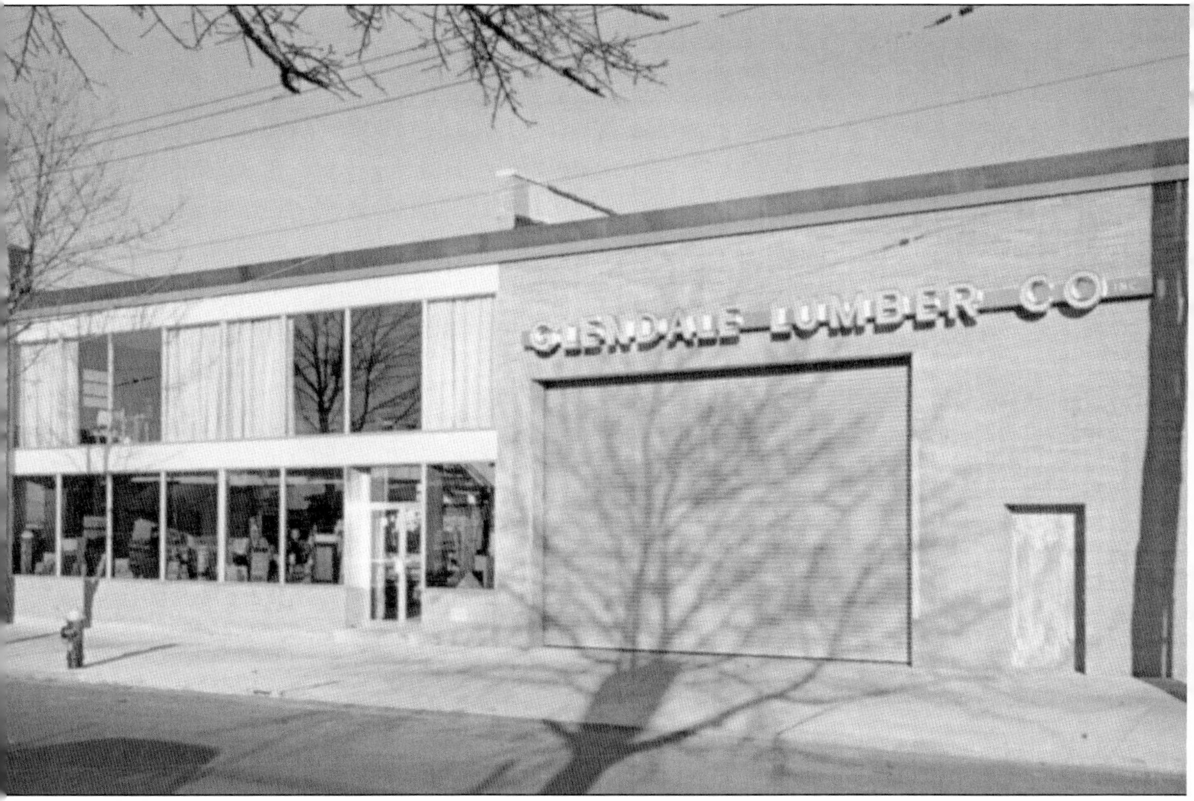

In 1960, Glendale Lumber was all but destroyed by a fire that engulfed the office and warehouse. The business was completely rebuilt, and the new facility was opened for business in 1961. It remains one of the oldest family-run businesses of its type and is ranked as one of the premier suppliers in the New York Metropolitan area, now being run by a fifth generation of the Wagner family. The postcard commemorates the new showroom and warehouse. (Courtesy of Lance Wagner.)

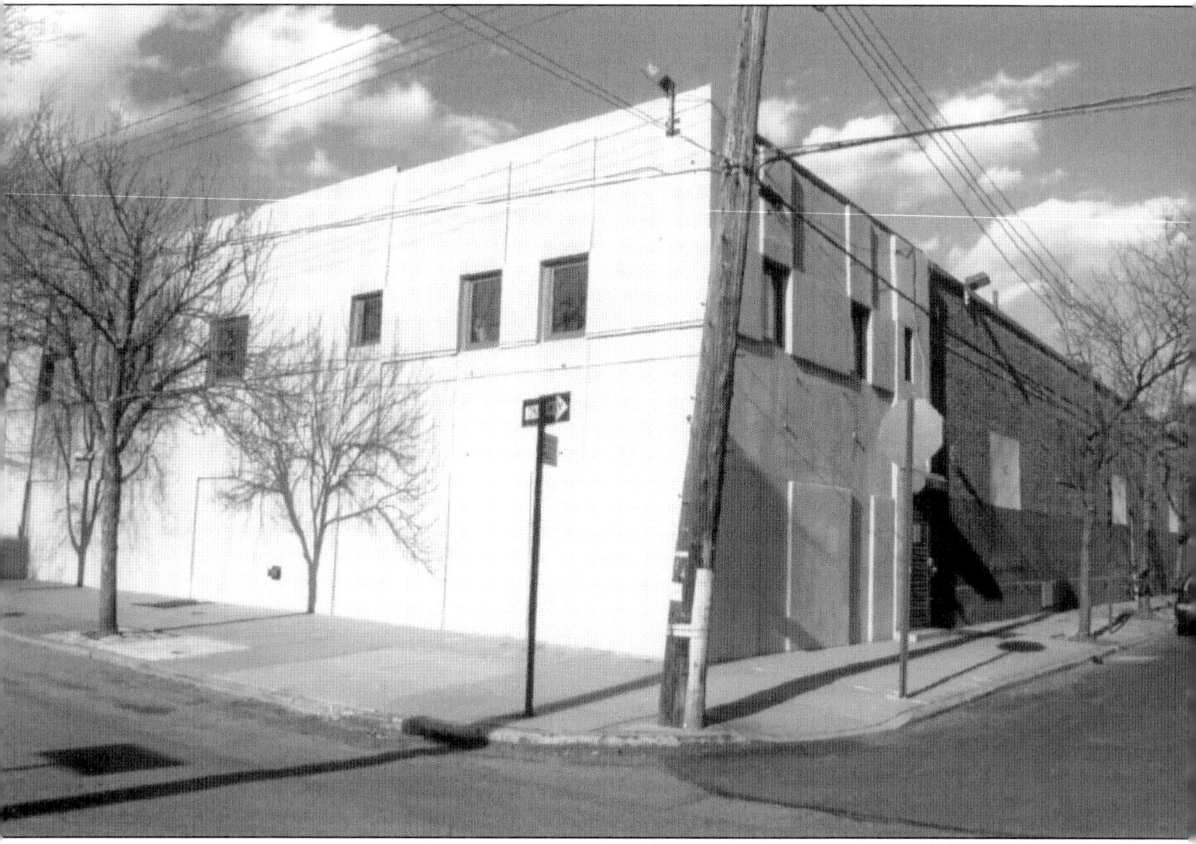

It has been a long time since Glendale was known for its picnic parks and small breweries, but part of that tradition is being revived in this nondescript building on Seventy-seventh Avenue and Seventy-sixth Street. It formerly housed the Kliegman Bros. laundry and dry cleaning business and, later, an imported food distributor. After a massive cleanup effort to remove hazardous waste from cleaning chemicals that are believed to have polluted the soil due to leaks in two storage tanks, the building now houses the Finback Brewery Company. The brewery produces a variety of specialty beers in small lots in the European tradition. It was founded by two college friends from Massachusetts, and they plan to open the Glendale facility to the public for beer tastings and other events that will help to incorporate it into the community and keep Glendale's beer-making tradition alive. (Courtesy of the author.)

Three

The Cemetery Belt

In 1847, New York State passed a law called the State Rural Cemeteries Act that sought to prevent the construction of any more cemeteries in Manhattan. A deadline was set for 1850, after which no further cemetery development would be allowed, but this created a problem because of the rapid population growth that New York City was experiencing. Developers in the cemetery industry began to look outside of the Manhattan limits for available land, and while parts of Westchester and Rockland Counties were also available, they seem to have preferred areas to the east, which included Brooklyn and Queens.

At that time, Glendale was in the process of evolving from a farming community to more of a residential and industrial area, but it still had large amounts of undeveloped land. As cemetery operators began to buy up much of this land, the town soon became almost surrounded by more than 10 cemeteries, occupying land that was adjacent to Metropolitan Avenue on the north and on both sides of Cypress Hills Street to the south. Forest Park and the Interboro Parkway would later be built in that general area as well.

Today, any drive through Glendale passes through areas surrounded by well-kept cemetery grounds, which in some ways contribute to the rural atmosphere of the town. Families of all faiths have the opportunity to choose the nonsectarian Cypress Hills Cemetery for burial of their loved ones or one of the many others catering to people of the Jewish, Catholic, Lutheran, and other Christian faiths. Among the notable people whose final resting places are in Glendale are actress Mae West, baseball great Jackie Robinson, and legendary magician Harry Houdini.

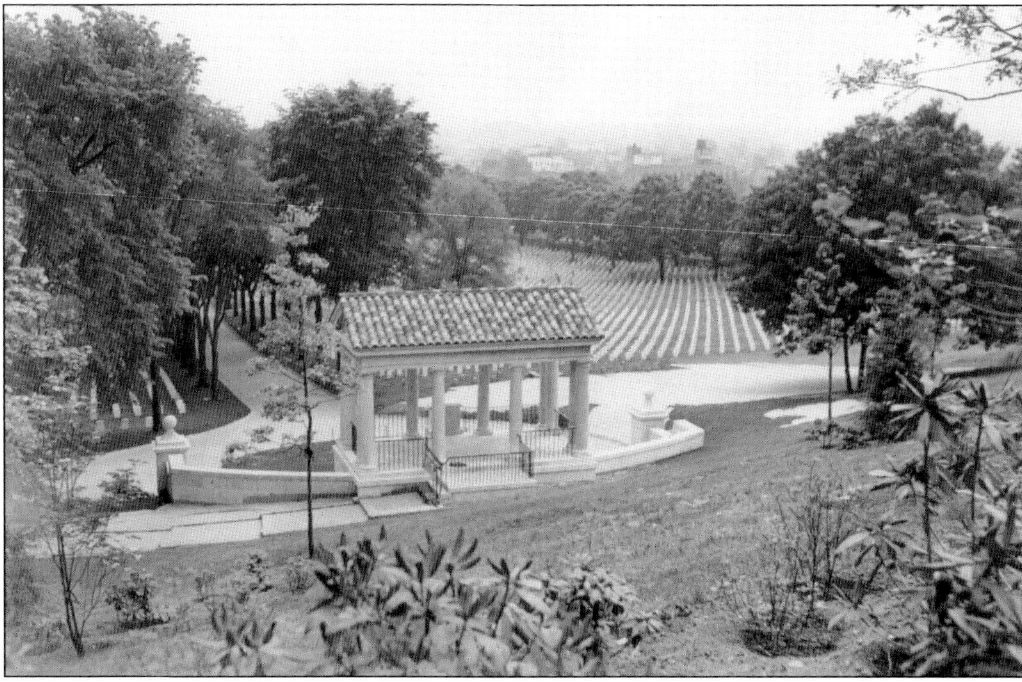

This 1939 photograph shows the beautiful landscaping throughout the Cypress Hills Cemetery and the rostrum built near the section dedicated to veterans' gravesites. Much of this work was done as part of a Works Progress Administration (WPA) project. (Courtesy of GRHS.)

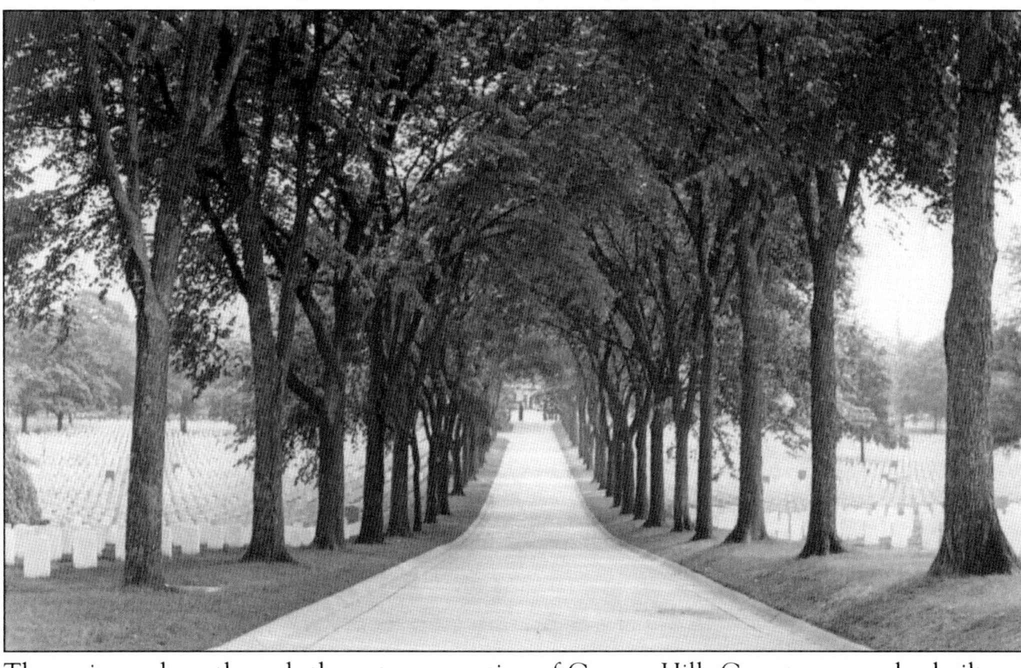

The main roadway through the veterans section of Cypress Hills Cemetery was also built as a WPA project, as seen in this additional 1939 photograph. In later years, as nearby Long Island developed and less space was available in Glendale, additional land for veterans' burials was set aside in the towns of Melville and Calverton. (Courtesy of GRHS.)

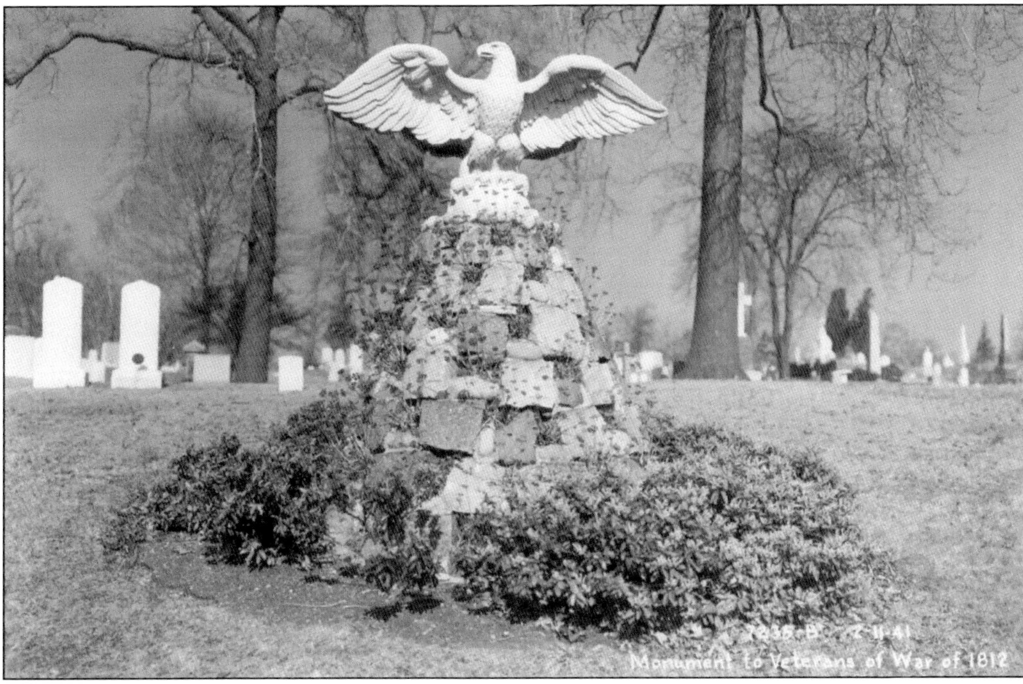

The Cypress Hills Cemetery also honors the war dead from previous conflicts where American service personnel gave their lives. This eagle-topped monument, seen here in a 1941 photograph, honors the veterans of the War of 1812. (Courtesy of GRHS.)

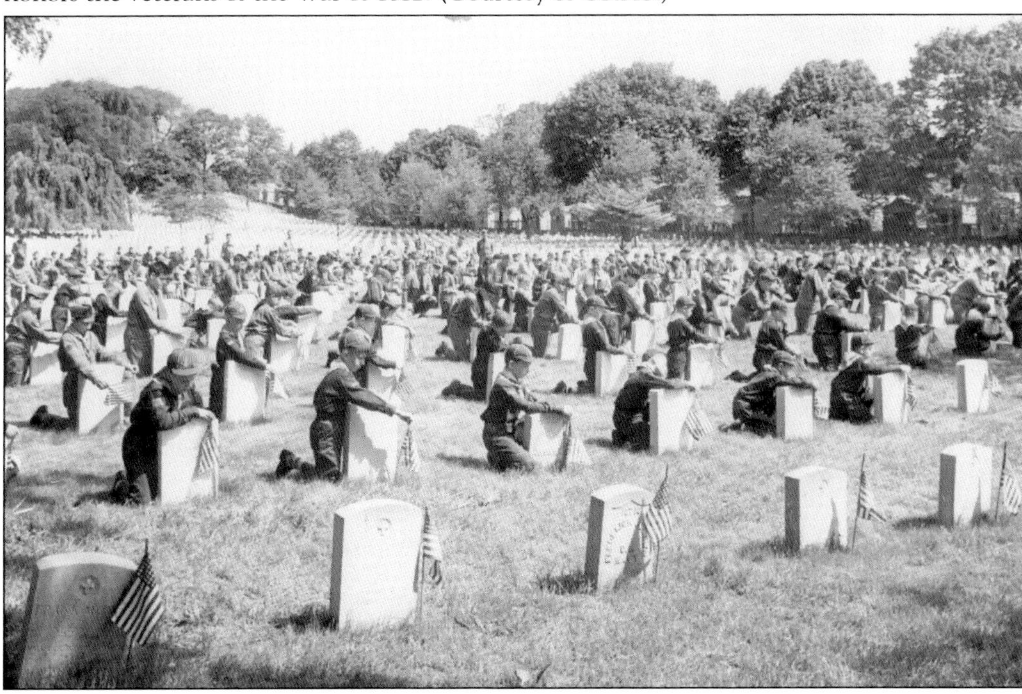

A long-standing tradition in many areas is to place flags on the graves of veterans on Memorial Day and the other holidays honoring military personnel. This 1953 photograph features a group of Cub Scouts performing that service at Cypress Hills Cemetery. (Courtesy of GRHS.)

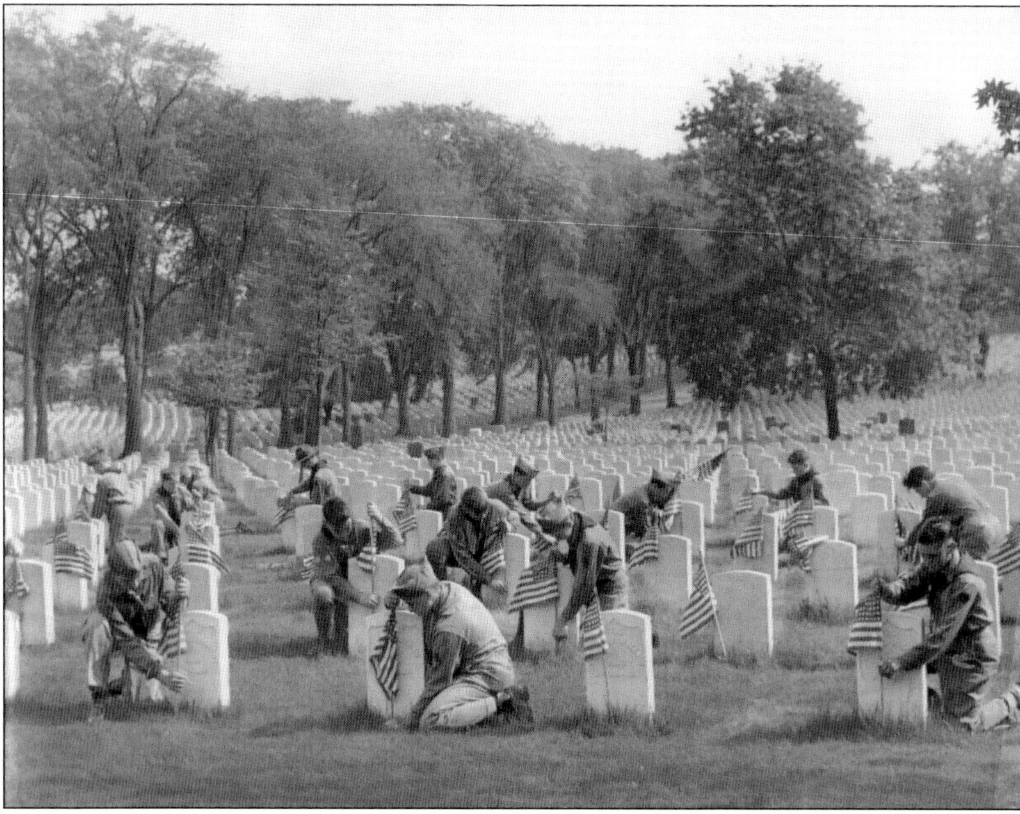

This second view of Scouts honoring veterans on Memorial Day is from 1945 and gives some indication of just how large the veterans section is at Cypress Hills Cemetery. The cemetery derived its name from the large stands of cypress trees that line its roadways. (Courtesy of GRHS.)

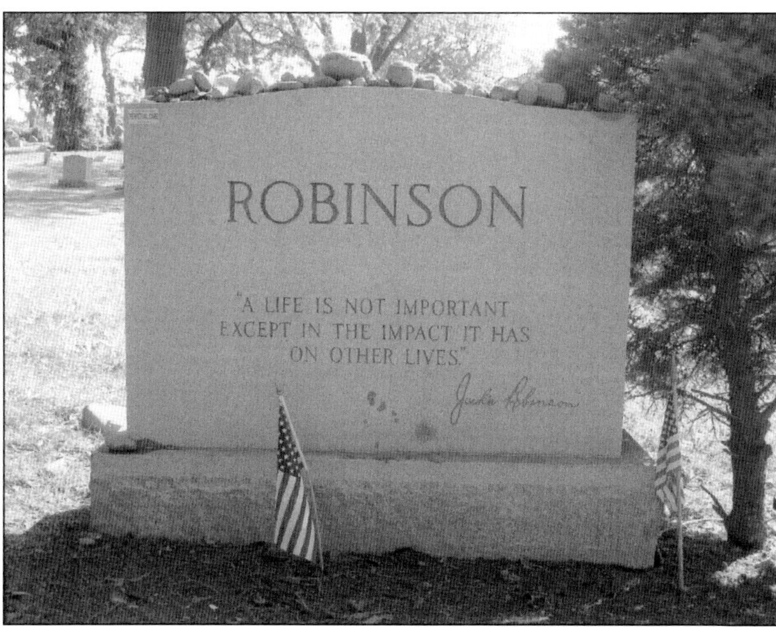

Baseball great Jackie Robinson, who broke baseball's color barrier, passed away in 1972 and is buried in the Cypress Hills Cemetery in Glendale. The nearby Interboro Parkway was renamed in his honor in 1997 and is now the Jackie Robinson Parkway. (Courtesy of the author.)

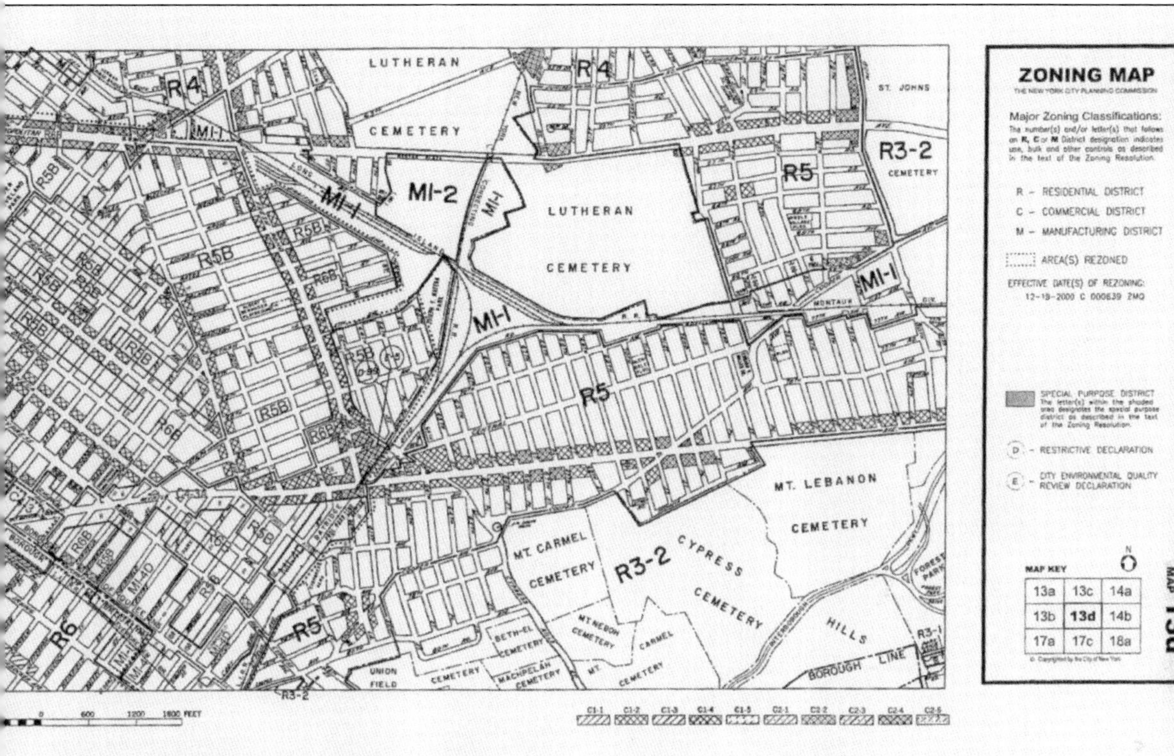

Glendale's zoning restrictions were changed just before this map was prepared by the New York City Planning Commission in 2000. It presents a vivid picture of how the cemeteries have prevented more industrial development of Glendale and why the term "cemetery belt" was created to describe the area surrounding the community. Metropolitan Avenue, bracketed by the Lutheran Cemetery, is on the top of the map, and Myrtle Avenue runs from left to right in the bottom half, showing no fewer than nine different cemeteries. The western border of Forest Park is seen in the lower right, with the renamed Jackie Robinson Parkway running right through Cypress Hills Cemetery. There was some controversy when the parkway was first built because its construction required the disinterment and reburial of hundreds of bodies that were buried along the proposed parkway route. (Courtesy of GRHS.)

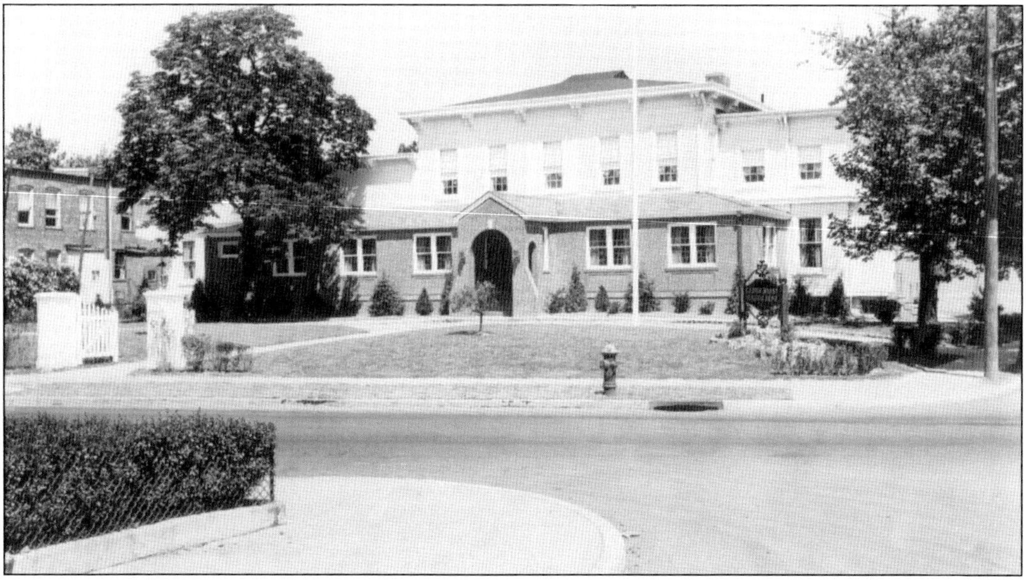

One of the premier funeral establishments in the Glendale area is the George Werst Funeral Home, seen here in 1935. The building dates back to the mid-1800s, when it was part of a plantation belonging to the Liggett & Myers Tobacco family. In the early 20th century, it was the home of a member of the Holzhauser family, and then, in 1910, it was purchased by William Hafner for his residence. (Courtesy of GRHS.)

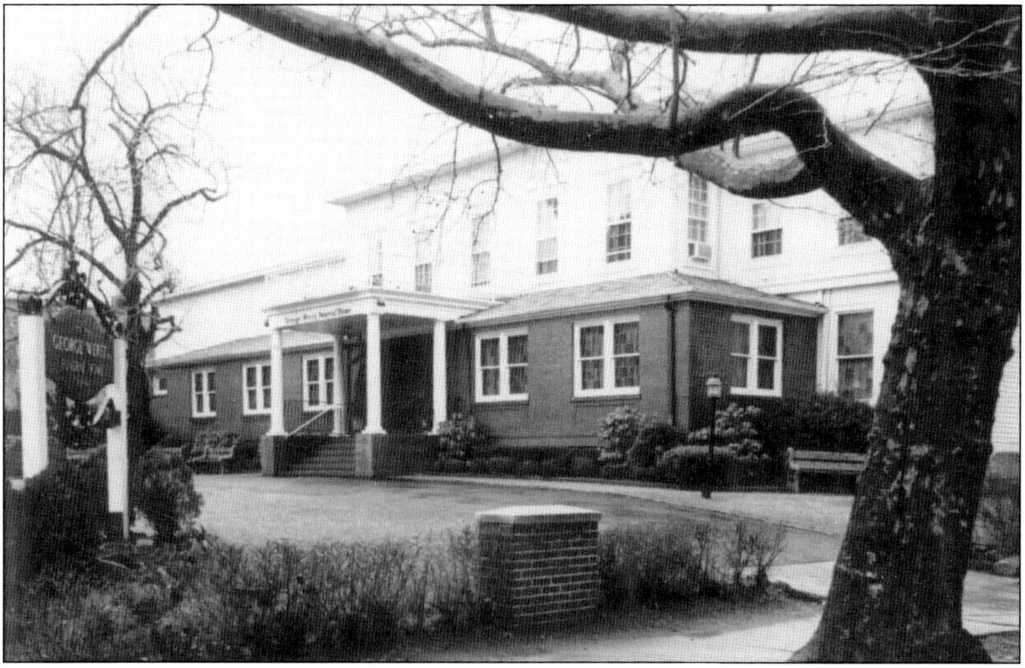

In the early years, the building was modified several times, and by the time of the Roaring Twenties, it was used as a clubhouse for the Glendale Squire Club. It was purchased in 1935 by George Werst and renovated again to make it more suitable as a funeral establishment. Most of the building remains unchanged from the time when this photograph was taken in 1976. (Courtesy of GRHS.)

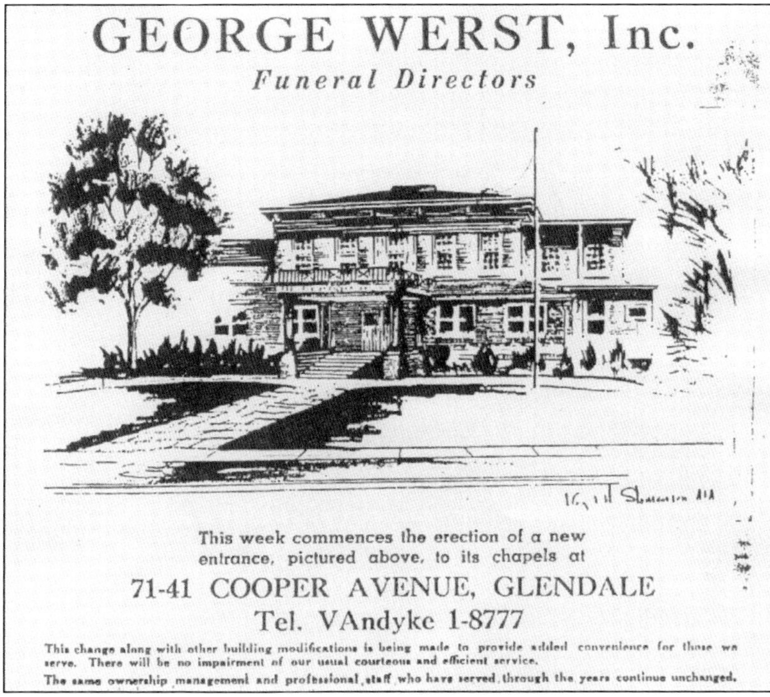

This 1960 advertisement from the *Ridgewood Times* indicates that the entrance has been enlarged and shows how it differs from the 1935 photograph. Note that the old telephone exchange from the days when they began with a word is "Vandyke," which was used to pay tribute to the Dutch origins of the area that became Glendale. (Courtesy of GRHS.)

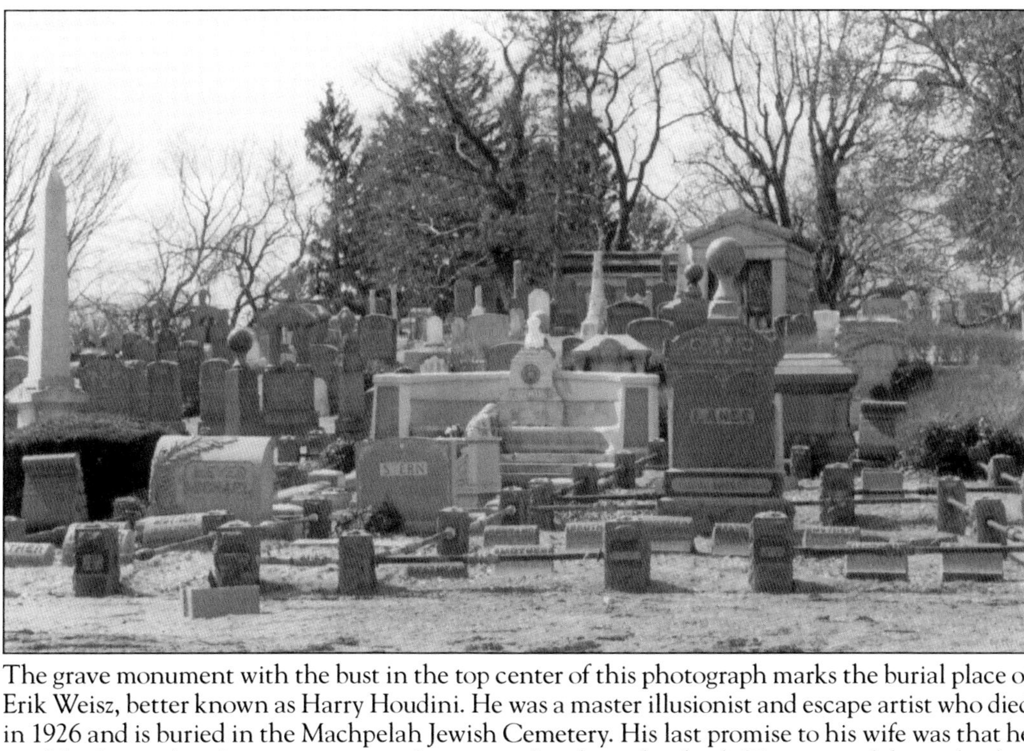

The grave monument with the bust in the top center of this photograph marks the burial place of Erik Weisz, better known as Harry Houdini. He was a master illusionist and escape artist who died in 1926 and is buried in the Machpelah Jewish Cemetery. His last promise to his wife was that he would achieve the ultimate escape and return to her from the dead. (Courtesy of the author.)

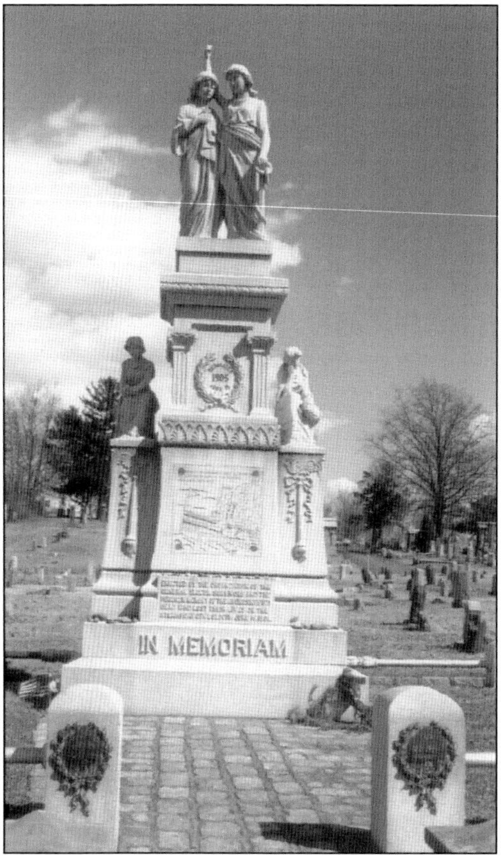

The steamship *General Slocum* left a pier in lower New York on June 15, 1904, loaded with members of various German heritage societies from Glendale and other New York City communities. They were bound for the North Shore of Long Island for a picnic outing, but the ship caught fire while still in the East River. Flames swept through the ship before the captain ran it aground near the Bronx shore, and 1,020 passengers lost their lives in the catastrophe. This monument near the Glendale entrance to the All Faiths Cemetery was erected in remembrance of those who were lost that day and features a graphic engraving of the ship in flames. (Both, courtesy of the author.)

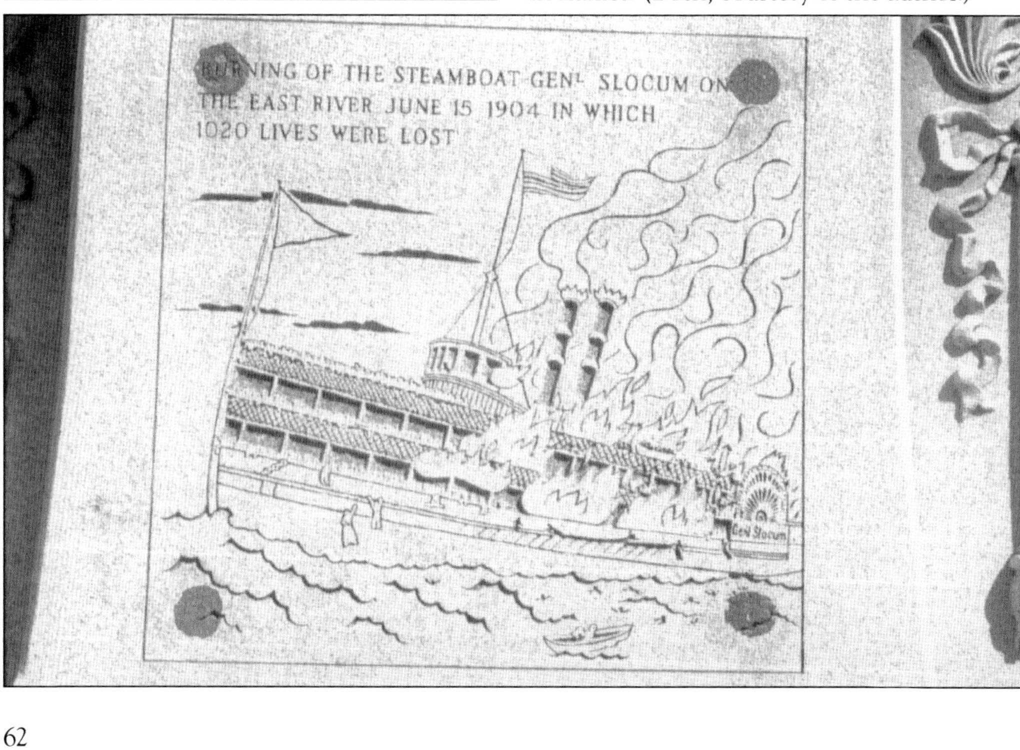

Four

Serving the Community

Glendale, like so many other old towns across the United States, places a high value on the concept of service to the community. There was a spirit of volunteerism that characterized its early days, as people stepped up and did what they could to help the community grow and help their neighbors. Through two world wars, Glendale residents served their country proudly, and many gave their lives in defense of our nation's freedom. The sacrifices of people from Glendale who served in those wars and in every other major conflict are commemorated throughout the community by the many monuments erected at various places in the town.

The people of Glendale placed a high priority on the education of their children and worked with the New York City school system to offer students a wide range of choices. Civic associations and numerous other organizations representing different cultural, ethnic, and business interests sprang up to give members of specific groups a voice in the community. The 104th Police Precinct and the Fire Department Engine Company No. 286 are looked upon as neighbors by the residents of Glendale and partners in protecting the community and preserving the rural charm and quality of life in this lovely part of New York City.

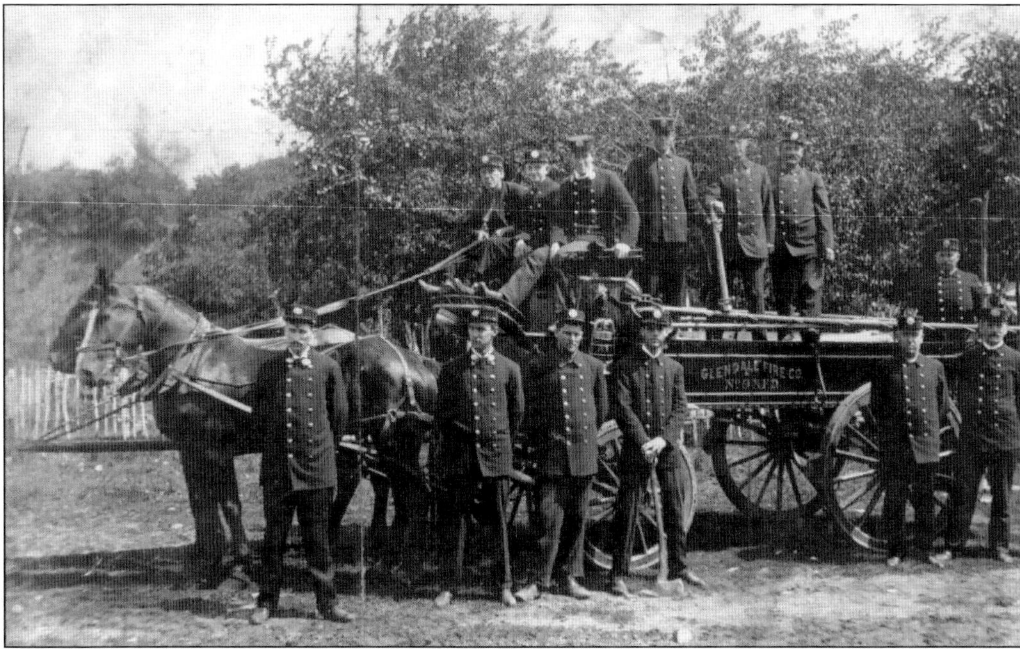

These two photographs from 1900 (above) and 1913 (below) show the men of the Glendale Fire Department, which was organized in 1896 and disbanded in 1913 when the New York City Fire Department took over their duties. In the days when an adequate water supply was not always available to fight fires, the brave volunteers of Engine Company No. 9 protected the Glendale community. Above is their original horse-drawn wagon, with pump handles on the side. The photograph below shows the evolution of firefighting equipment in 1913, with the steam-powered pumper in the background. (Both, courtesy of GRHS.)

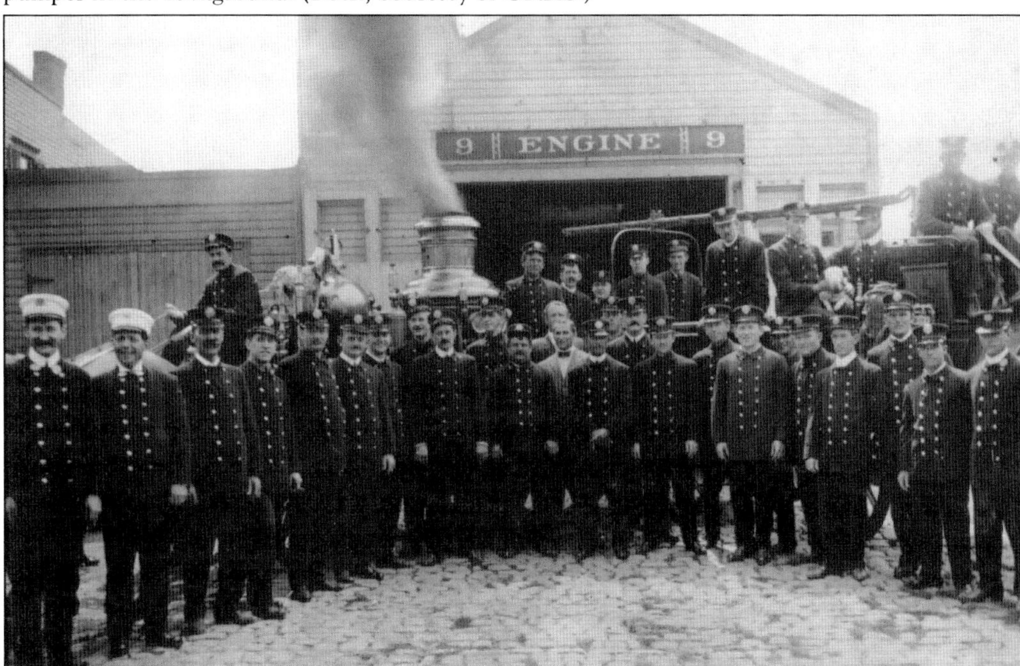

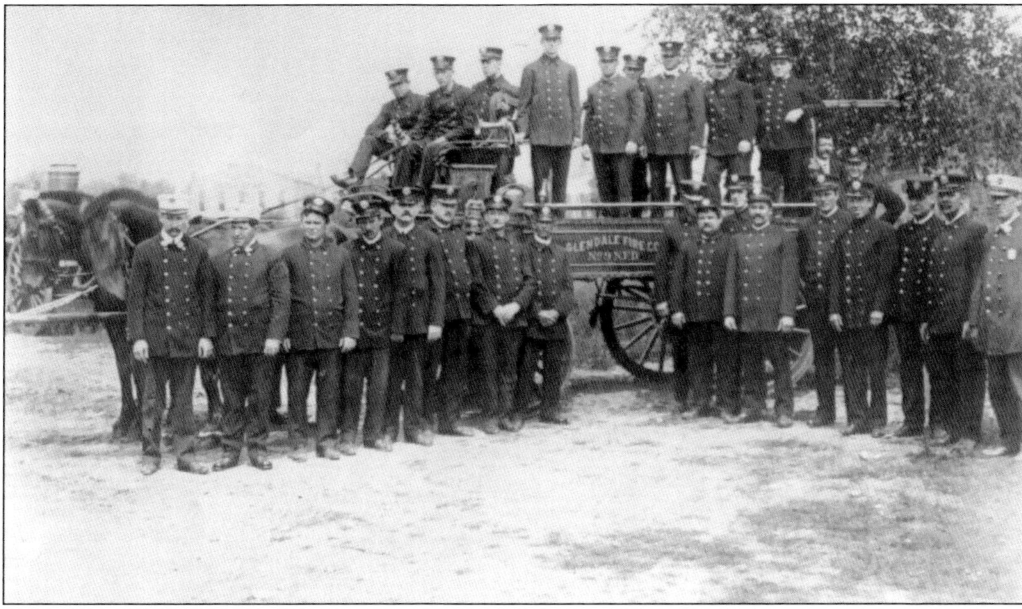

In this photograph, the old name *Newtown* is used because when the fire company was first formed, Engine Company No. 9 was part of the larger organization responsible for Glendale and the other communities that made up the town of Newtown. (Courtesy of GRHS.)

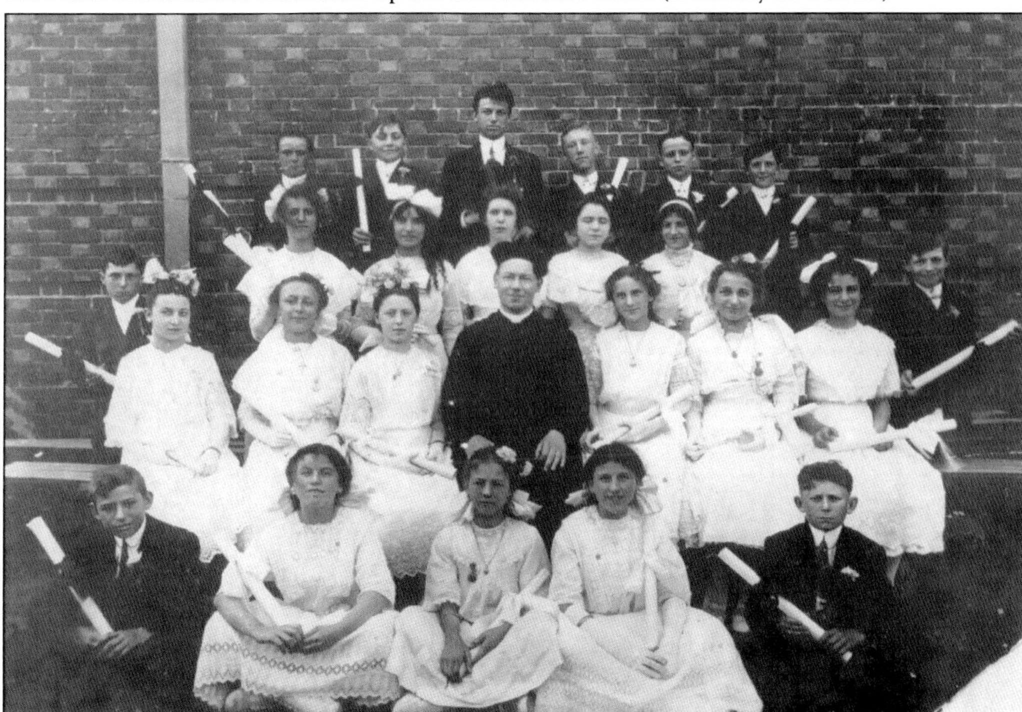

The St. Pancras parochial school graduating class of 1912 is shown here, and though he is unidentified in the photograph, the priest in the middle of the group may be Fr. Francis O. Siegelack, the first pastor. The church and school were once housed in the same building until the church was moved out of the basement in 1909. (Courtesy of GRHS.)

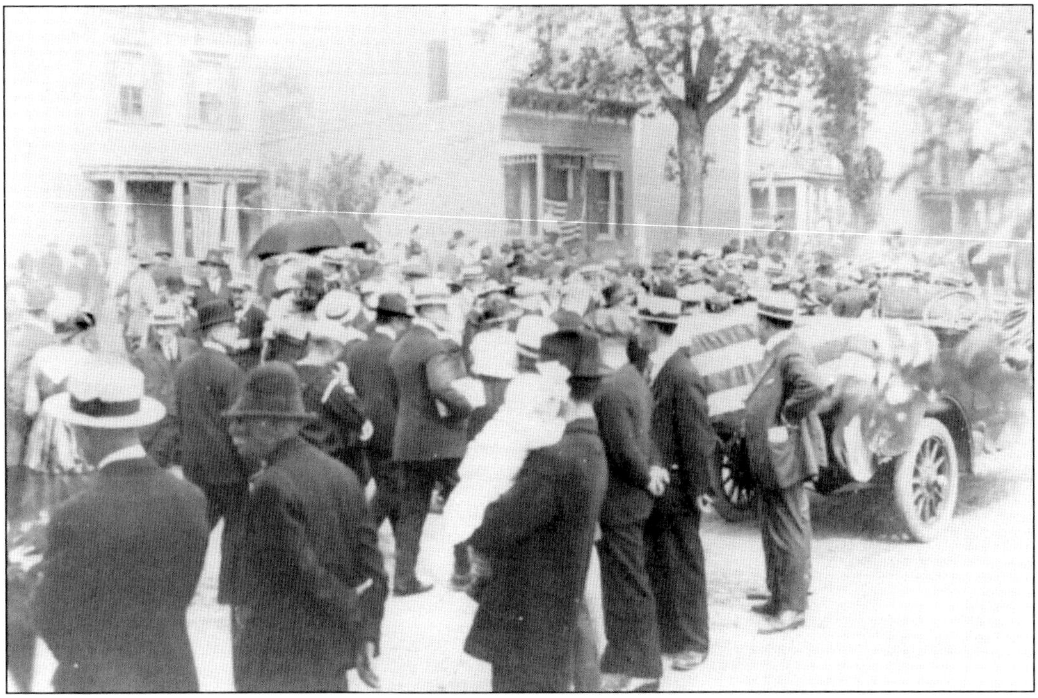

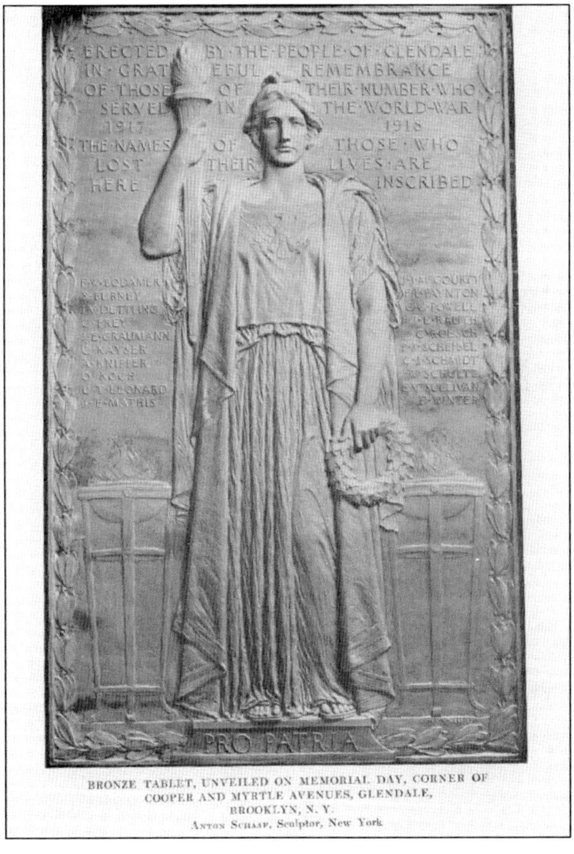

This 1917 photograph shows World War I draftees from the Glendale community marching off to war. An early motorcar draped with a flag is seen leading their march up an unidentified street. Many would not return, and their names are inscribed on the honor roll of the World War I memorial dedicated after the war in 1922. (Courtesy of GRHS.)

The World War I memorial and honor roll erected at the intersection of Cooper and Myrtle Avenues is shown in this 1922 photograph. For many years, a small cannon stood on the grass just in front of the tablet, but it was later removed. During the holiday season, a Christmas tree is now placed there and decorated in memory of the sacrifices made by Glendale families. (Courtesy of GRHS.)

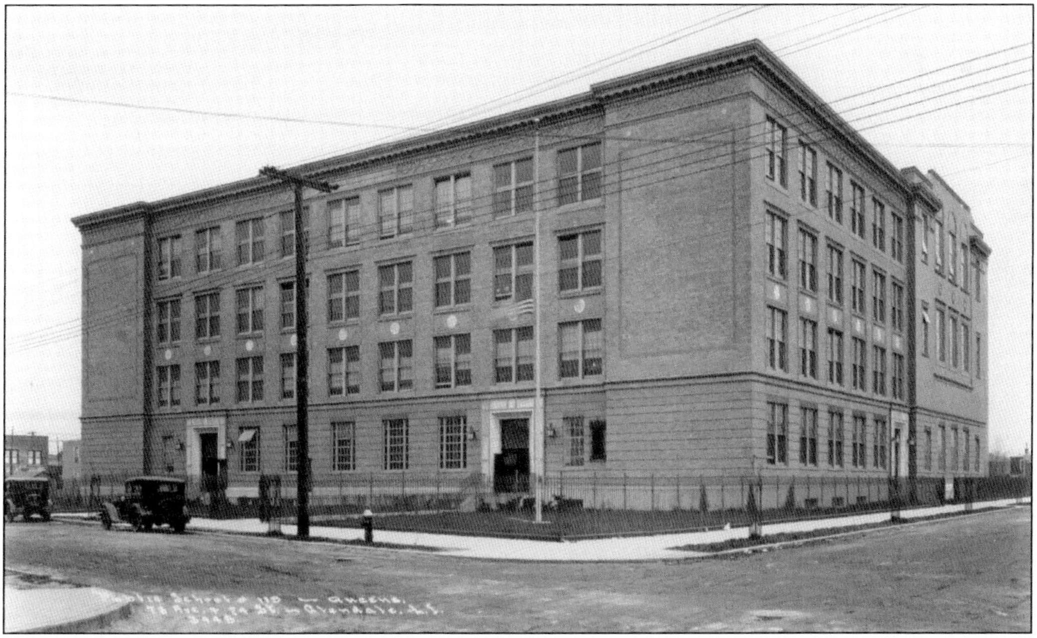

This fortress-like edifice is Public School No. 119, seen around the time it was built in 1929. It is located at the intersection of Seventy-eighth Avenue and Seventy-fifth Street and taught kindergarten through eighth grade until 1961. At that time, it was converted to a junior high school, teaching grades seven through nine to children from Glendale and the adjacent communities of Ridgewood and Middle Village. (Courtesy of GRHS.)

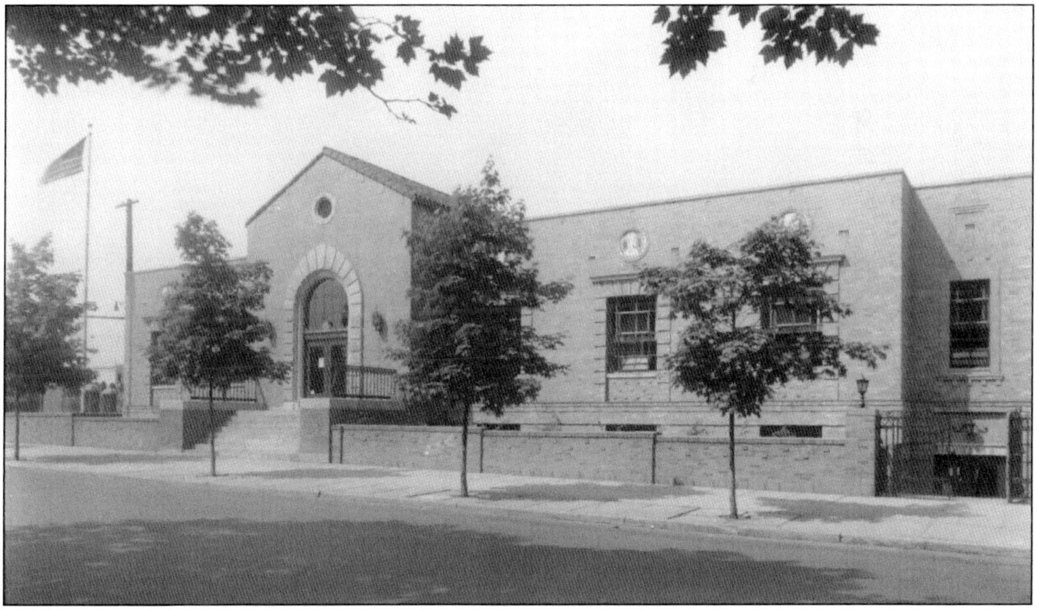

The first library service in Glendale was established in 1911 and designated the Glendale Branch, but it was located in a shoe store on Myrtle Avenue near Cooper Avenue. Over the years, it was moved to a variety of locations, one of which was nothing more than a shack attached to a pickle factory. The present library, shown here, was built in 1937 as part of a WPA project. (Courtesy of GRHS.)

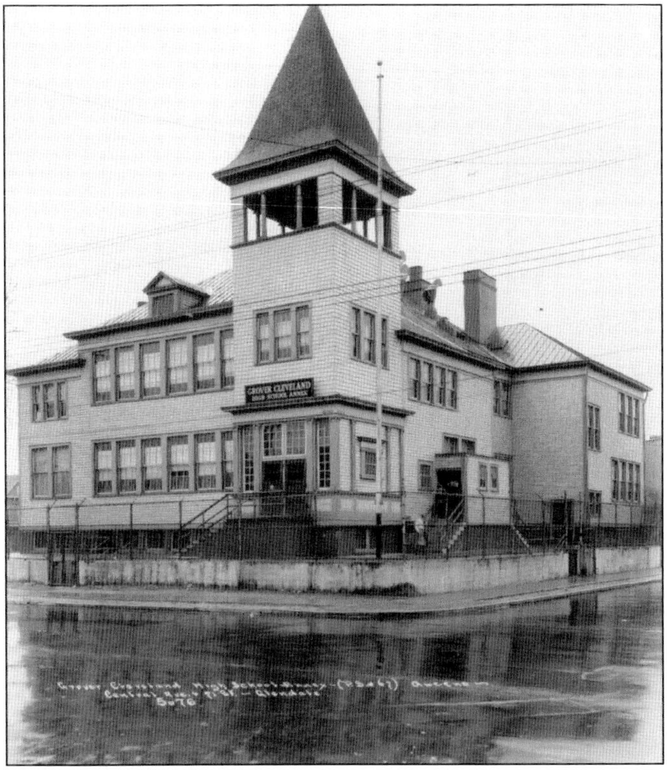

Since Glendale did not have its own high school, many of its students attended nearby Richmond Hill High School and Grover Cleveland High School in Ridgewood. In 1938, this building at Central Avenue and Seventy-first Street was designated as the Grover Cleveland High School Annex, and it served in that capacity until 1940. (Courtesy of GRHS.)

In another fine example of the architecture of the period, Public School No. 91 was built in 1915 at the corner of Central Avenue and Sixty-eighth Place. At that time, the streets were named Folsom Avenue and Fosdick Street, and John Wesley Drumm (of the prominent Drumm family) was its first principal. (Courtesy of GRHS.)

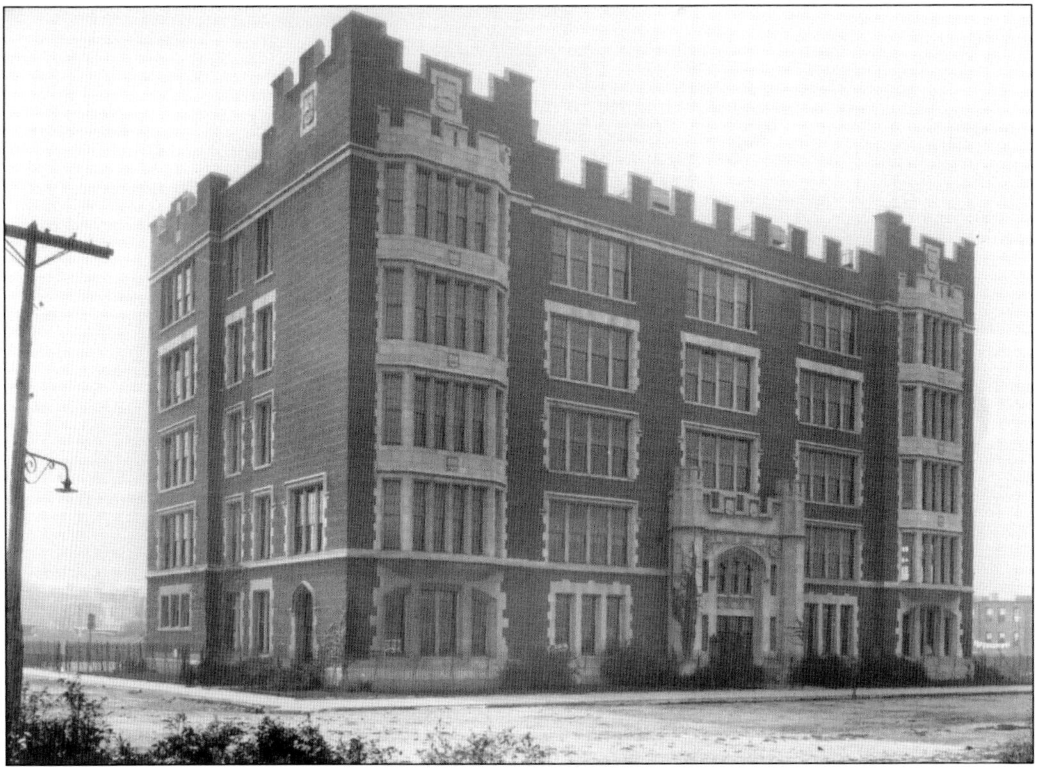

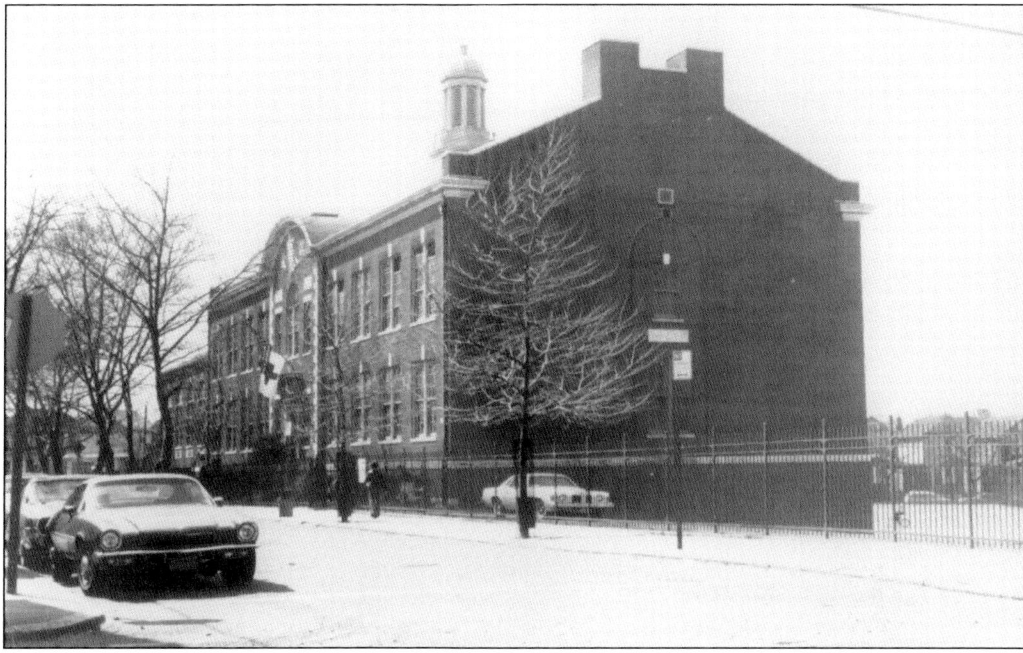

Public School No. 113, located at 87-21 Seventieth Avenue, was erected in 1928 and is shown here in 1976 after earlier construction work to widen the street was completed. The building has remained relatively unchanged, and it had an enrollment of 476 students when this photograph was taken. (Courtesy of GRHS.)

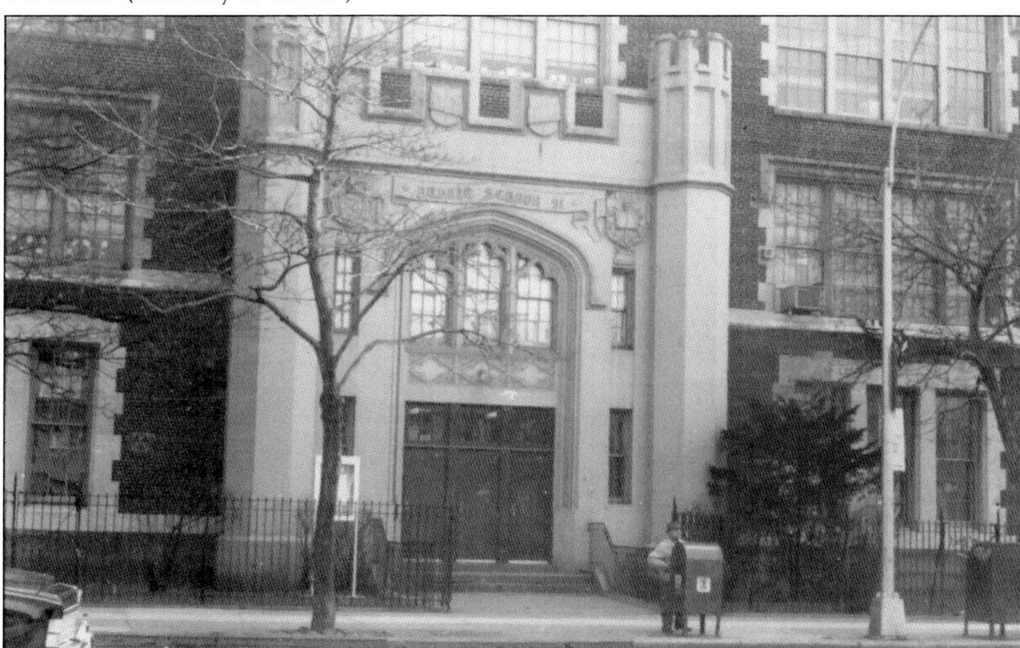

This later view of Public School No. 91 from 1976 highlights the interesting architecture, with its castle-like towers and parapet surrounding the main entrance. At the time of this photograph, 791 students were passing through these doors each day. (Courtesy of GRHS.)

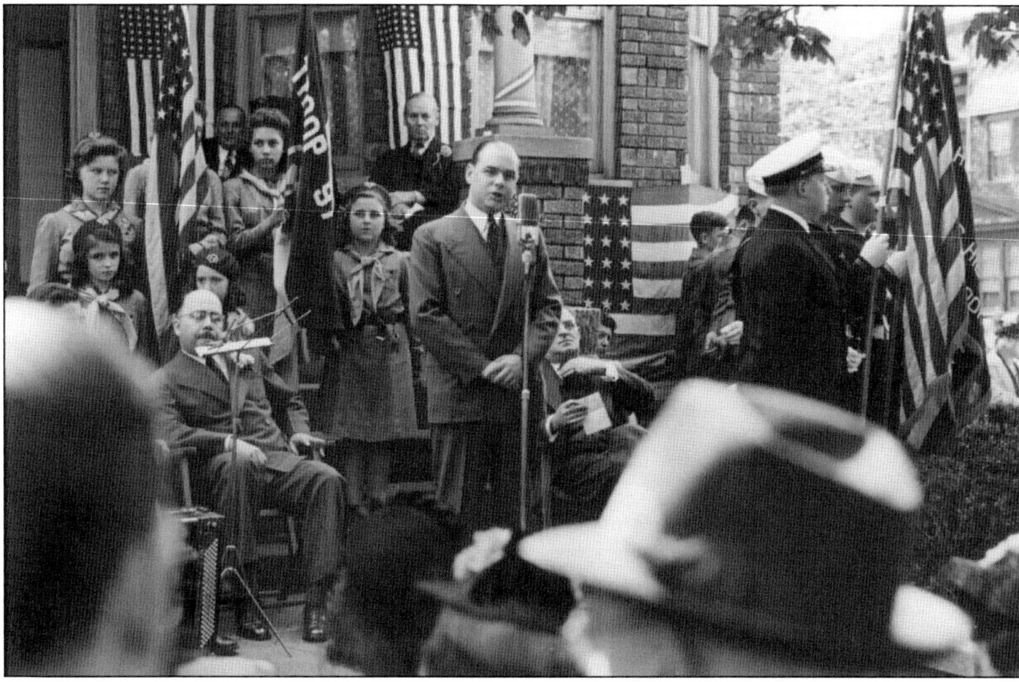

In this 1943 photograph, former state assemblyman and Republican Party leader George Archinal speaks at the dedication of the World War I memorial. Archinal ran unsuccessfully for the office of Queens borough president and for the US Congress. He died in Glendale in 1983 at the age of 87, after a lifetime of service to the community. (Courtesy of GRHS.)

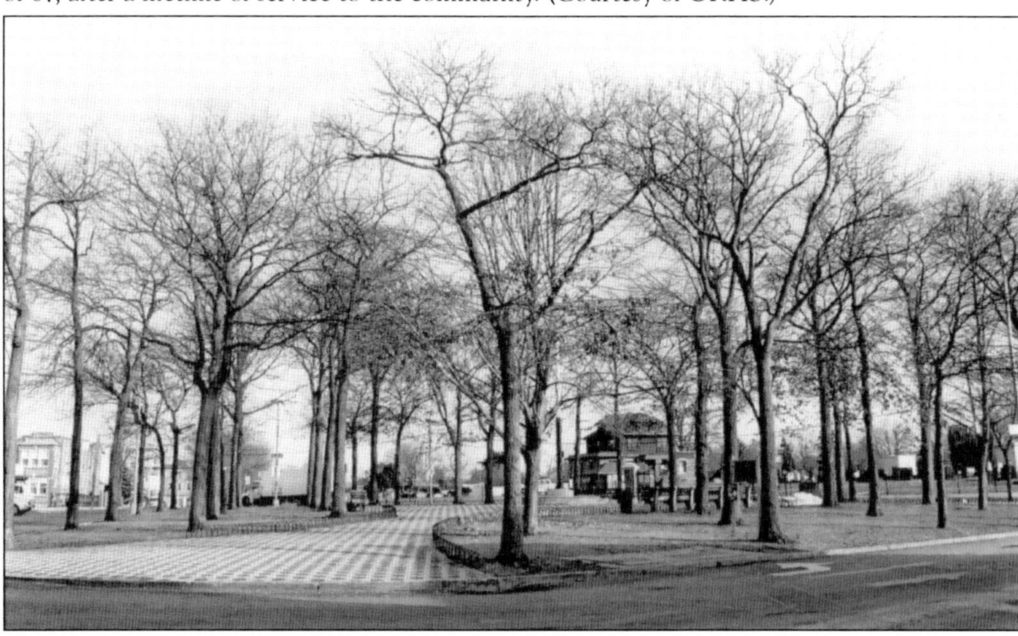

Drumm Triangle, sometimes called Drumm Park, is a small bit of New York City parkland at the intersection of Cypress Hills Street and Cooper Avenue. It was built in 1932 and named after local educator John Wesley Drumm, who was the principal of Glendale's Public School No. 91 from 1915 until 1929. (Courtesy of the author.)

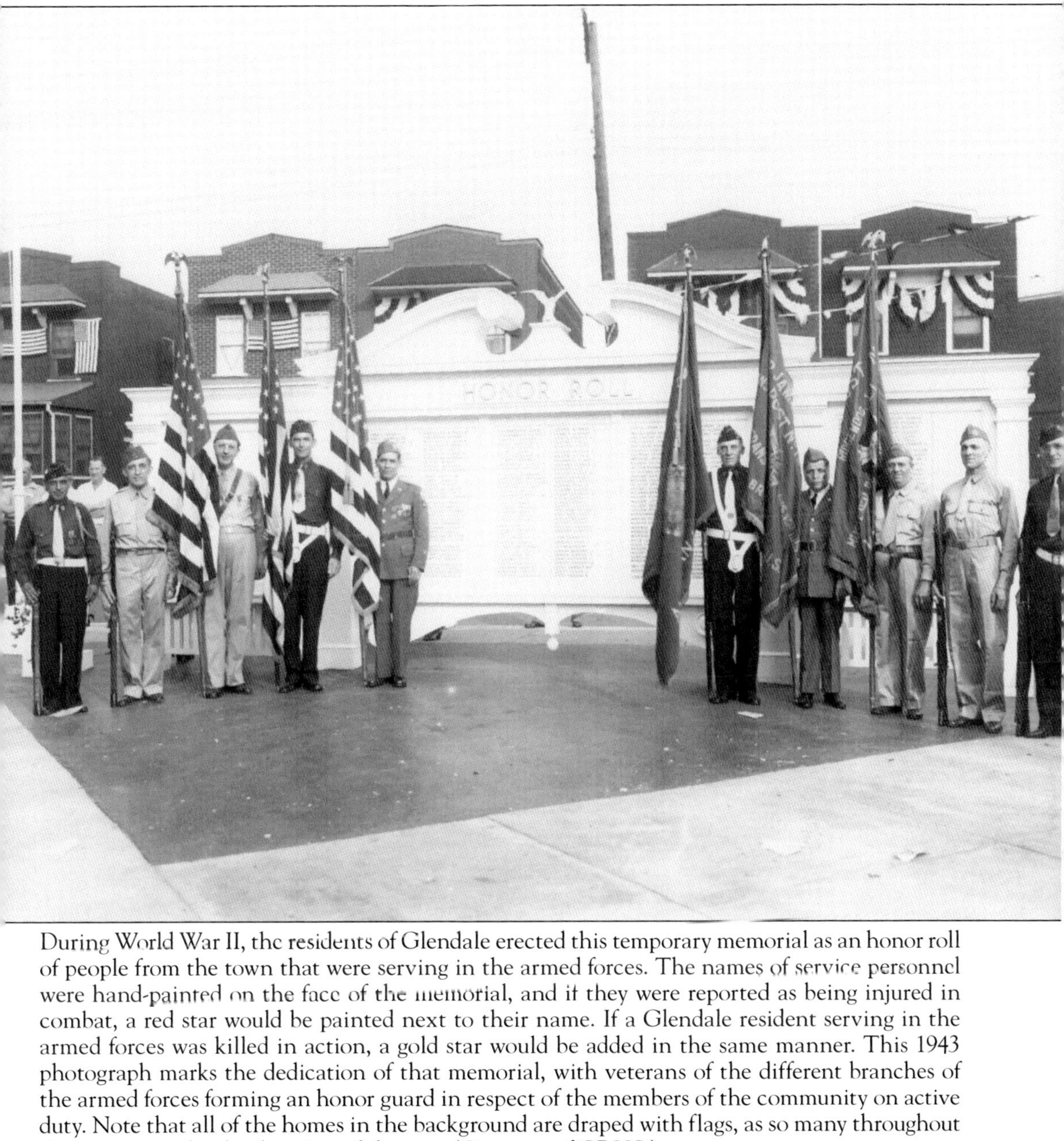

During World War II, the residents of Glendale erected this temporary memorial as an honor roll of people from the town that were serving in the armed forces. The names of service personnel were hand-painted on the face of the memorial, and if they were reported as being injured in combat, a red star would be painted next to their name. If a Glendale resident serving in the armed forces was killed in action, a gold star would be added in the same manner. This 1943 photograph marks the dedication of that memorial, with veterans of the different branches of the armed forces forming an honor guard in respect of the members of the community on active duty. Note that all of the homes in the background are draped with flags, as so many throughout the town were for the duration of the war. (Courtesy of GRHS.)

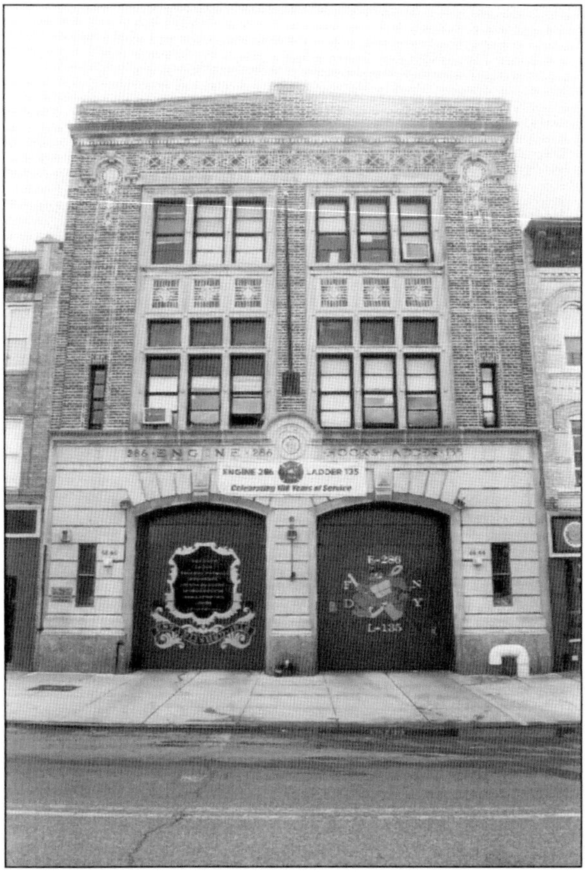

The Glendale firehouse was built in 1913 and houses Engine Company No. 286 and Ladder Company No. 135 of the New York City Fire Department. Prior to the present location on Myrtle Avenue at Sixty-sixth Street, the fire companies operated out of a facility at Cooper and Myrtle Avenues. In addition to protecting the Glendale community, firemen assigned to the Glendale companies are frequently called upon to assist other units in adjacent parts of Brooklyn that are regarded as higher-risk fire areas. The designs painted on the firehouse doors pay tribute to the fire companies' history of distinguished service and include what appears to be a ninja turtle decked out in a fireman's hat rushing to someone's aid. (Both, courtesy of the author.)

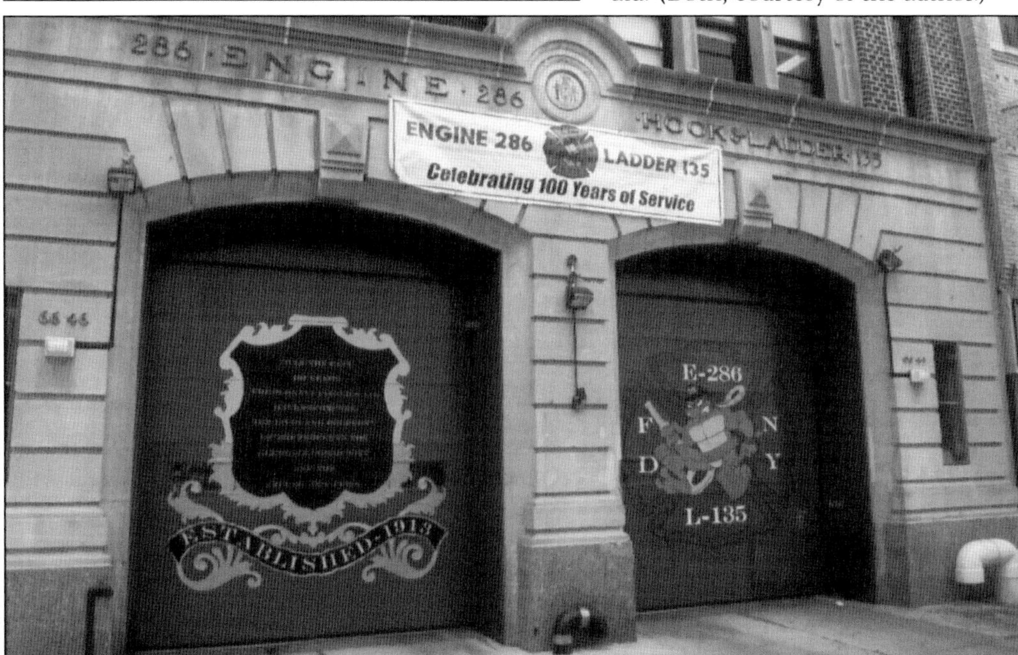

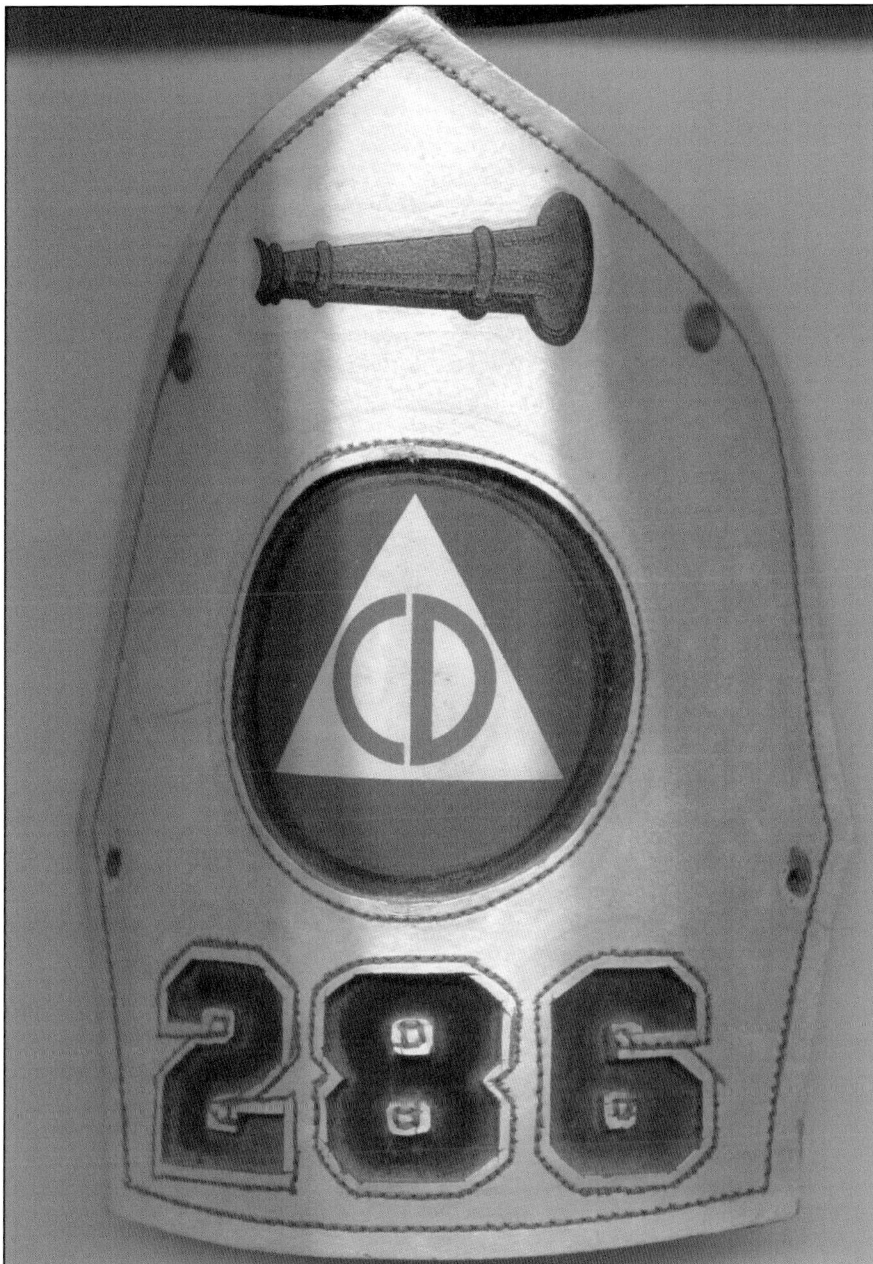

During World War II and the Cold War era, volunteers from the Glendale community assisted the regular firemen and served as civil defense firemen. They wore red, round steel helmets similar to those worn by air raid wardens and performed many of the duties of the regular firemen. Safety regulations prohibited them from entering a building at a fire scene, but they responded to the calls along with the regulars, handled fire hoses at the scene, and assisted with crowd control. In many ways, they functioned like the volunteer firemen that were protecting residents in the rural communities outside of New York City. This helmet shield from that era shows the civil defense logo and the assignment of the author's father to Engine Company No. 286. (Courtesy of the author.)

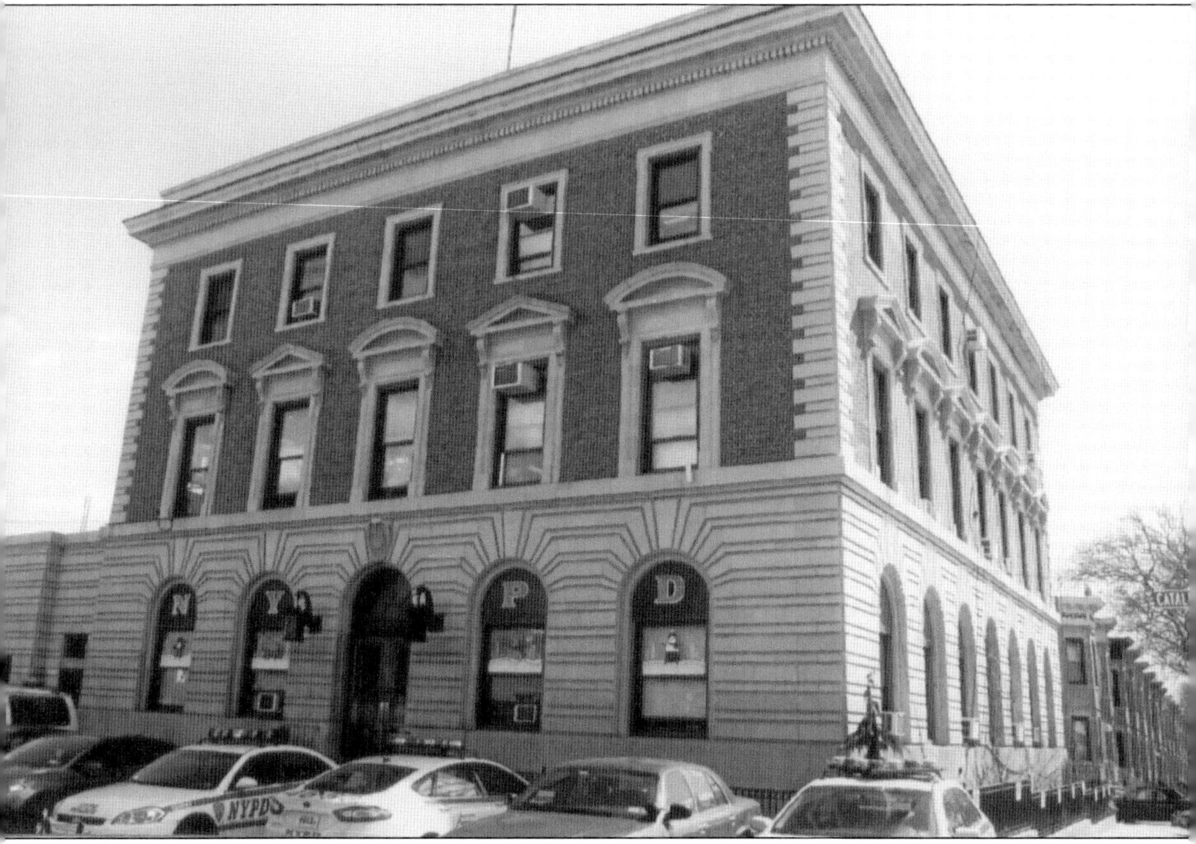

When Queens County and New York City were consolidated in 1891, a police precinct was instituted for the Glendale area and headquartered on Catalpa Avenue at Sherman Street. The present building, shown here, was built in 1925, and the precinct designation was changed from No. 285 to No. 54. After another reorganization of the New York City Police Department structure in 1929, a final change in designation was made, and it has remained Precinct No. 104 to this date. The building is located near the border between Glendale and Ridgewood, and while Glendale residents regard it as their own, the area of responsibility for the police force assigned there includes Glendale and Ridgewood as well as the adjacent communities of Middle Village and Maspeth. (Courtesy of the author.)

Five

DINING AND RECREATION

As Glendale continued to develop but still retained its rural atmosphere, in stark contrast to its reputation as a place full of cemeteries, it became a very popular leisure destination for people from the more congested parts of New York City. The influence of its early German population was visible throughout the community in its many picnic parks and beer gardens, which drew in visitors. Names like Schuetzen Park, Schmidt's Woods, Pfleghardt's hotel, and the Seuffert Bandshell all traced their origins back to German families but catered to people of all nationalities, as Glendale's reputation as a playground grew.

To preserve some of the land from further development, New York City began purchasing land from numerous owners in 1895, and three years later, when the last of a total of 538 acres were transferred to the city, Forest Park was born. Local taverns, movie theaters, and bowling alleys added to the tourist attractions that provided entertainment to local residents and others who sought to spend their leisure time in a place that offered opportunities not available in Brooklyn or Manhattan. Few people could resist the appeal of an afternoon of picnicking on acres of green parkland or enjoying a bratwurst and beer in an outdoor beer garden with its traditional German music.

They came by train or trolley or private motorcar to see the local baseball teams play in Farmer's Oval, enjoy a concert in Forest Park, or sample the German cuisine in one of the many new restaurants. Glendale had arrived with a character all its own, much of which is still in evidence today.

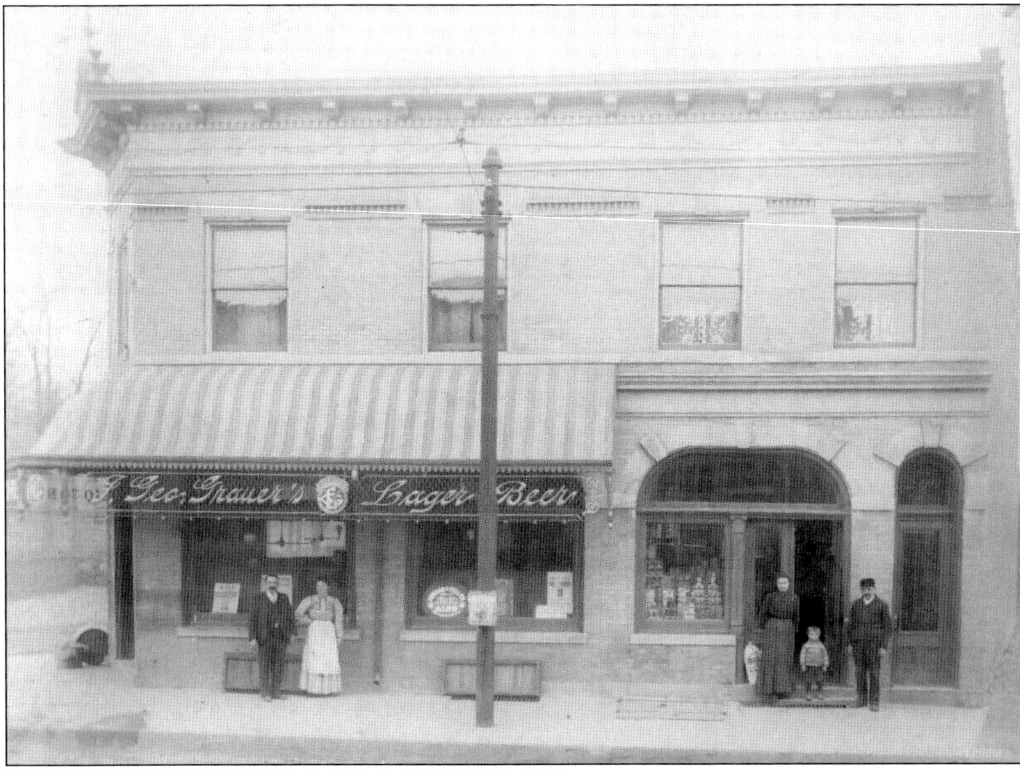

An excellent example of a Glendale watering hole was Fogarty's Saloon, located at Seventy-ninth Street and Cypress Avenue and shown in this 1906 photograph. Of particular interest in the picture is the name "J. George Grauer Lager Beer," shown over the entrance to the tavern. Grauer had been a part owner in a picnic grounds and decided to become a brewer in 1891. He underestimated the amount of ice that he would need for his brewery and was forced to build an ice plant as well. Unfortunately, the brewery was operating at a loss when Grauer died in 1908. His wife sold it to S. Liebmann Sons, who also distributed Rheingold Beer, but she kept the ice plant, which continued to operate profitably until the introduction of electric refrigerators many years later. (Courtesy of GRHS.)

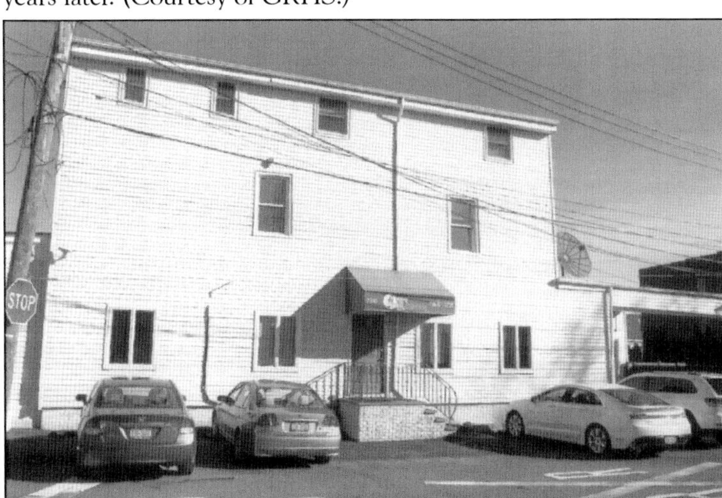

Wood's Inn, at Seventy-third Street and Edsall Avenue, was another old Glendale tavern, and the building is still standing today. It dates back to the 1830s and originally housed a tavern on the ground floor and rooms for rent on the upper two floors. At the time of this writing, it is the office of a cartage company, and local folklore claims that the building is haunted. (Courtesy of the author.)

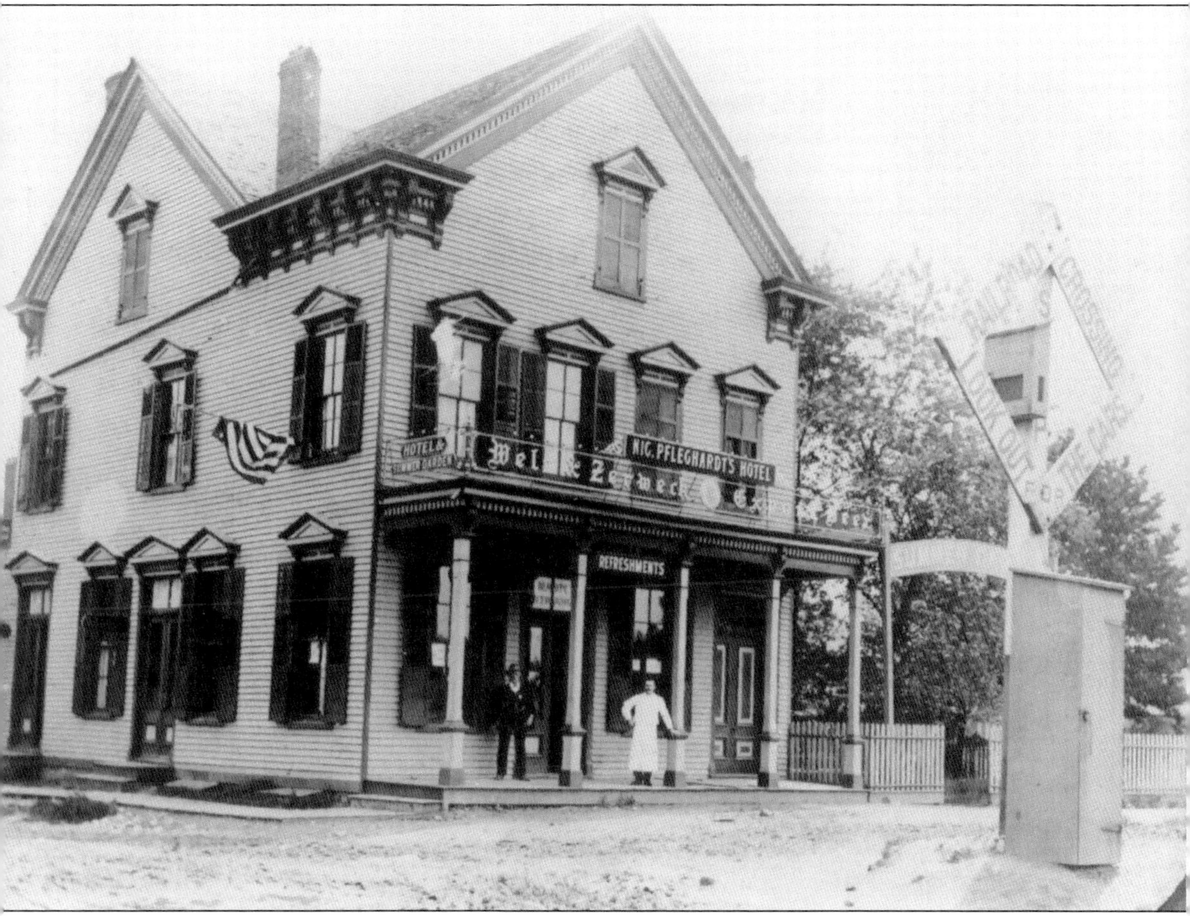

Nicholas Pfleghardt's hotel, located at Seventy-second and Edsall Avenues, dated back to 1885. The photograph describes it as a "hotel and summer garden." Situated where it was within walking distance of the old Glendale railroad station, it was a convenient stop for thirsty travelers on their way to have fun in Glendale. (Courtesy of GRHS.)

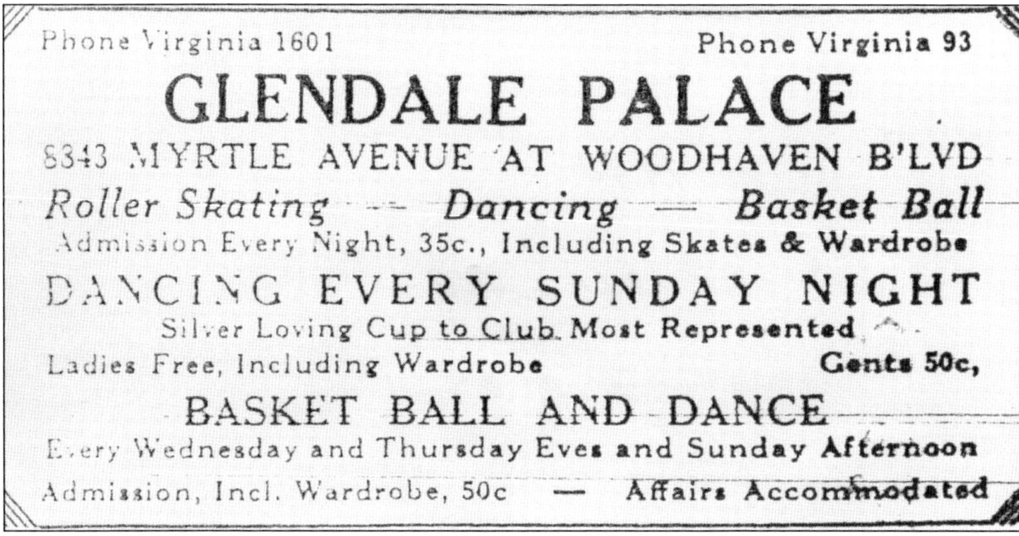

Phone Virginia 1601 Phone Virginia 93

GLENDALE PALACE

8343 MYRTLE AVENUE AT WOODHAVEN B'LVD

Roller Skating — Dancing — Basket Ball

Admission Every Night, 35c., Including Skates & Wardrobe

DANCING EVERY SUNDAY NIGHT

Silver Loving Cup to Club Most Represented

Ladies Free, Including Wardrobe **Gents 50c,**

BASKET BALL AND DANCE

Every Wednesday and Thursday Eves and Sunday Afternoon

Admission, Incl. Wardrobe, 50c — Affairs Accommodated

The Glendale Palace took out this newspaper advertisement in 1930 to let potential customers know just how much fun was in store for them during an evening at the Palace. Roller-skating, dancing, and basket ball (before it became one word); what more could a fun-loving Brooklynite want? The emphasis on "wardrobe" and why ladies received one for free is a bit of a puzzle. (Courtesy of GRHS.)

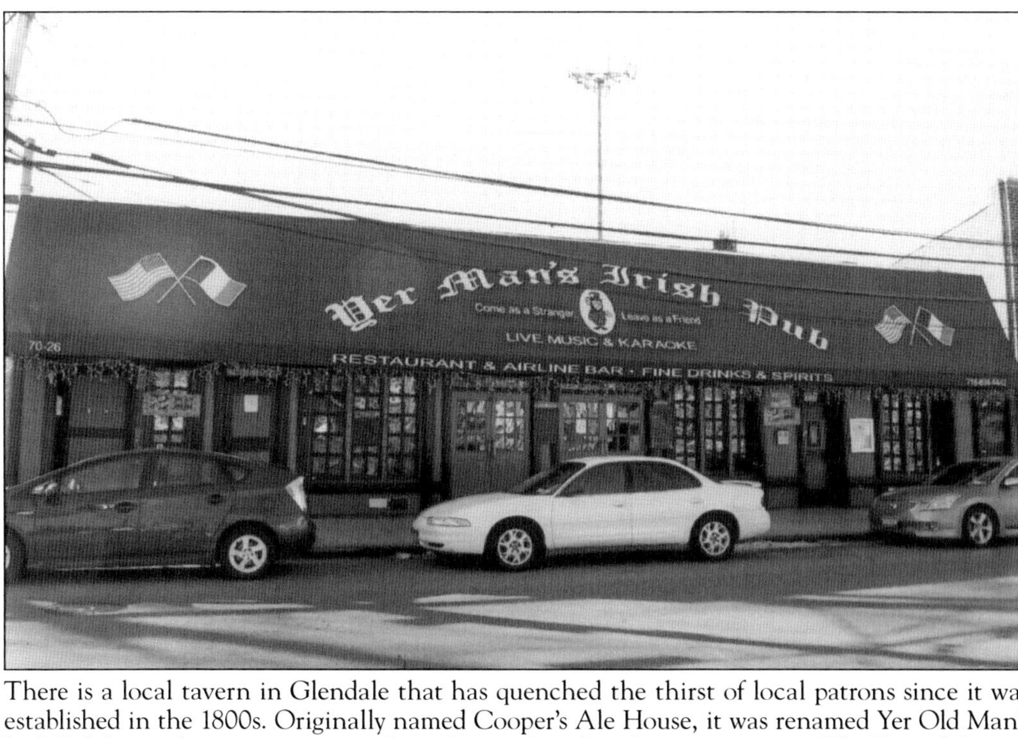

There is a local tavern in Glendale that has quenched the thirst of local patrons since it was established in the 1800s. Originally named Cooper's Ale House, it was renamed Yer Old Man's Irish Pub by a subsequent owner and was featured in the television program *The King of Queens* as a neighborhood bar. (Courtesy of the author.)

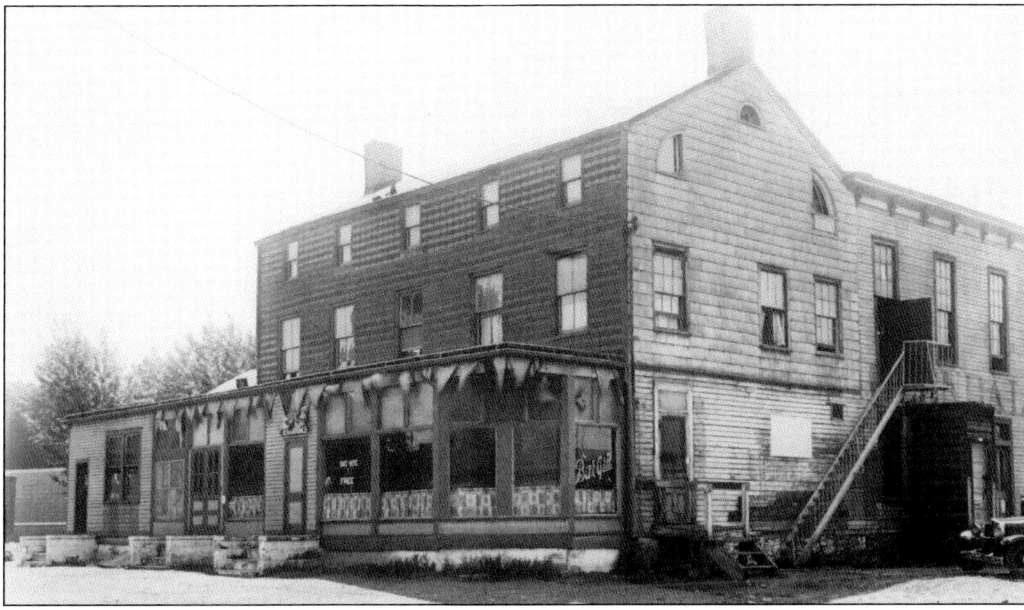

The building shown in this 1934 photograph was originally the Nicholas Wyckoff farmhouse, but it was later converted to a hotel and bar by a member of the Hillen family. The hotel included a picnic park on the property, and in later years, it was renamed Doty's Tavern by Dorothy Hillen, whose nickname was "Doty." The building was unfortunately demolished in 1970. (Courtesy of GRHS.)

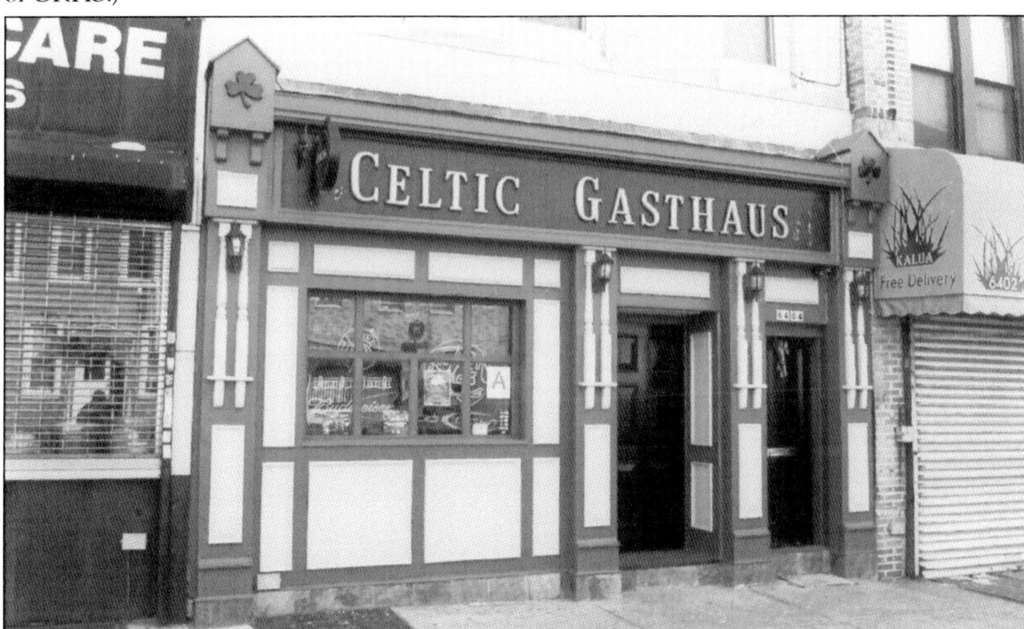

This building, located at 64-04 Myrtle Avenue for many years, was a reminder of Glendale's German heritage. As early as the 1950s, it was a tavern called the Golden Eagle, which featured live music on the weekends. It became Hans Gasthaus in 1994, and the most recent owners have changed the name again, presumably to honor two of the largest ethnic groups in Glendale. (Courtesy of the author.)

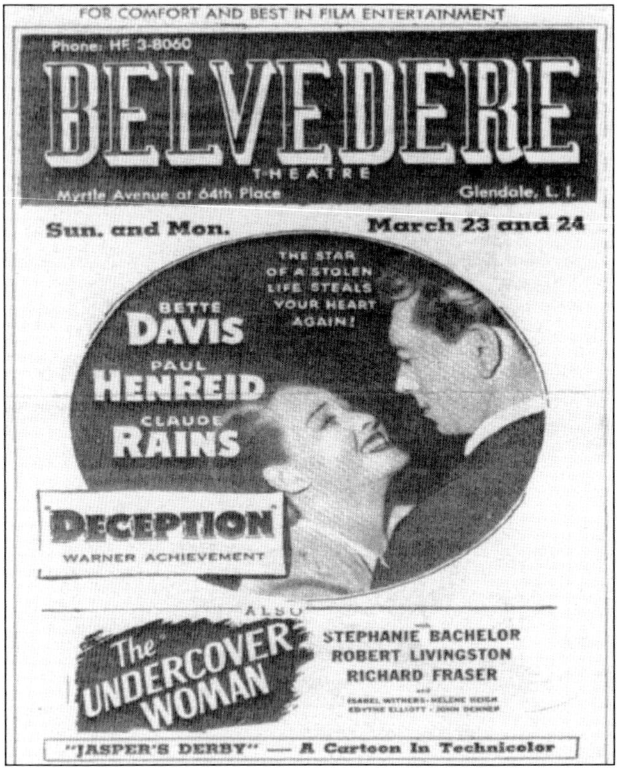

There seem to be no photographs available of the old Belvedere Theater, which stood at the corner of Myrtle Avenue and Sixty-fourth Place in the 1940s and 1950s. It joins the Acme and Glenwood Theaters, also on Myrtle Avenue, in being almost forgotten. This old poster reminds of the days when a double feature, previews, cartoons, and a short action serial could be seen for the bargain price of 25¢ in the 1950s. (Courtesy of GRHS.)

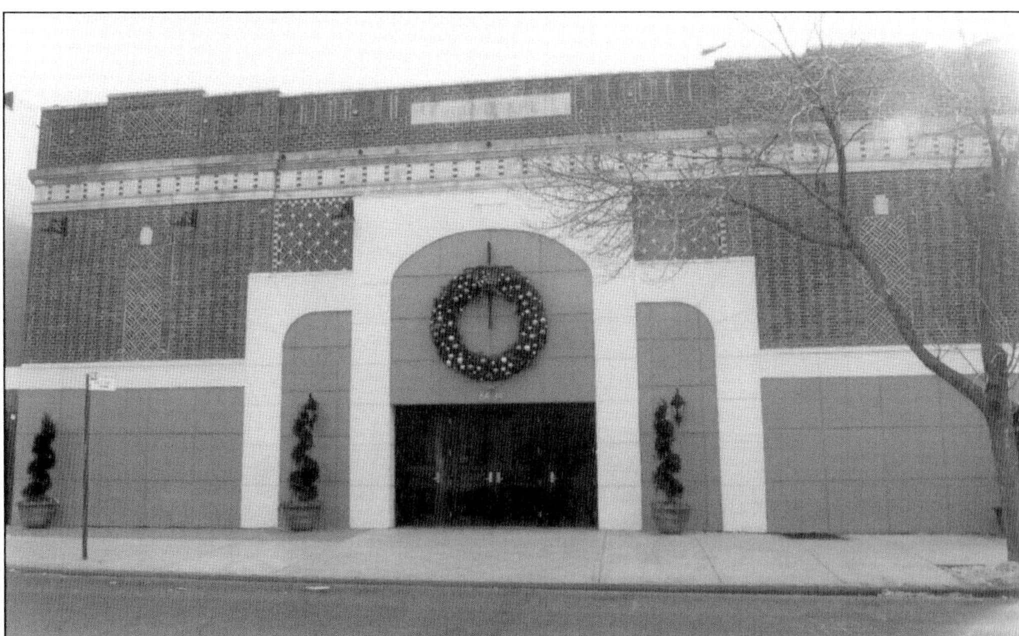

The Belvedere Theater building still stands today. After some years as a furniture store, it was converted to a Baptist church, and it continues to serve the Glendale community in that capacity. Removing the old marquee gave the building a more contemporary appearance, but the center section over the entrance still has the name Belvedere carved into it. (Courtesy of the author.)

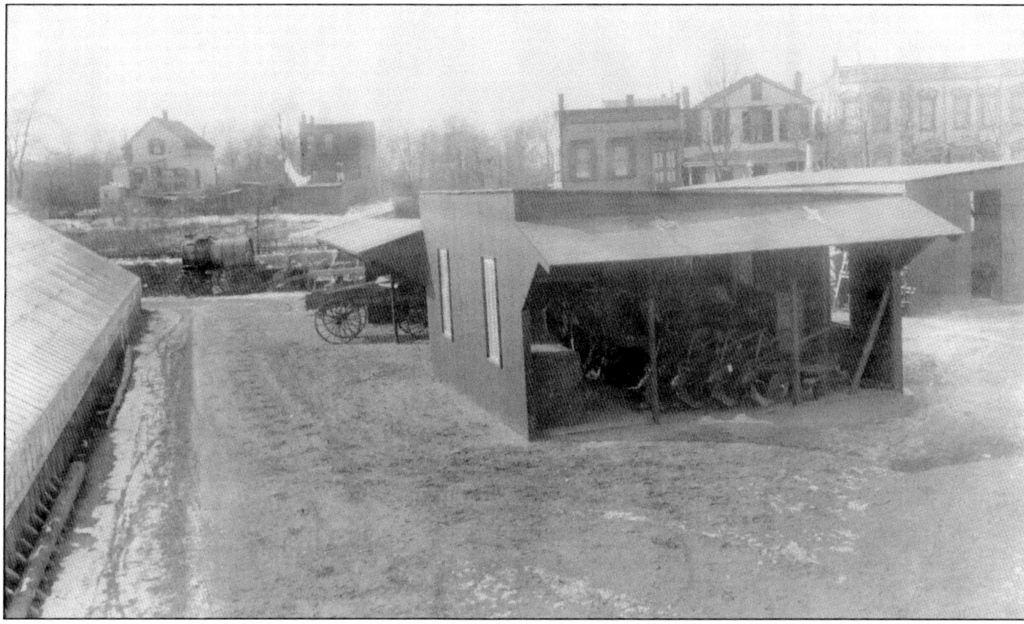

These two old photographs show some of the early construction in the days when Forest Park was being built, from 1895 to 1898. Temporary sheds were set up to house the horse-drawn construction and land-clearing equipment and the building materials that would create the roadways and park buildings. Many of the old houses in the background were later purchased and then torn down since the developers needed a total of 124 privately owned parcels of land to complete the project. Their efforts turned 538 acres of undeveloped land into beautiful parkland. (Both, courtesy of GRHS.)

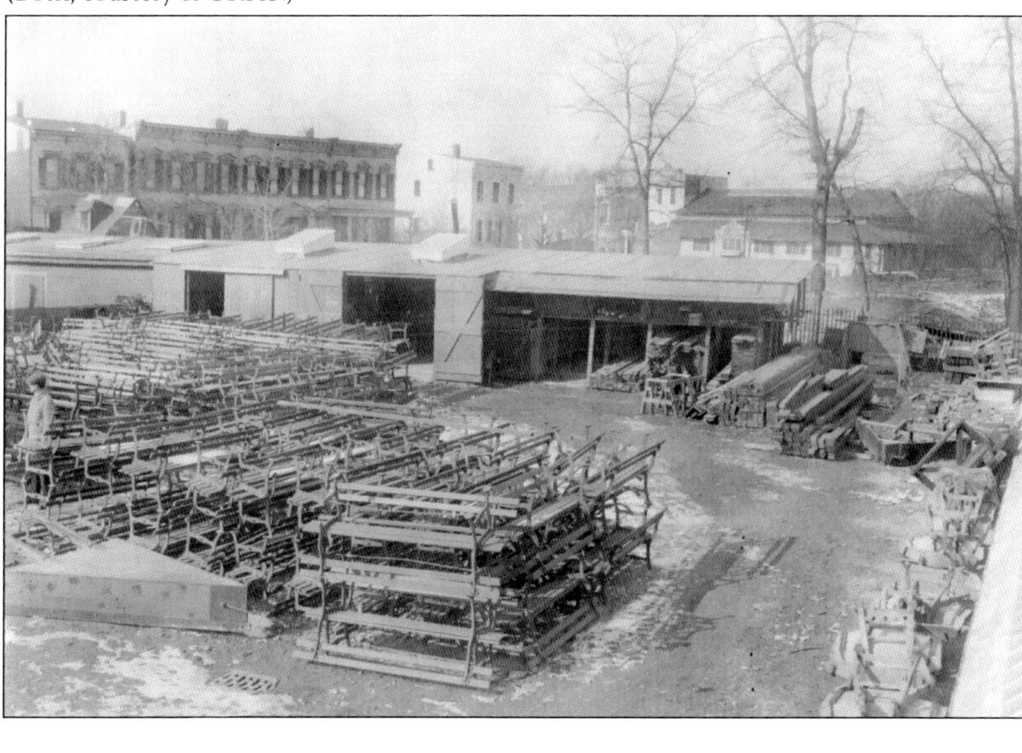

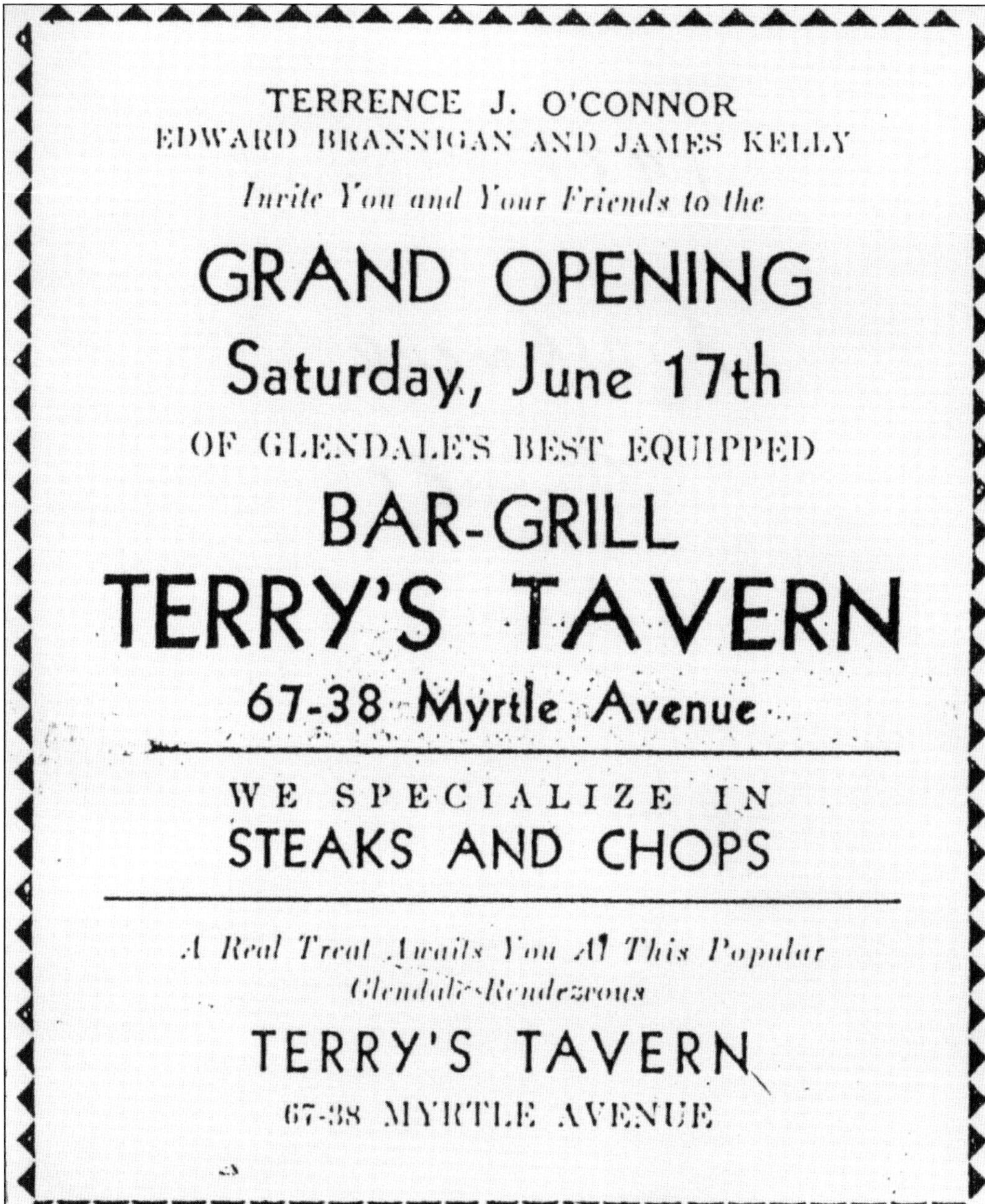

In this undated advertisement from the *Ridgewood Times*, Terry's Tavern attempts to lure in new customers by promising, "A Real Treat Awaits You at This Popular Glendale Rendezvous." Knowing that Terry had the best-equipped bar and grill in Glendale gave it quite an appeal. (Courtesy of GRHS.)

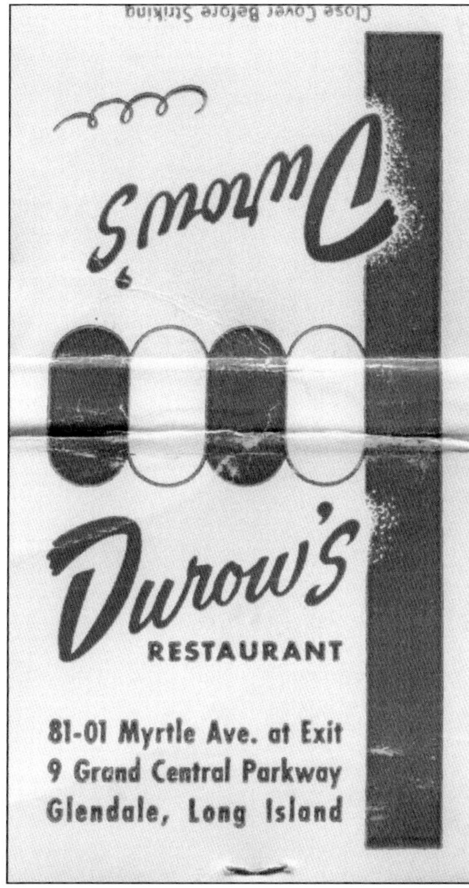

One of the premier restaurants and catering halls in Glendale from the 1940s until the 1970s was Durow's, located at the corner of Eighty-first Street and Myrtle Avenue. Like so many other local dining establishments, Durow's had been preceded over the years by other restaurants at that same location. At one time, it was Happy's Night Club, and then Victor Koenig's Restaurant, until it was sold in 1944 to Heinz Durow. Durow's, like so many other German restaurants in Glendale, was known for its sauerbraten and for the elaborate party that it staged every New Year's Eve. When word of mouth was not enough, Durow's resorted to the matchbook cover advertising that was so popular in the 1940s and 1950s. (Both, courtesy of the author.)

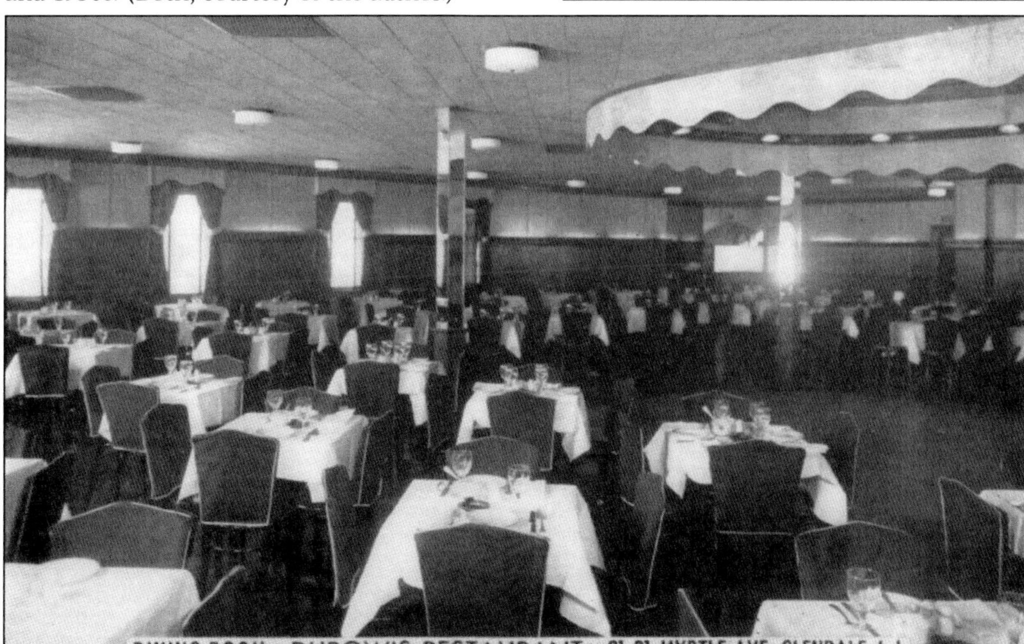

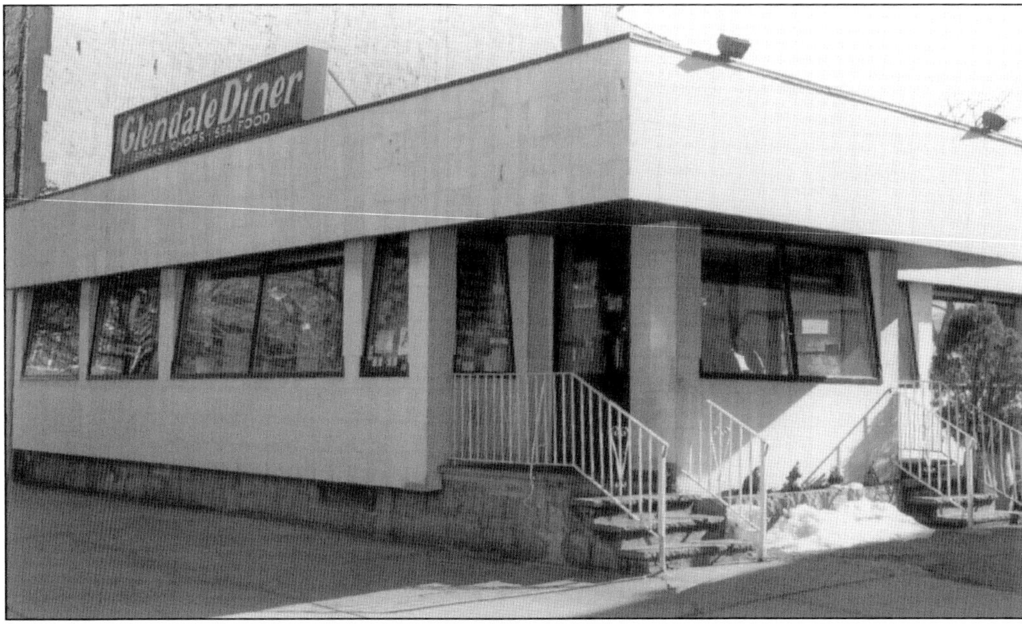

During its early years, from the 1940s to the 1960s, the Glendale Diner, which is still in operation, was known as Bob's Diner. Like many other restaurants in Glendale, Bob's claimed that its sauerbraten was the best. When it got too late for a sauerbraten dinner, many a late-night partygoer stopped by at Bob's Diner for a cup of coffee and the early-morning breakfast that was available at any time. The photograph above shows the diner as it looks today, while the earlier photograph below illustrates the more traditional look for a diner, but the general shape of the building was very similar. The advertising on the wall of the adjacent building was removed, and Krug's Bread Company is no longer in business. (Above, courtesy of the author; below, courtesy of GRHS.)

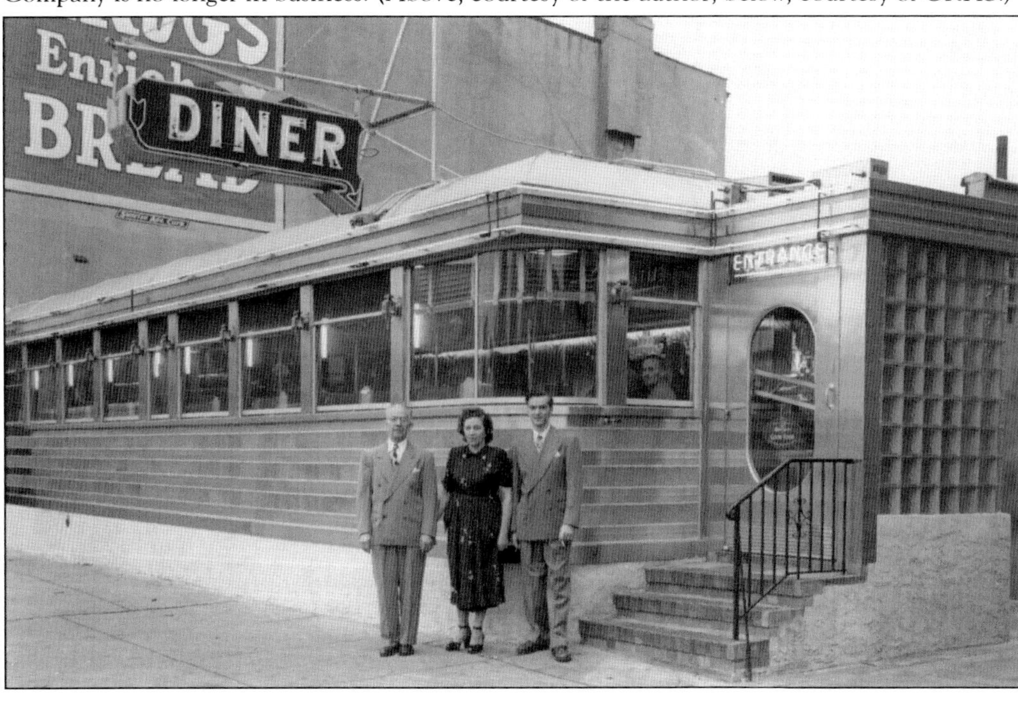

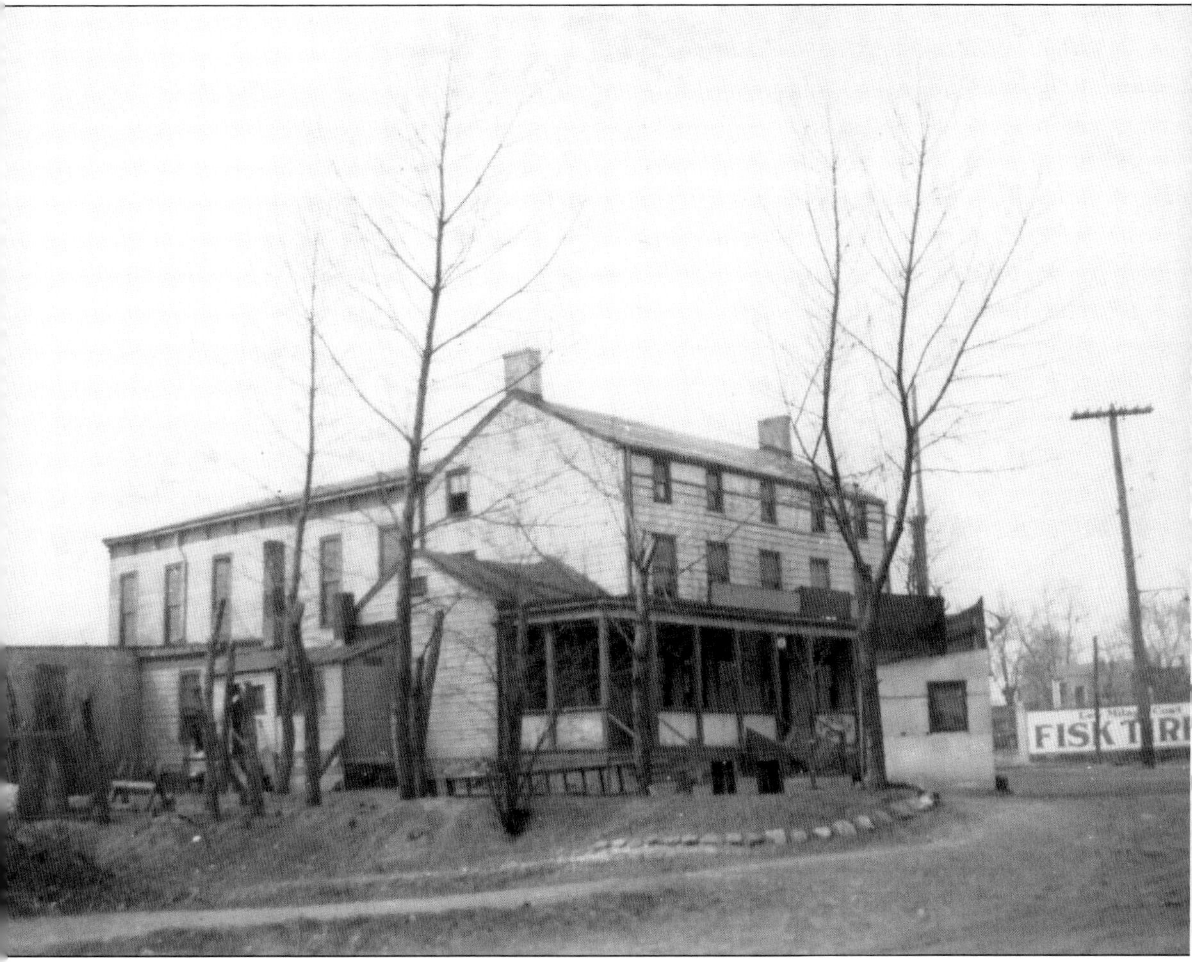

This 1923 photograph shows the old Glendale Hotel, located at Cooper Avenue and Seventy-fourth Street. Even though it appears to be the first hotel to use Glendale as part of its name, it has been forgotten in most historical records of the town. It is clear that the area was still very rural in nature, with no paved streets or sidewalks and no place to even park a car. (Courtesy of Queens Borough Public Library.)

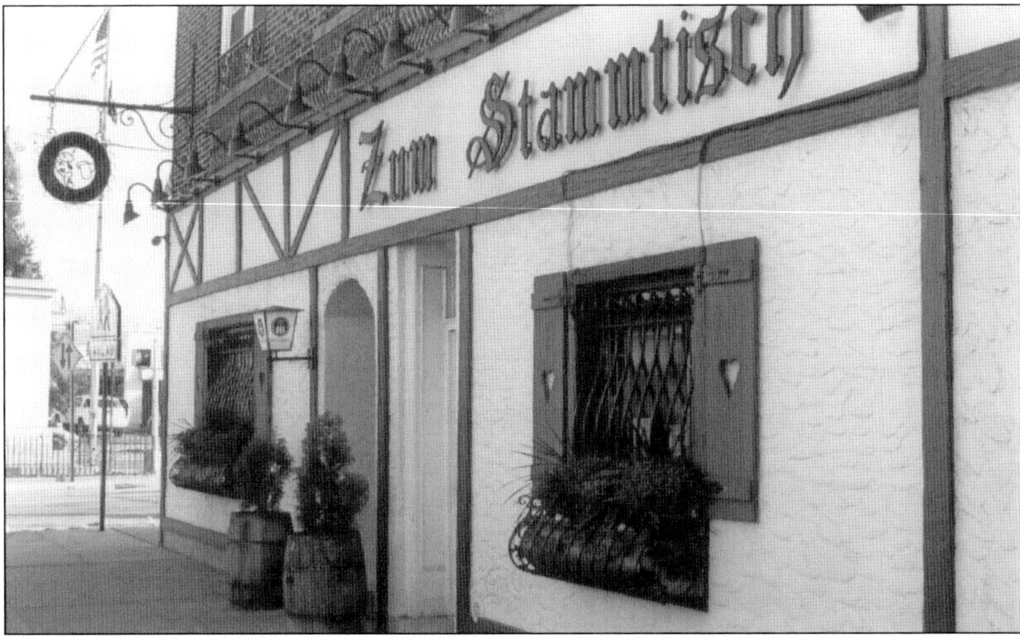

Glendale's most renowned German restaurant is Zum Stammtisch, located near the corner of Cooper and Myrtle Avenues. Rated by Zagat and operating at the same location since 1972, it was founded by John Lehner, who had been a coppersmith in Germany. He immigrated to the United States in the 1950s and opened this restaurant with two other partners. Owning a restaurant had been Lehner's dream since he left Germany. After several years, he bought out his partners, and when he passed away, the operation of the restaurant was taken over by his two sons. The name of the restaurant means "family table" in German, and they recently opened a retail store (below) to allow patrons to bring home traditional German specialties for their own family's table. (Both, courtesy of the author.)

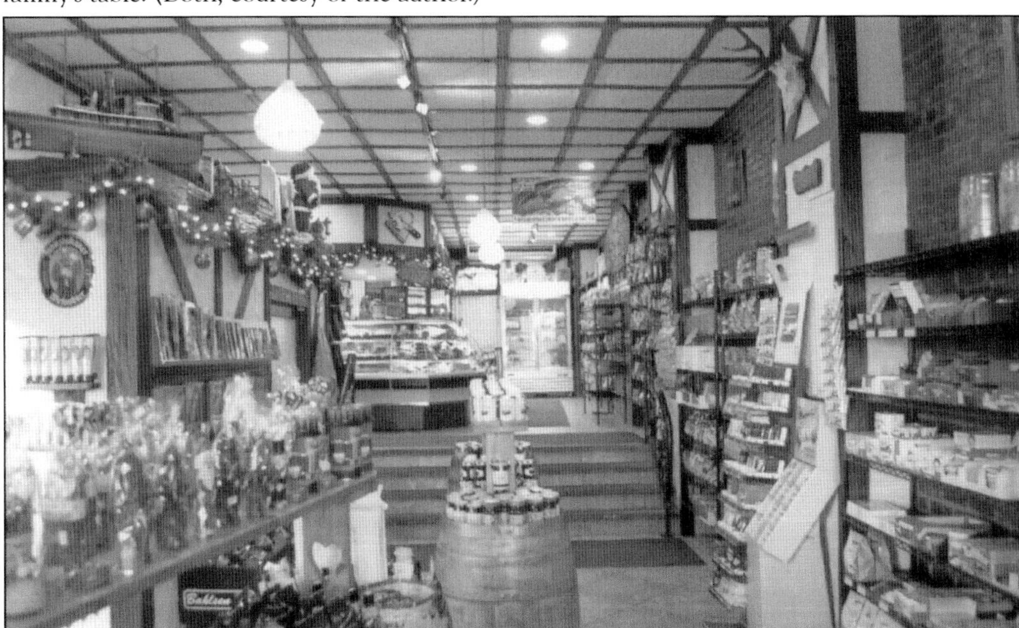

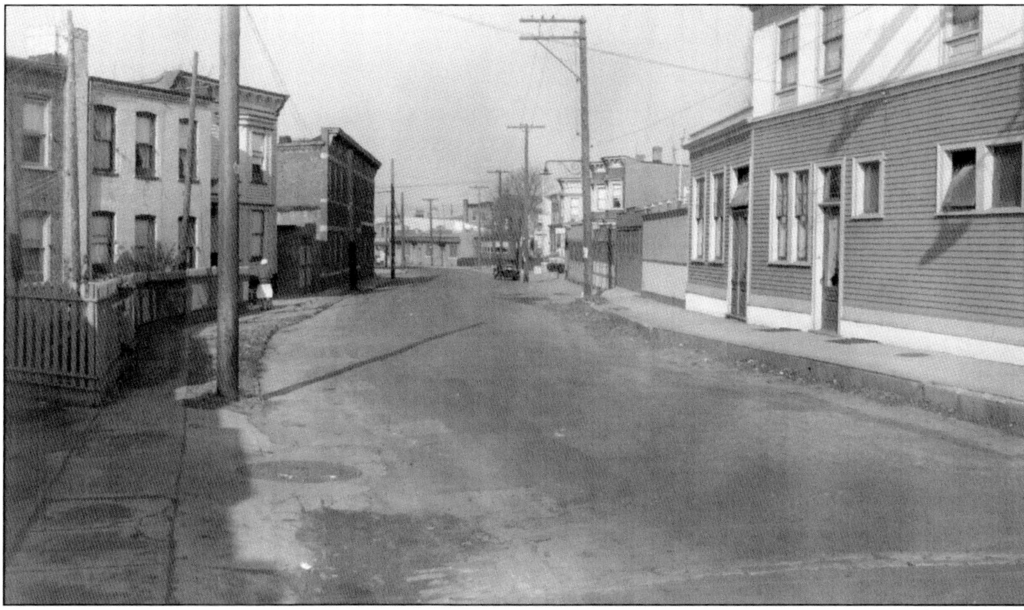

At the corner of Cooper Avenue and Cypress Hills Street is a building that is presently being used as a Serbian social club, according to the sign over the front door. Another part of Glendale history that seems to be lost is the fact that, for many years, this building was known as the Welcome Inn. Beginning in the early 1940s, it was a catering hall that hosted weddings and a variety of other functions. The author has fond recollections of family weddings, Christenings, and anniversary parties held at the Welcome Inn, as well as other functions that included New Year's Eve celebrations and dinners held there by the local Boy Scout troop to mark the advancement of Cub Scouts into Boy Scout Troop No. 383. (Above, courtesy of GRHS; below, courtesy of the author.)

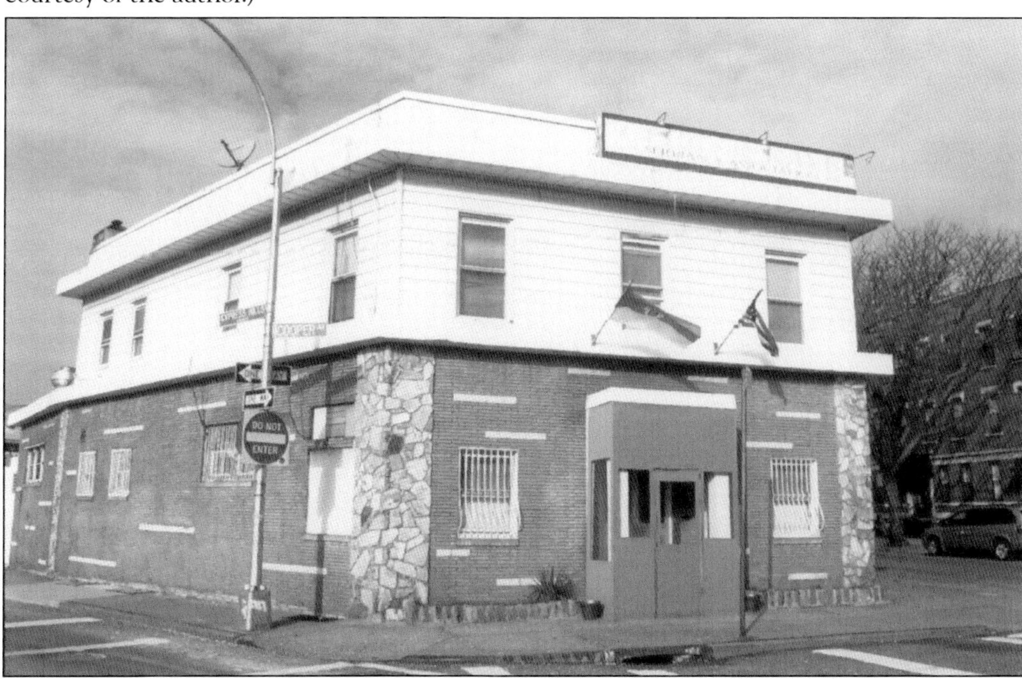

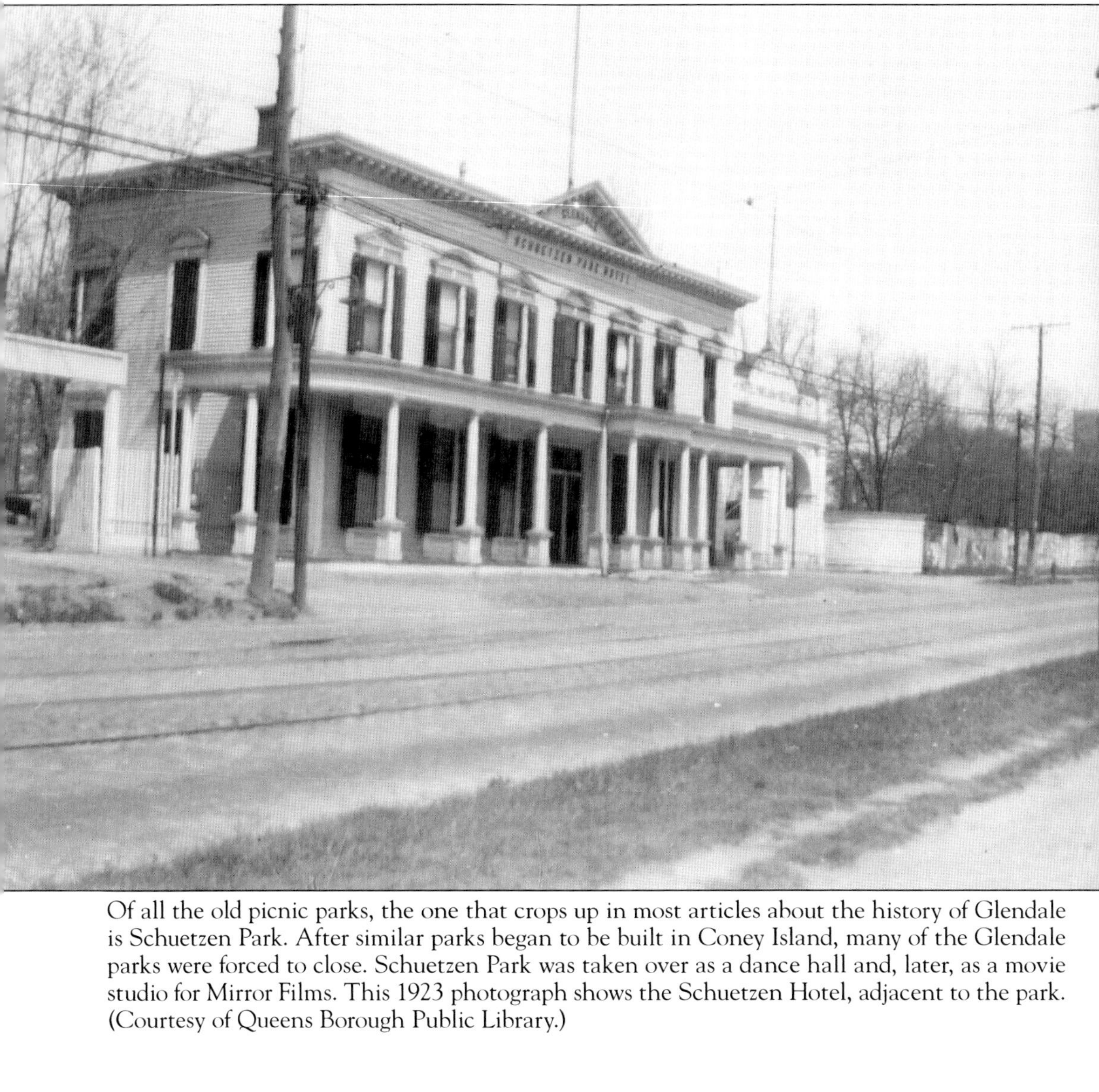

Of all the old picnic parks, the one that crops up in most articles about the history of Glendale is Schuetzen Park. After similar parks began to be built in Coney Island, many of the Glendale parks were forced to close. Schuetzen Park was taken over as a dance hall and, later, as a movie studio for Mirror Films. This 1923 photograph shows the Schuetzen Hotel, adjacent to the park. (Courtesy of Queens Borough Public Library.)

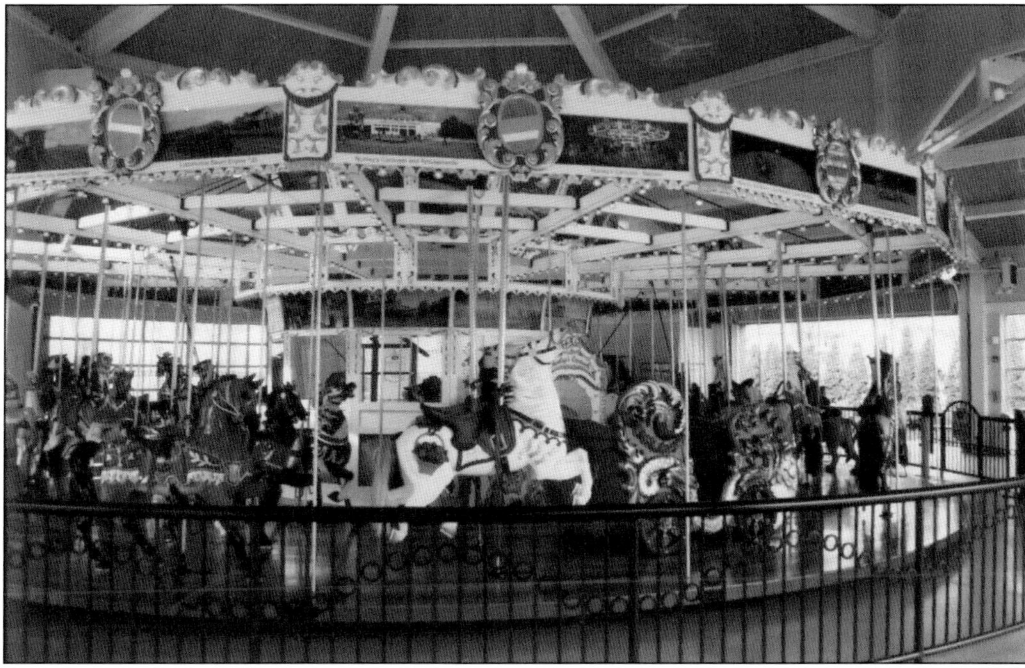

The present carousel operating in Forest Park was first crafted in 1890, while the animals were built later in 1903. It was the work of master carver Daniel Carl Mueller and is one of only two examples of his work still in existence. Another carousel did operate in Forest Park for a number of years, but it burned down in 1966. A search for a replacement turned up the present carousel, which had been in use in Dracut, Massachusetts, in 1903, but was later taken apart and stored. It features 49 horses, a lion, a tiger, a deer, and two chariots, and is listed in the National Register of Historic Places. (Above, courtesy of New York City Parks Department; below, photograph by the author.)

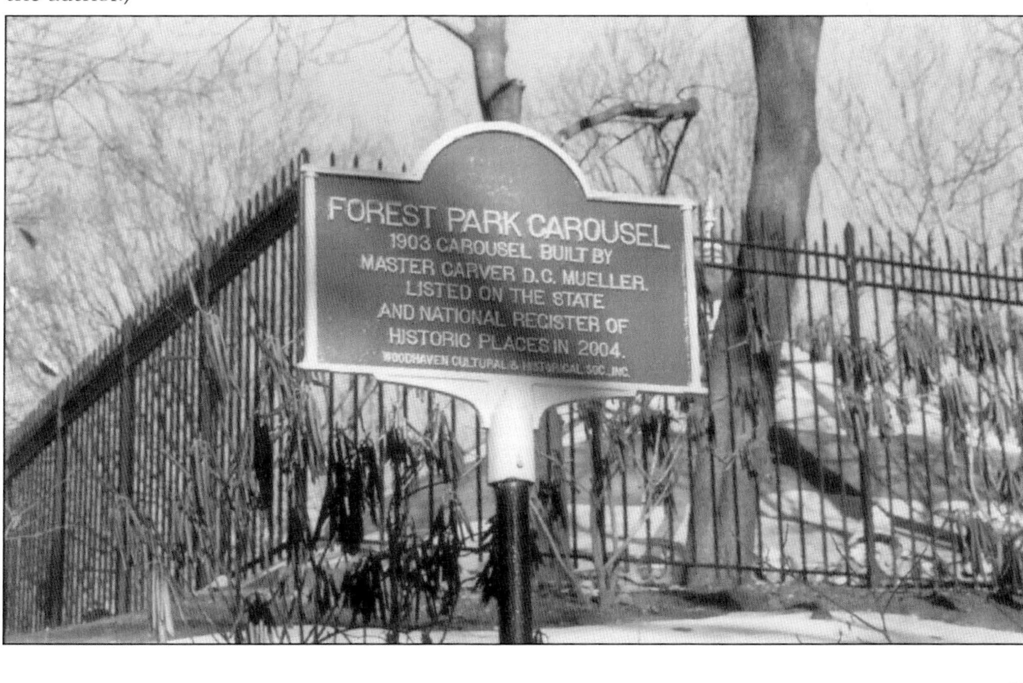

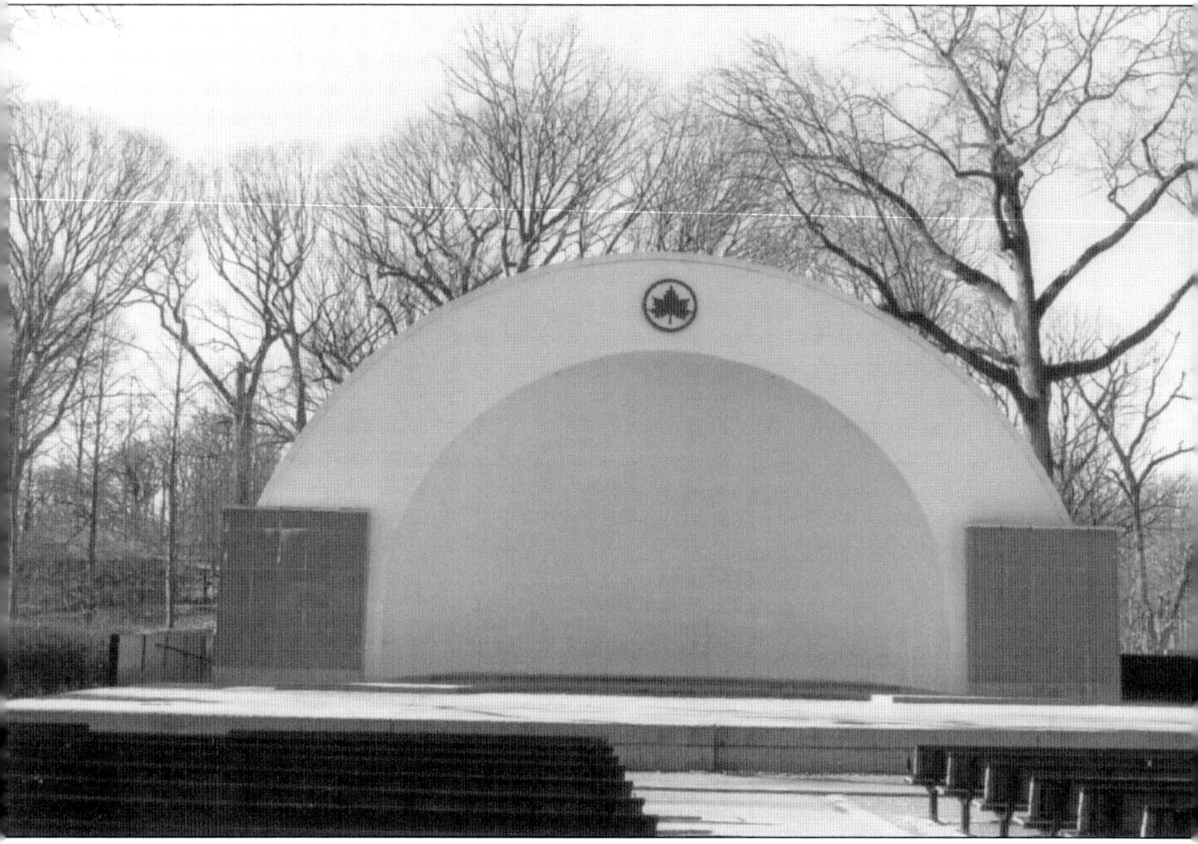

Another prominent landmark in Forest Park is the George Seuffert Bandshell, built in 1920 to accommodate the Seuffert Band, which performed outdoor concerts in the park. It seats 3,500 people and was renovated in 1999 to improve the sound system, lighting, stage, and landscaping. It continues to entertain residents from all over Queens County with concerts, movies, and other types of live performances. (Courtesy of the author.)

Six

TRANSPORTATION

Without a doubt, the development of Glendale followed the rails—two different kinds of rails carrying two different types of vehicles. For its industrial growth, Glendale owes its success to the Long Island Railroad. The tracks running in and out of the community brought in all of the building materials that went into the homes and factories, the coal that fueled the engines of industry and warmed the homes of Glendale residents, stone, block, and cement to pave the roads, and pipe and iron fixtures to create the sewer system and indoor plumbing. It also brought in many of the things that Glendale residents used each day while going about their daily lives.

The same railroad tracks also carried away products manufactured by early Glendale industries, particularly those doing business in the new Atlas Terminal industrial park. Companies there manufactured toys, brushes, airplanes, paper products, safety matches, textiles, china, lubricants, and other goods that fueled the industrial growth of the nation in the beginning of the 20th century.

At one time, there was even a Glendale passenger station for the Long Island Railroad, so that in the days of the famous picnic parks and beer gardens, people from Brooklyn and all parts of the surrounding area could hop a train to escape the noise and congestion of New York City and enjoy a day of boating, picnicking, or fine dining in one of Glendale's many restaurants.

For those that did not live as far away or have access to the railroad, the Myrtle Avenue trolley provided an enjoyable scenic ride to the playground that Glendale was becoming. Beginning a day's outing with a relaxing trolley ride made the area a popular destination for people from neighboring Brooklyn communities and from the eastern villages of Jamaica and Richmond Hill.

The trolley rails are long gone today, but the railroad tracks remain. Most trains do not even stop in Glendale any longer, but the community is alive and still growing, proud of its heritage and the part that transportation played in it.

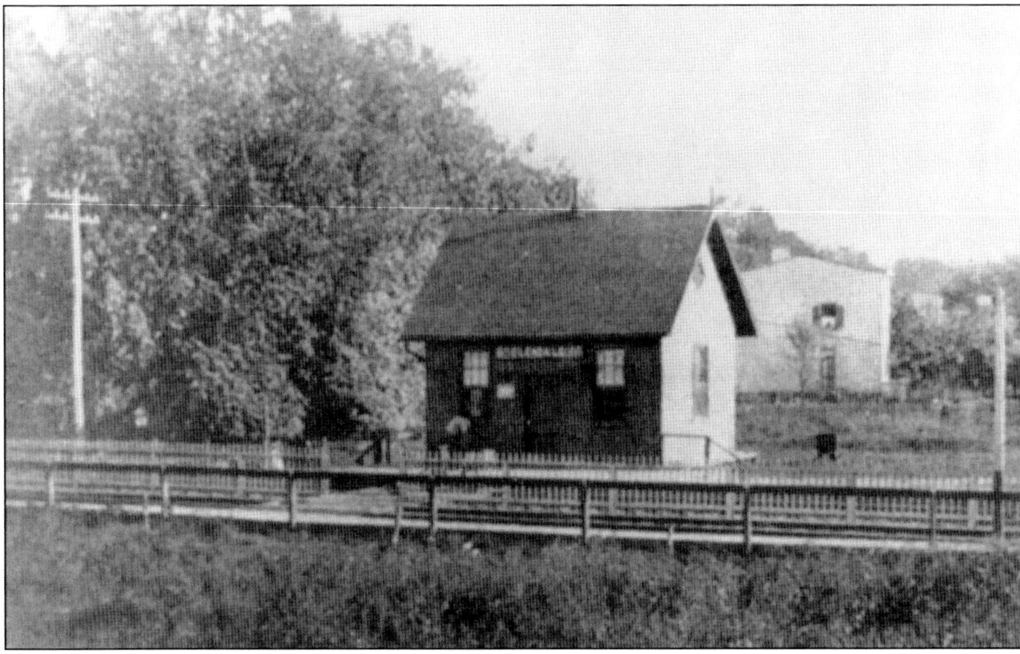

This amazing photograph is from 1893 and shows the original Glendale station for the Long Island Railroad. The records indicate that it was destroyed in the 1950s, but they do not provide any specific details about how or why that happened. (Courtesy of Queens Historical Society.)

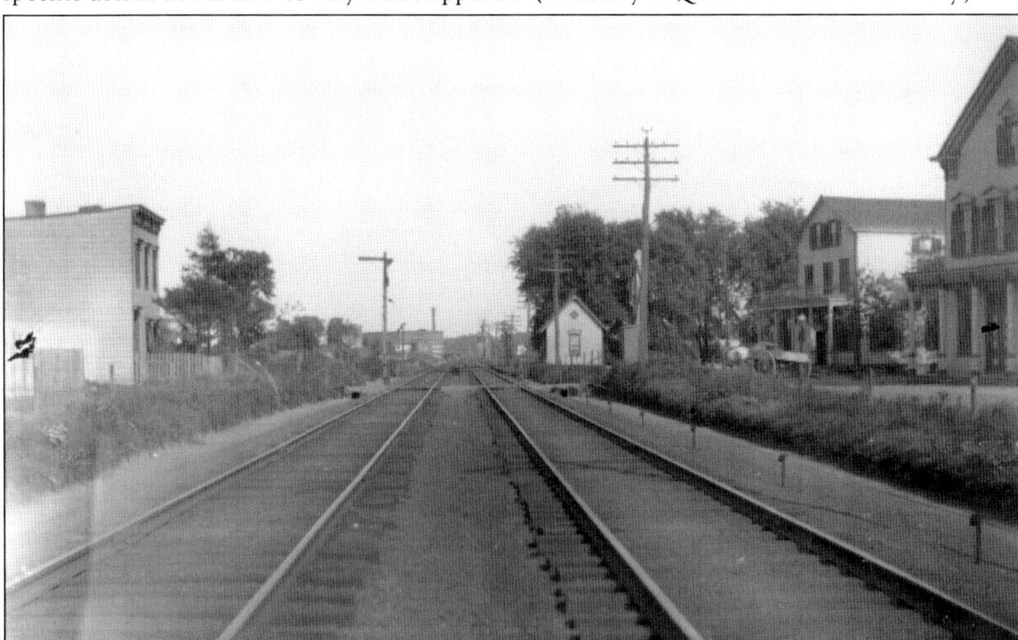

The Long Island Railroad route through Glendale was fully developed by the time this 1906 photograph was taken. The view shown is looking east near Seventy-second Place, past the mixture of private homes and guesthouses that line the tracks. After the station building was torn down, the platform was still used, but if the engineer did not see any passengers waiting on the platform, the train would not make the Glendale stop. (Courtesy of GRHS.)

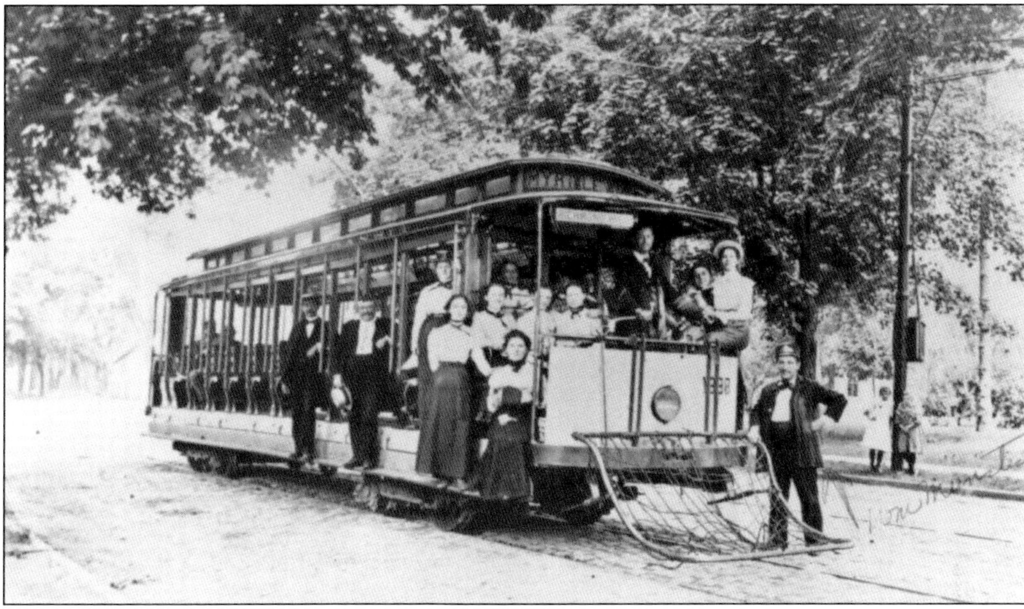

There is a sense of merriment in this 1895 photograph of the Myrtle Avenue trolley and conductor William Munster with his passengers, who may be on their way to an outing at one of Glendale's picnic parks. The main street through Glendale was named for all of the myrtle trees that lined it and that are prominent in the image. (Courtesy of GRHS.)

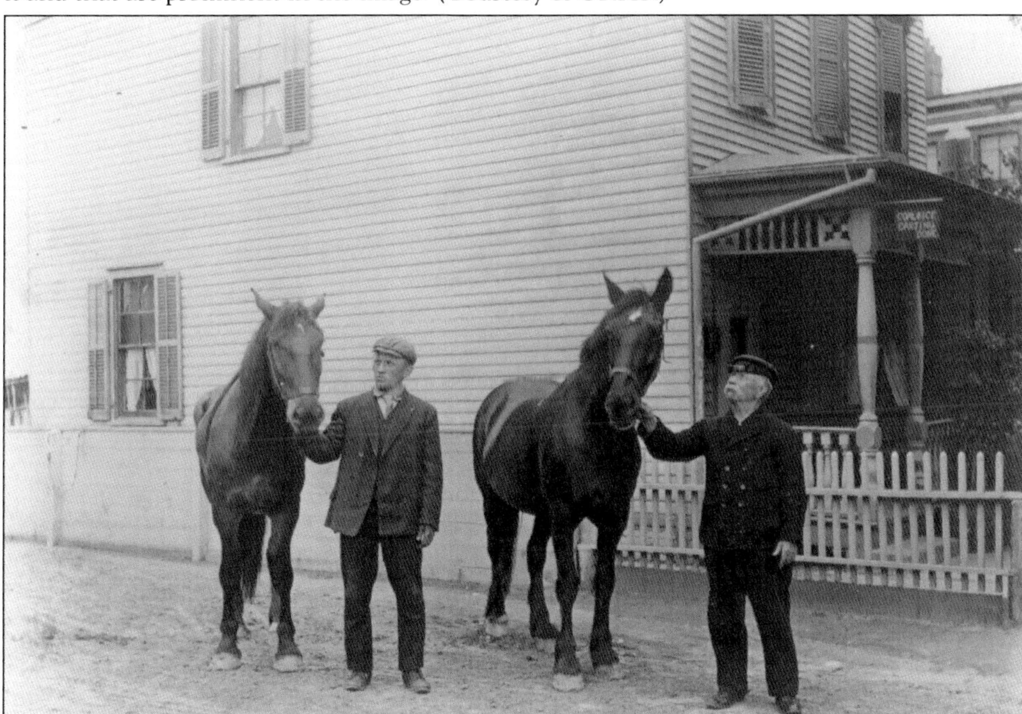

Not all of the transportation in Glendale was by rail, however, as this 1915 photograph of William and Jacob Keller shows. They are proudly displaying the horses that they used for their local carting business, which is advertised on the small sign over the front porch. (Courtesy of GRHS.)

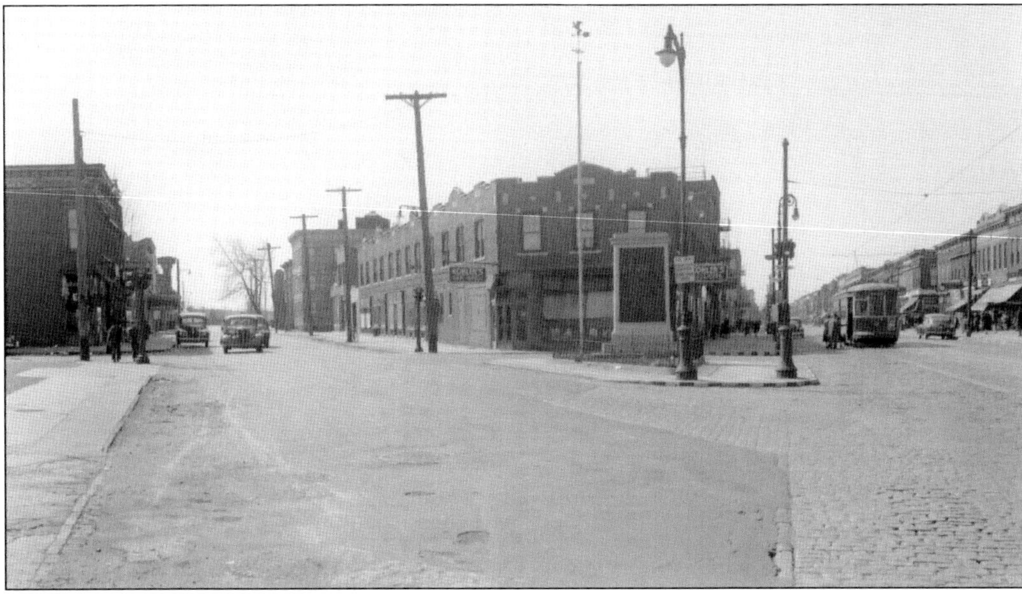

The intersection of Cooper and Myrtle Avenues is shown here in 1945, with the Myrtle Avenue trolley making its way past what would become the Zum Stammtisch restaurant in later years. Children traveling on the trolley from the western end of Glendale to St. Pancras School were able to ride the trolley for one nickel, as long as they had a special student pass. (Courtesy of GRHS.)

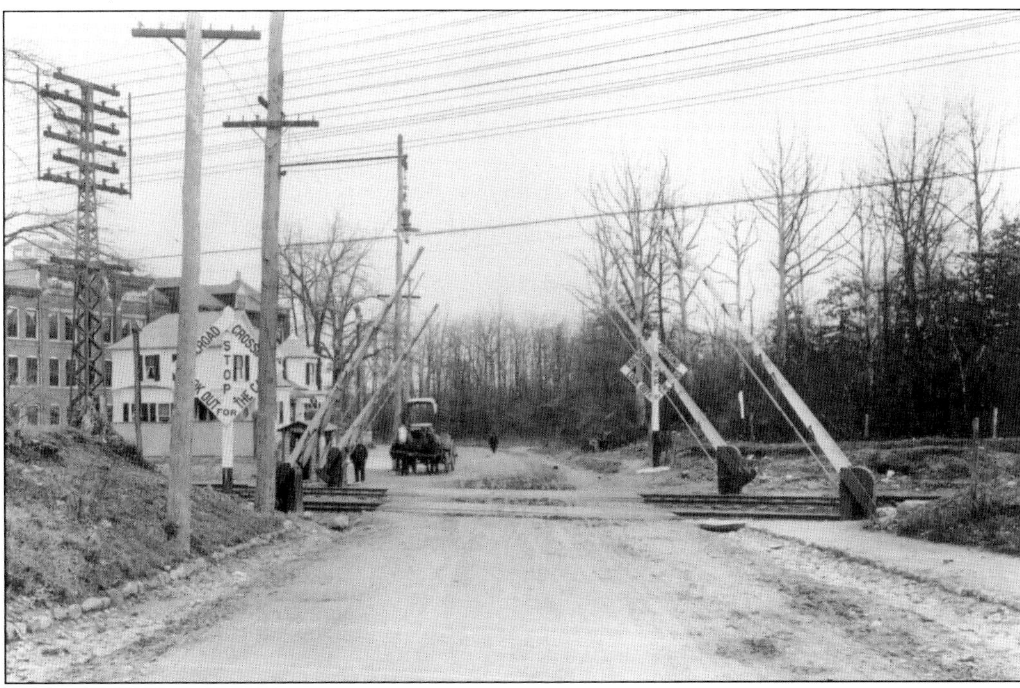

This 1911 photograph shows traffic about to cross the railroad tracks at Trotting Course Lane. The fact that the traffic consists of only one horse-drawn wagon seems appropriate in view of the name of the street crossing. At that time, the gates required an operator to open them, and he is seen here standing outside of the small shack on the far side of the racks. (Courtesy of GRHS.)

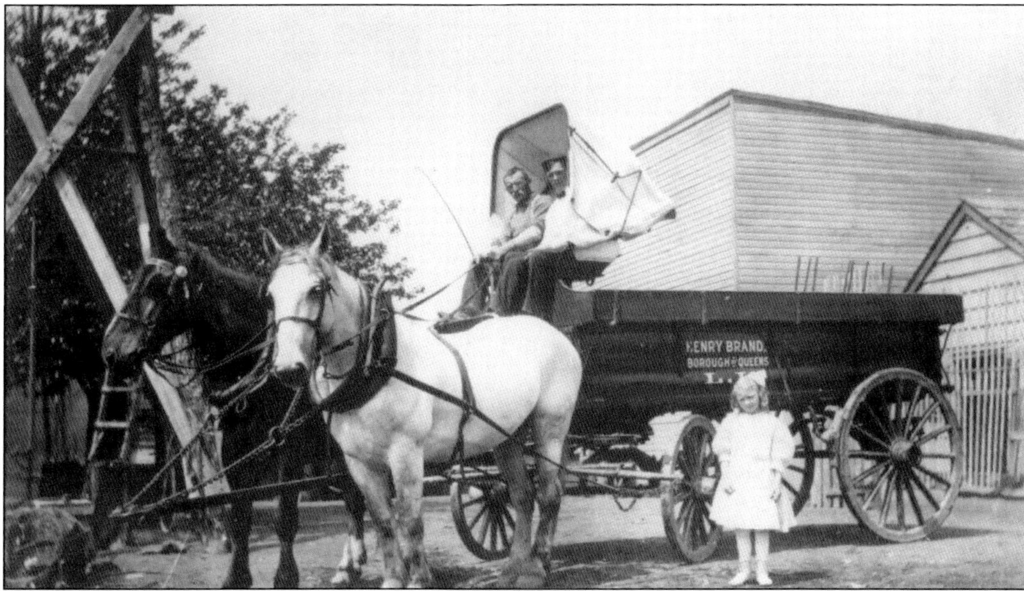

This undated photograph is an example of a local business still using a horse-drawn delivery wagon to transport its goods. The name "Henry Brand" is displayed on the wagon, with its unusual pairing of one black and one white horse, and the young lady shown is likely a member of the Brand family. (Courtesy of GRHS.)

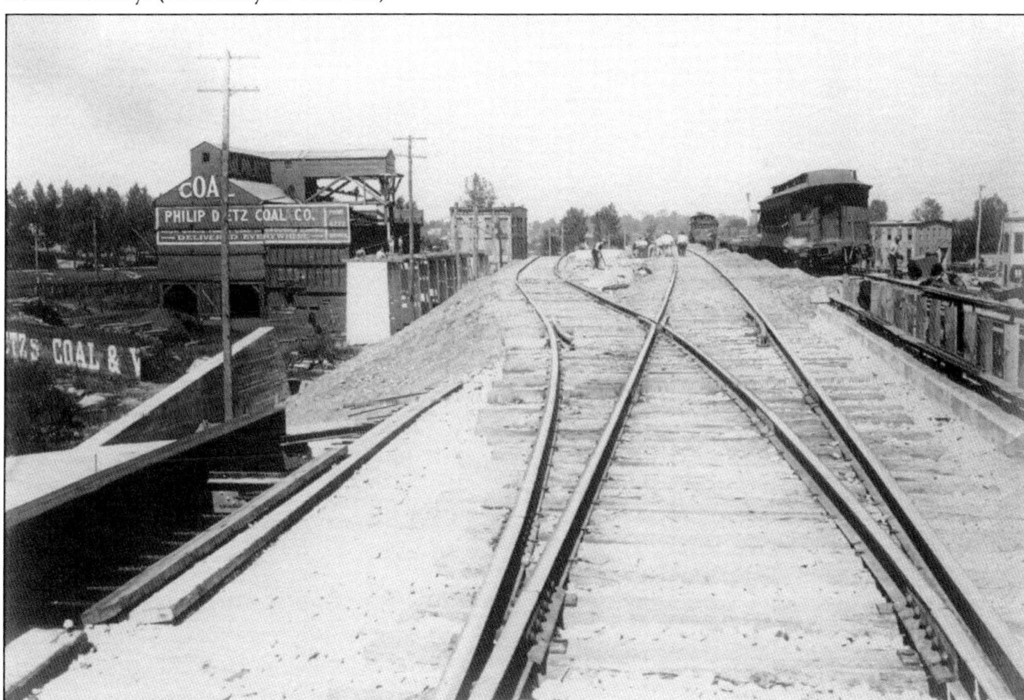

The Dietz Coal Company building shown on the left indicates that this 1913 photograph was taken in the vicinity of Cypress Hills Street and Fresh Pond Road. The tracks branch off to the left to enter the Dietz yard, and the factory on the right is the Ivanhoe Tobacco Company plant. (Courtesy of GRHS.)

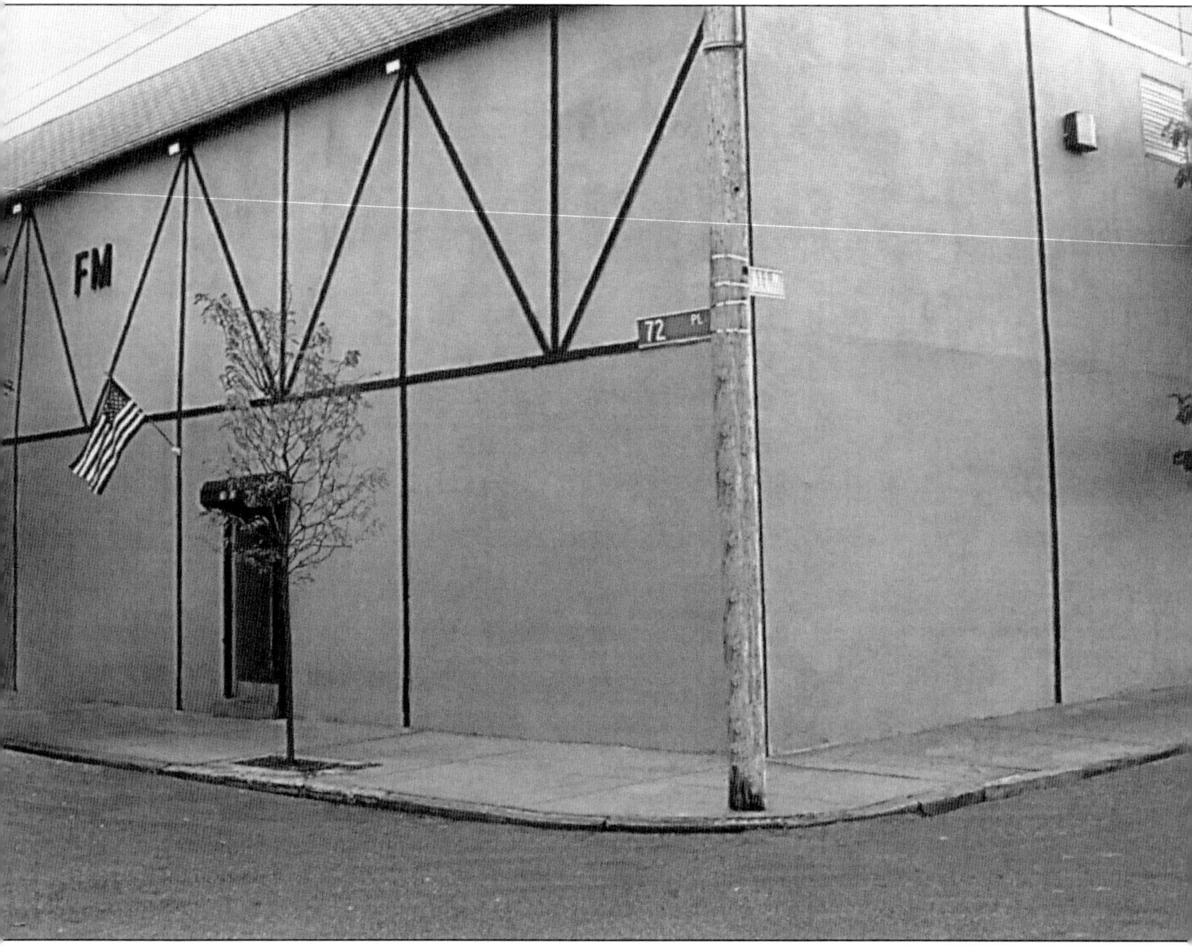

Easy access to freight transportation played a pivotal role in the expansion of one of Glendale's early manufacturers. Founded in 1929 by Frederick Mink Sr., the company carved out a niche for itself in the market for brushes in a variety of industries. FM Brush Company became known for its unique style of brushes for cosmetic, art, theatrical, medical, and craft industries. The company continues to be known throughout the world for the excellence of its products and employs more than 350 people in its US and overseas operations. It continues to manufacture its brushes by hand in a manner that makes them their own art form. Amazingly, members of the original Mink family continue to serve in key management positions in the company, more than 85 years after it began during the early years of the development of Glendale.

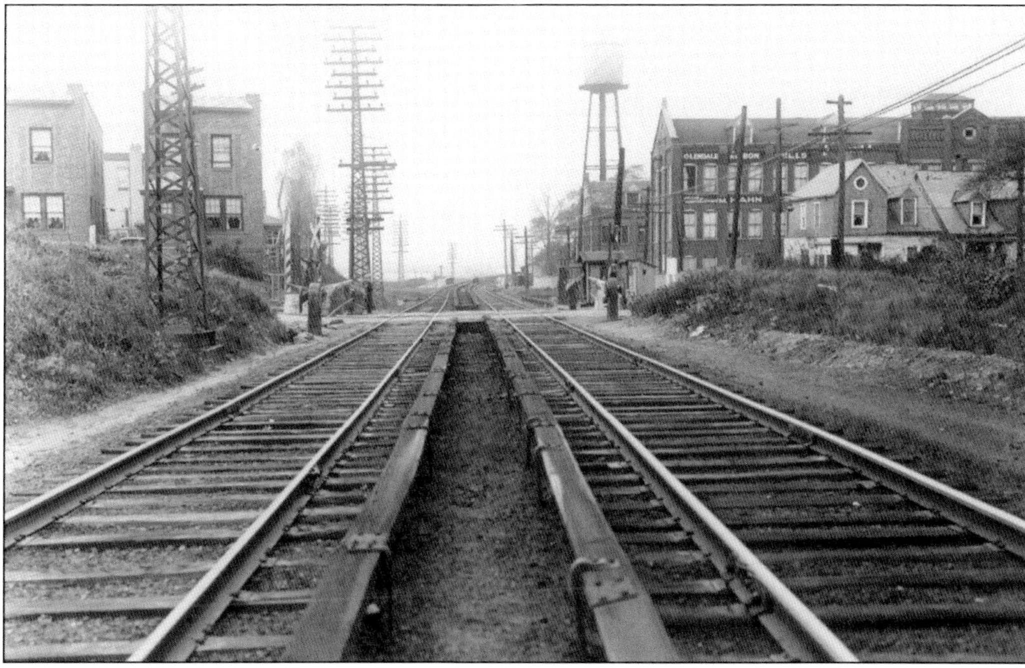

While the image on page 94 shows a horse-drawn wagon at the Trotting Cross Lane railroad crossing, this later photograph from 1935 shows the result of 24 years of industrial development. The little shack is still there, but the crossing gates were automated by this time. (Courtesy of GRHS.)

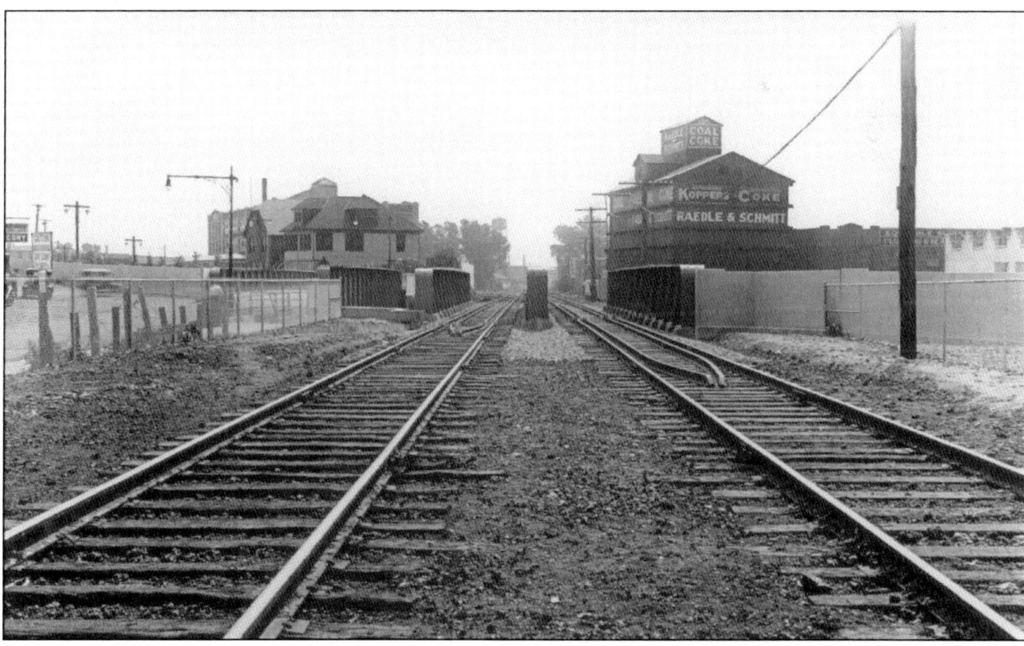

With no other fuel source at the time, 1930s Glendale relied on coal and its byproduct, coke, for all of its energy needs, and only the railroad could bring them there. This 1935 photograph shows a huge storage facility operated by the Koppers Company, with the rail line and switching mechanism that would divert the coal cars off to their siding. (Courtesy of GRHS.)

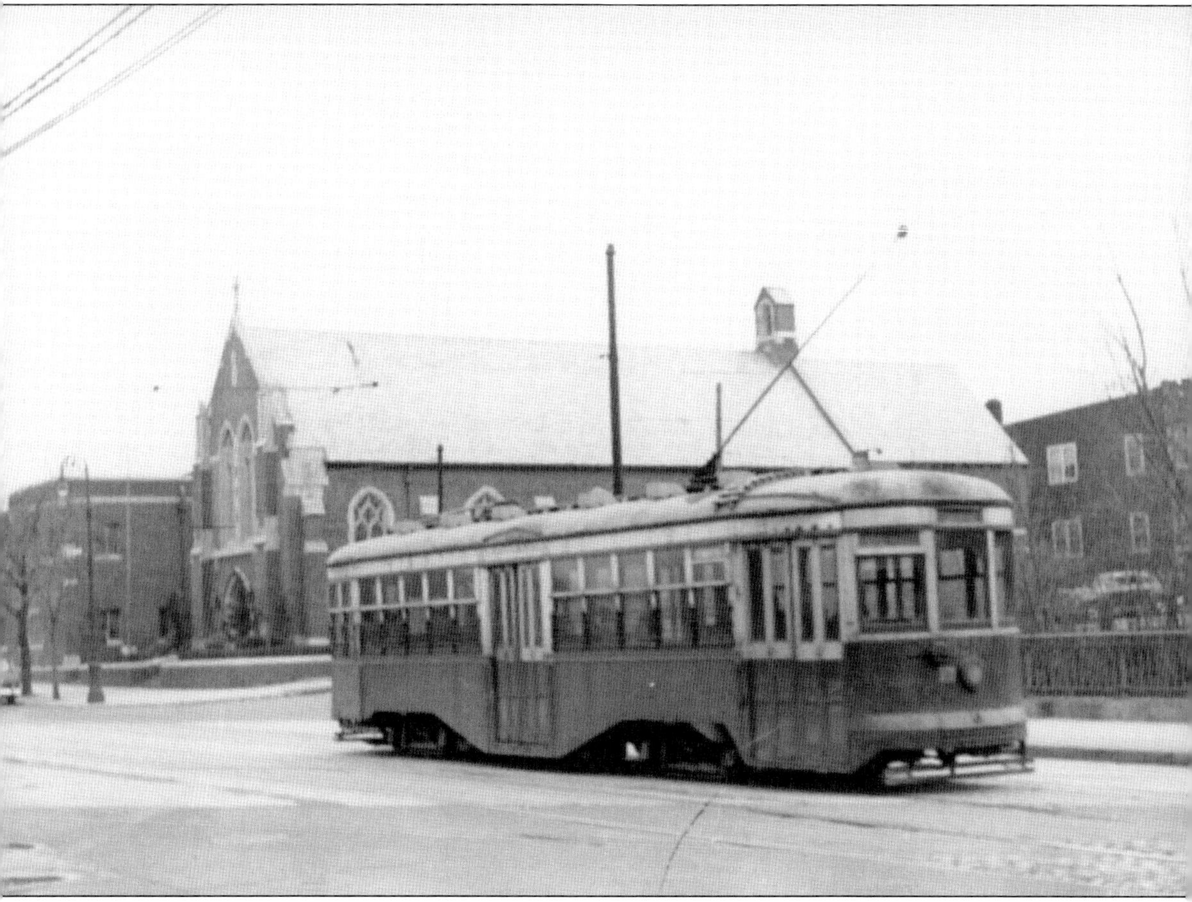

By 1948, the trolley lines serving Glendale were electrified and operated by Brooklyn Manhattan Transit (BMT). They ran up and down Myrtle Avenue and allowed transfers to separate lines such as the Cypress Hills Line and the Lutheran Line, both of which took passengers to some of the area's cemeteries. (Courtesy of GRHS.)

Seven

Celebrating Diversity

While the area known today as Glendale had its origins in the early Dutch and English colonies, for much of that period, it was mostly farmland. Glendale's development lagged behind that of the surrounding areas that were part of Greater Ridgewood, but when its time came, it was early German and Irish immigrants that took advantage of the opportunities that this open land offered. One of the earliest Irish farmers was Patrick Lyons, who acquired 35 acres near where the parkway is today and turned it into a cattle and hog farm.

While many German immigrants flocked to the Glendale/Ridgewood area and also became farmers, others made their mark in different ways. The great picnic parks and restaurants for which the area was so well known were opened by families with names like Scheible, Walter, Pfleghardt, and Deckelmann. The community that they created brought even more German immigrants into early Glendale.

As the town grew, so did the spiritual needs of its people, and many of the early churches catered to people of the Lutheran faith, which was so prominent in the German community. Later years saw the addition of Baptist, Methodist, Catholic, and United Christian churches in Glendale, as people of Italian, Hispanic, and Eastern European descent moved into the area. Today, with the creation of synagogues and places of worship for other faiths in the surrounding communities, all of the people of Glendale have the opportunity to practice the faith of their choice. This diversity is reflected in some of the cemeteries surrounding Glendale as well, where different sections are set aside for specific ethnic and religious groups.

The Glendale of today is a mixture of cultures and ethnic backgrounds, all joined together by an appreciation for what the town has to offer. Its people may get on a train each day to go off to work in Manhattan or some other part of the New York area, but they return home at night to a quieter, more welcoming part of New York, which never strayed too far from what it started out to be.

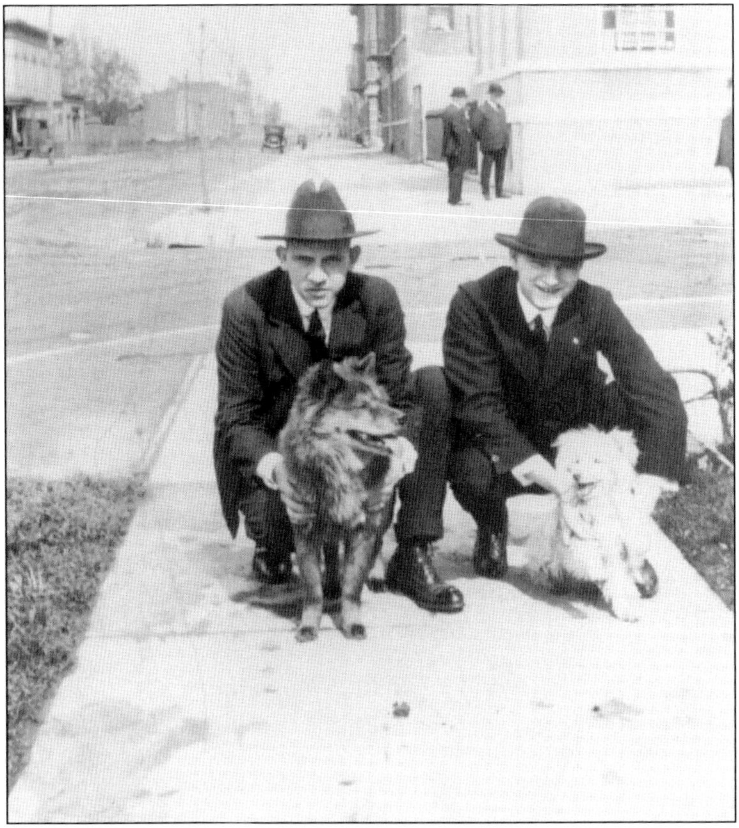

Two members of an early Glendale German family, the Wengler brothers, are pictured here in a 1920 photograph. Even though the uniform of the day for those times was a dark suit and white shirt, note their different choices in how to wear their hats and the obvious different choice in the type of dog each one preferred. (Courtesy of GRHS.)

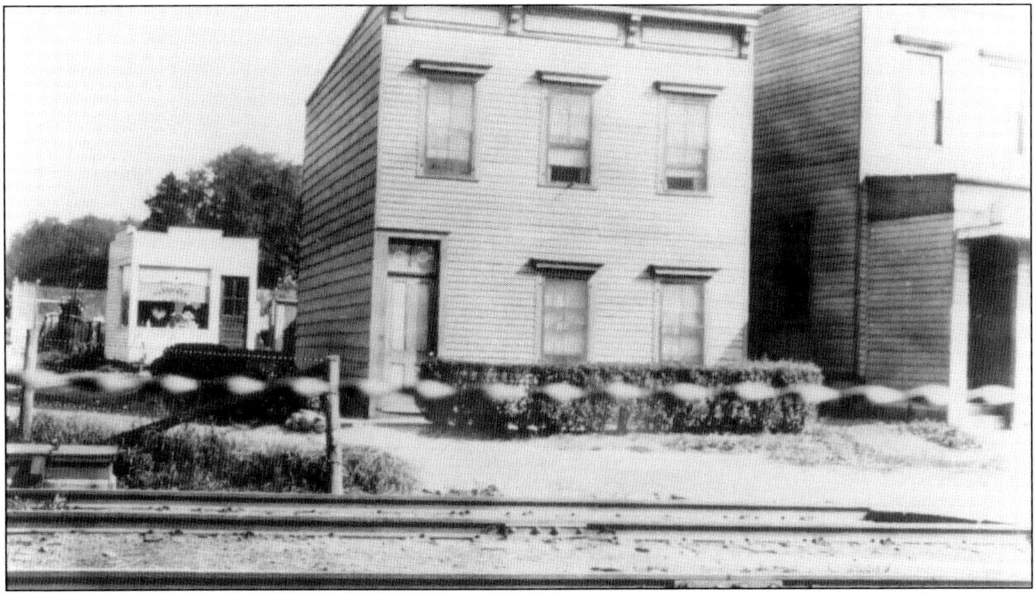

Even though the choice of location was not ideal, Margaret Nicke apparently managed to operate a florist shop out of her home in 1925 by using the shed-like building in the rear of the house at 73-01 Edsall Avenue. As the caption in this photograph indicates, the building was still standing as late as 1988. (Courtesy of GRHS.)

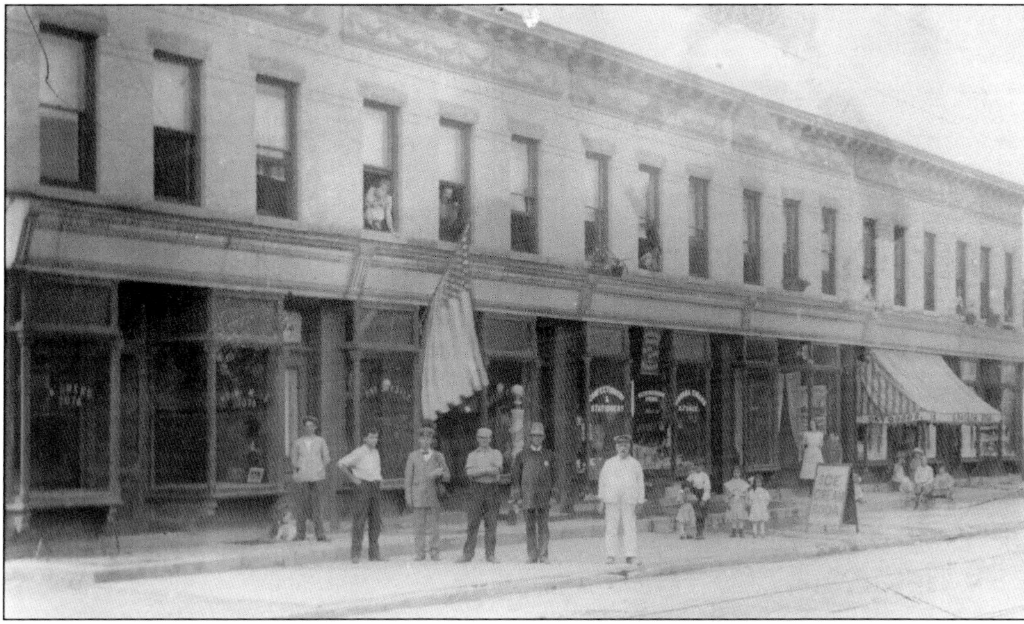

The quality of this 1905 photograph is starting to suffer, but it presents a wonderful picture of the diversity of the old Glendale community. A couple of young men stand by as a mailman, a policeman in a London Bobby–type helmet, and a milkman in white all pose for the camera. Everyone seems to have just stopped what they were doing, including the children standing by the ice cream sign behind the main group. Word must have spread quickly about a picture being taken, because even the apartment dwellers on the second floor made sure that they were leaning out their open windows so they would be included in the shot. (Courtesy of GRHS.)

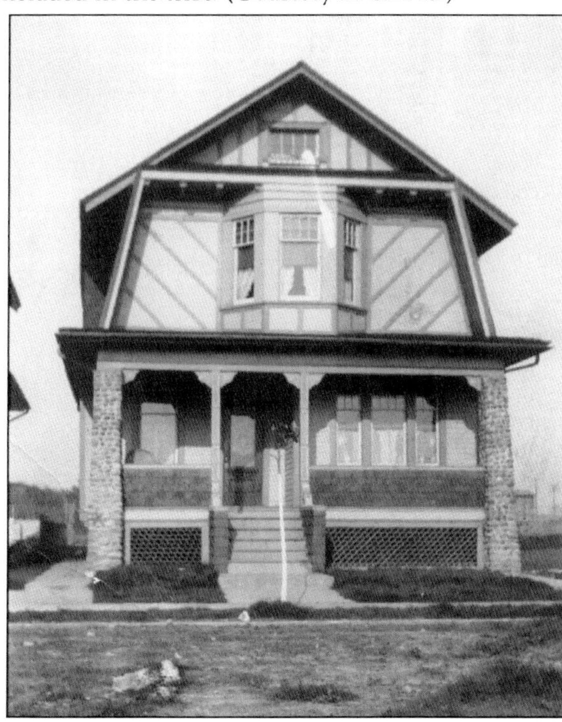

John A. Fischer was a builder and developer who constructed a number of homes of this type during the Glendale building boom. This 1911 photograph shows one of the homes on Seventy-ninth Street, which may have been the one that Fischer himself lived in for many years. (Courtesy of GRHS.)

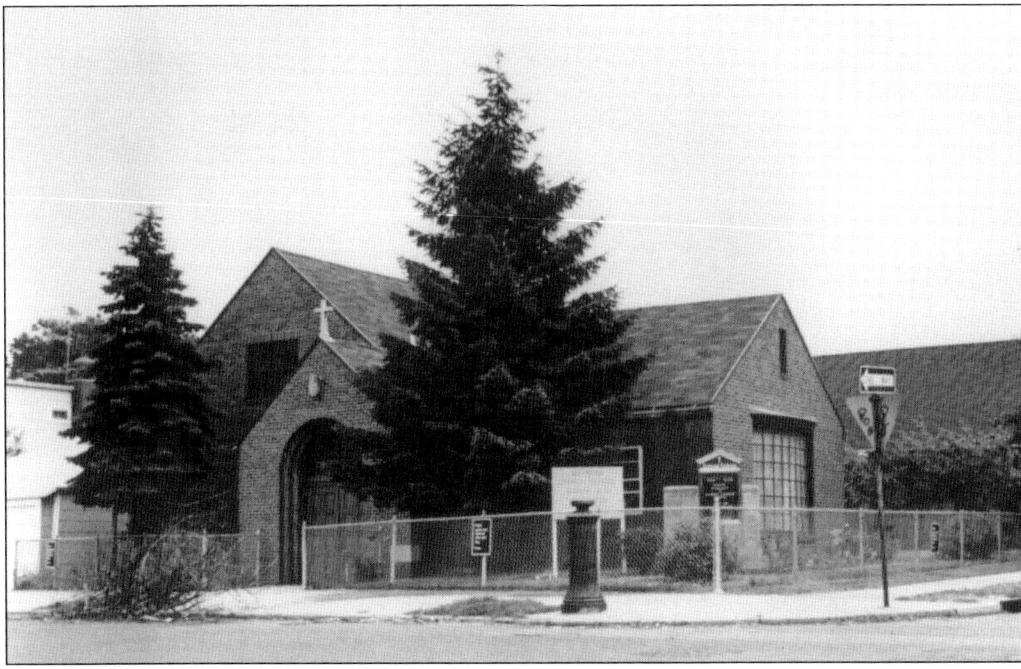

The Evangelical Lutheran Church of the Ascension, situated on Seventy-eighth Street, was organized in 1924 with the Reverend George U. Preuss as its first pastor. Following the death of Reverend Preuss in 1937, his son assumed leadership of the congregation until his retirement in 1970. (Courtesy of GRHS.)

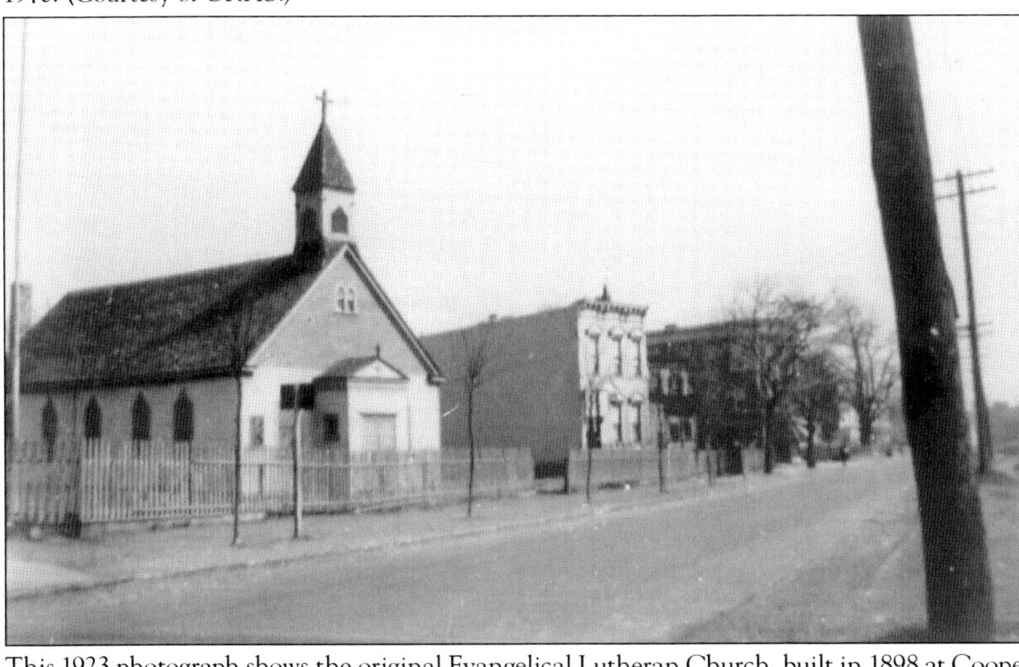

This 1923 photograph shows the original Evangelical Lutheran Church, built in 1898 at Cooper Avenue and Seventy-first Street. The building was later converted to a parish hall when a new church was built in 1920, but it was closed in 2002, and the congregation was absorbed by other Lutheran parishes in the area. (Courtesy of GRHS.)

The United Methodist Church of Glendale is a result of the merger of two different churches with two different ethnic backgrounds. The Christ Church of Glendale–United Methodist, of English origin, dates back to 1896. It merged with the Glendale United Evangelical Brethren (of German origin) founded in 1912. Pictured here in 1976 is their present church on Central Avenue and Sixty-sixth Street. (Courtesy of GRHS.)

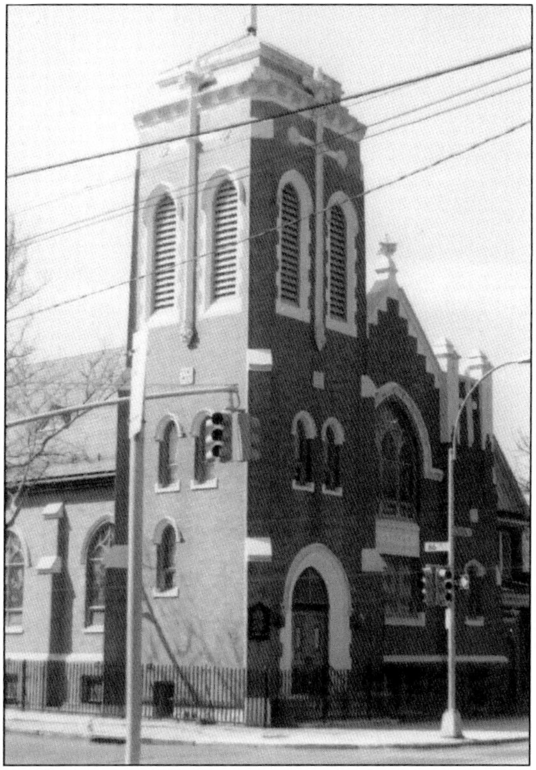

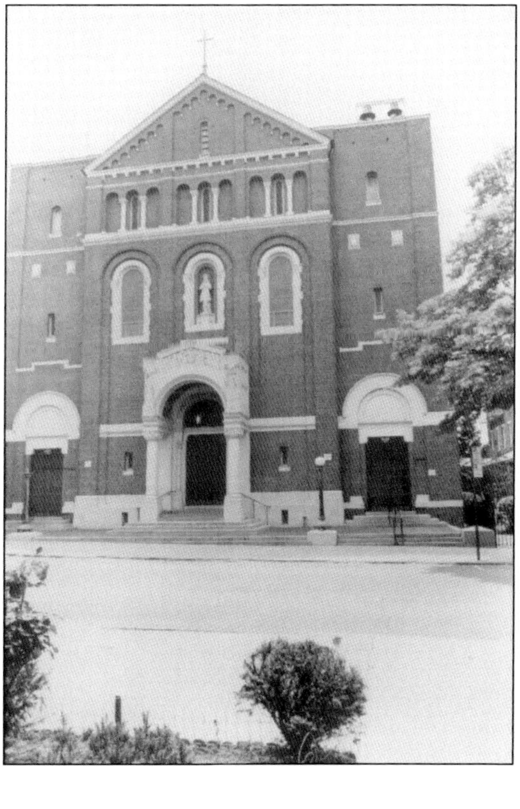

The population growth and building boom of the late 1890s increased the Catholic population of Glendale but gave them no place of worship within the community. The alternatives were St. Brigid's in Ridgewood or St. Margaret's in Middle Village, but with transportation as it was in those days, attending services there was easier said than done. This brought about the beginnings of St. Pancras parish in 1899. (Courtesy of GRHS.)

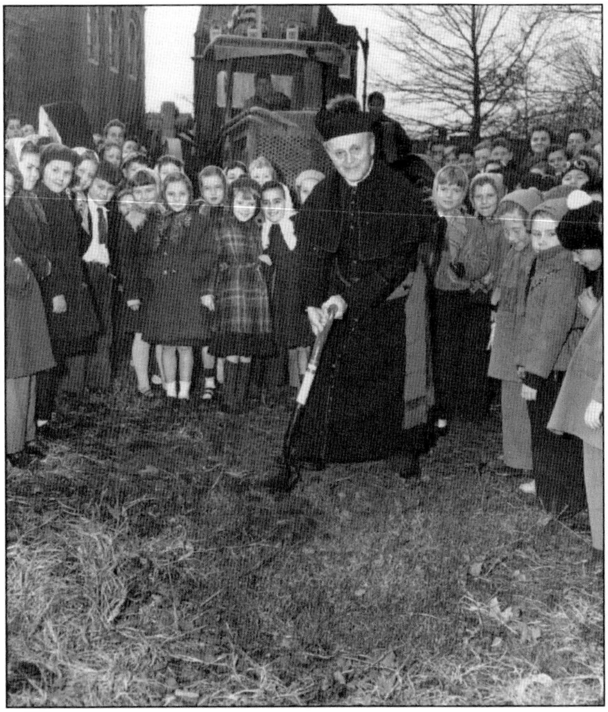

Initially, St. Pancras Roman Catholic Church merely functioned as an out-mission for St. Margaret's, with services being conducted in the local firehouse. It became an independent parish in 1904, operating out of a small building on Myrtle Avenue that also functioned as a school. It was not until 1909 that the present church, built in the Roman Basilica style (preceding page), was built on Sixty-eighth Street. The 1950 photograph on the left shows Msgr. Herman Pfeiffer breaking ground for the new school, surrounded by some of its future students. The 1940 photograph below shows the parish rectory, which was built in 1917, being moved to its present location next to the church. (Both, courtesy of GRHS.)

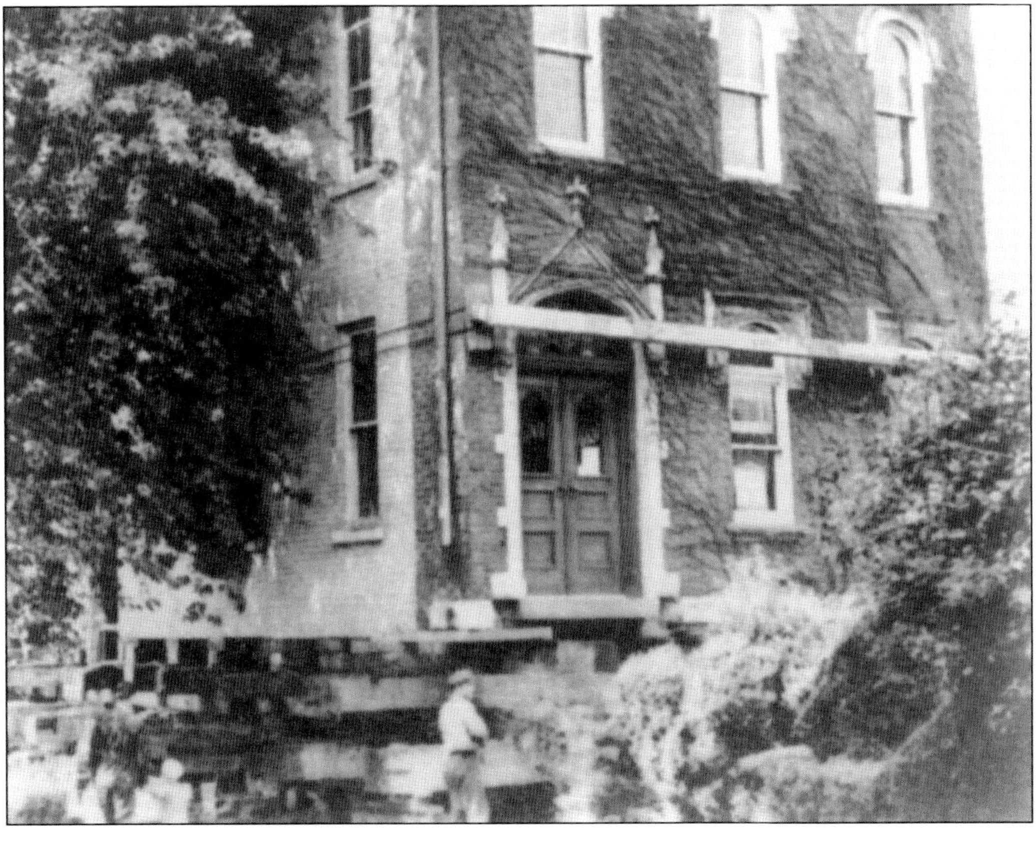

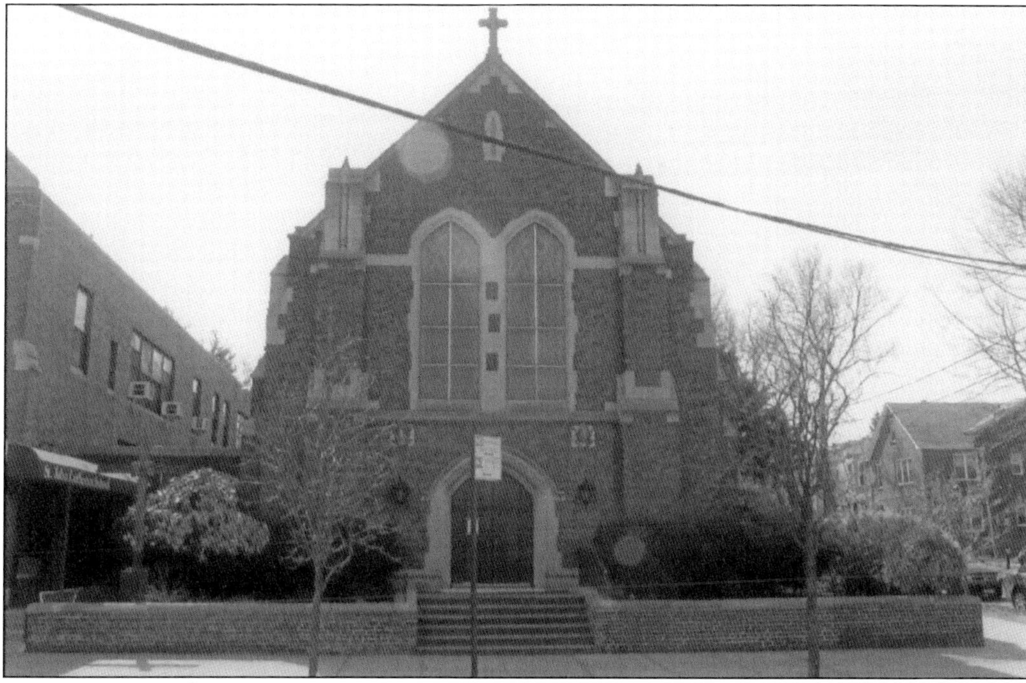

The predominantly German population of early Glendale made the Lutheran faith the predominant religion in the area and brought about the creation of several Lutheran parishes. The St. John's Evangelical Lutheran Church was founded in 1844 at the home of local resident Carl Mertz. In the early days, their services were held in Public School No. 3, but they were able to move into their own building in Brooklyn in 1846. By 1884, the congregation had grown to more than 1,500 members, so a second site was chosen on Maujer Street (also in Brooklyn), and a new church was built. As growth continued and the parish required a larger church, the present church, located on Myrtle Avenue at Eighty-eighth Street, was built in 1926. (Above, photograph by the author; below, courtesy of GRHS.)

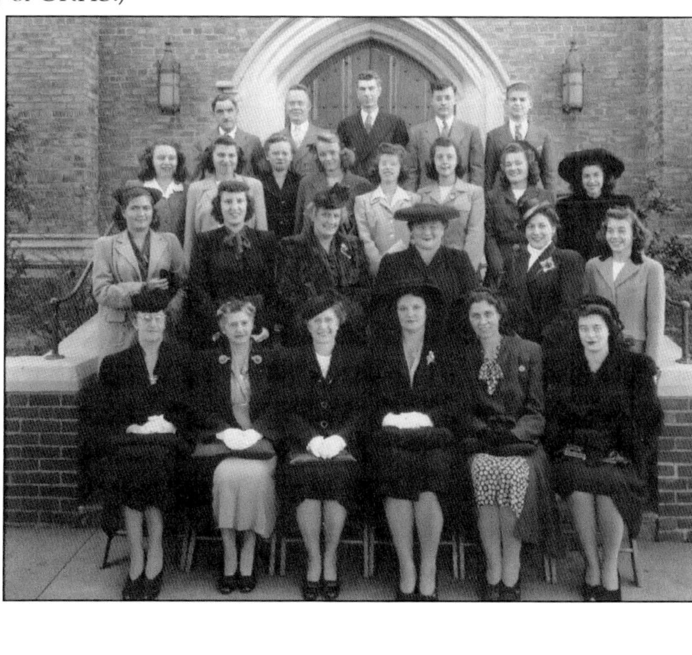

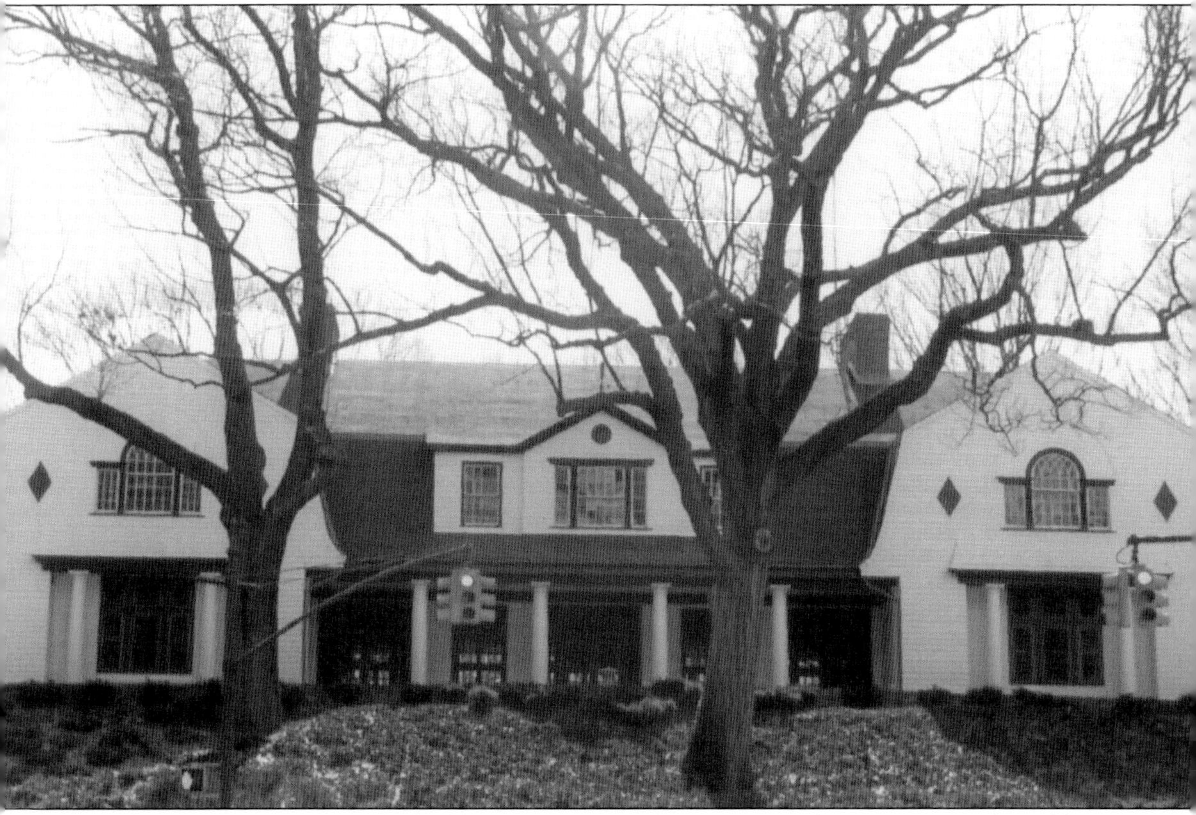

There is a magnificent old building on Forest Park Drive near the entrance to the golf course that was designed to pay tribute to the early Dutch influence in the Glendale area. It was built in 1905 in a Dutch Colonial Revival style and was the clubhouse for the first nine-hole golf course. The building is named Oak Ridge, and it is set in a beautiful grove of red and black oak trees on the crest of a mass of rock called the Harbor Hill Moraine. The property was purchased from landowner David Leggett by the Brooklyn Department of Parks, who then commissioned the architectural firm of Helmle, Huberty & Hudswell to design the structure. It presently serves as an administration building for the park, the home of the Queens Council for the Arts, and a community center. (Courtesy of the author.)

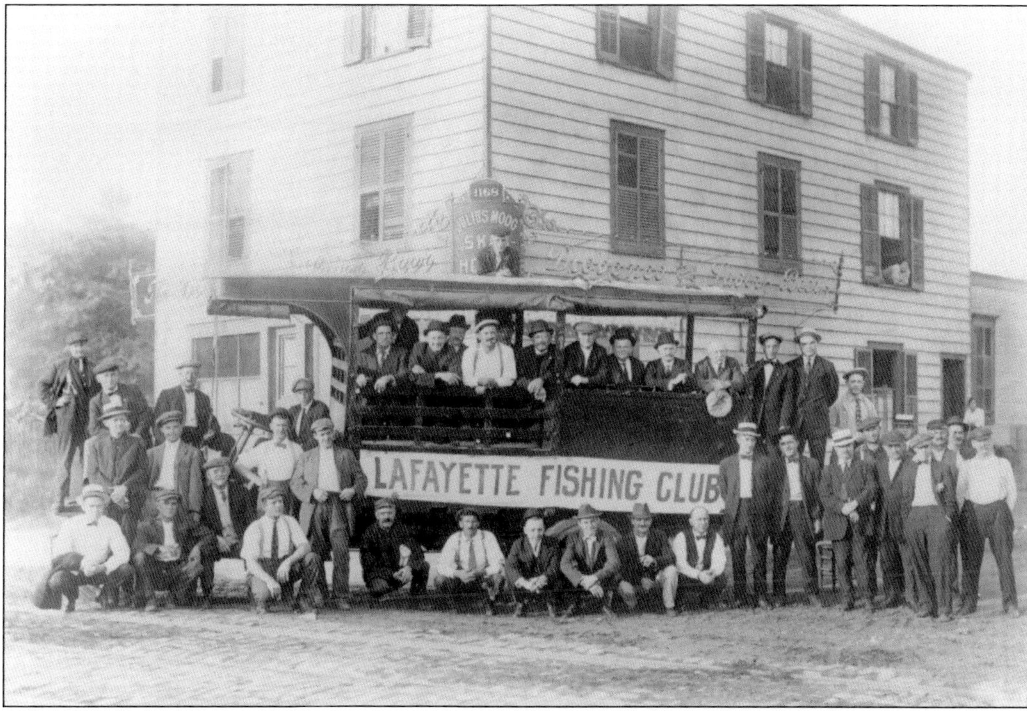

The Lafayette Fishing Club held its meetings at Julius Moog's saloon on Seventy-ninth Avenue, which was named Lafayette Street at the time. Saloon keepers like Moog frequently served in official capacities for local sporting clubs, filling the position of treasurer or some other elected office. (Courtesy of GRHS.)

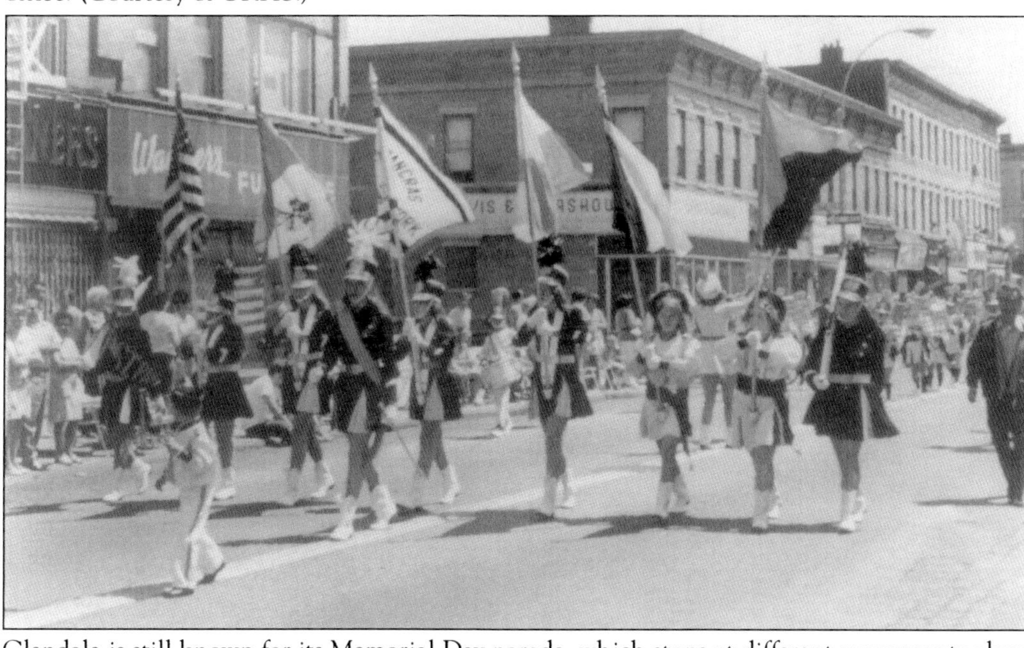

Glendale is still known for its Memorial Day parade, which stops at different monuments along the Myrtle Avenue route to pay tribute to the town's war veterans. This 1973 photograph shows a local school band marching past the corner of Sixty-sixth Street. (Courtesy of GRHS.)

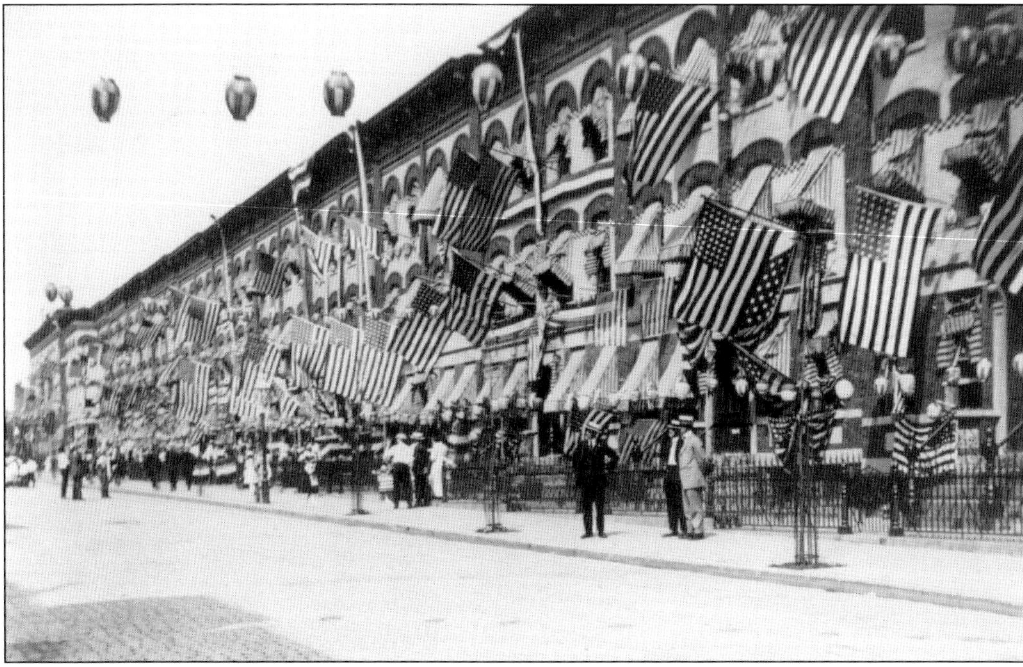

This undated photograph from the 1920s or 1930s shows a flag-lined street and residents who appear to be waiting for a parade. Judging by the period clothing, they may be celebrating the old Armistice Day holiday, commemorating the end of World War I. (Courtesy of GRHS.)

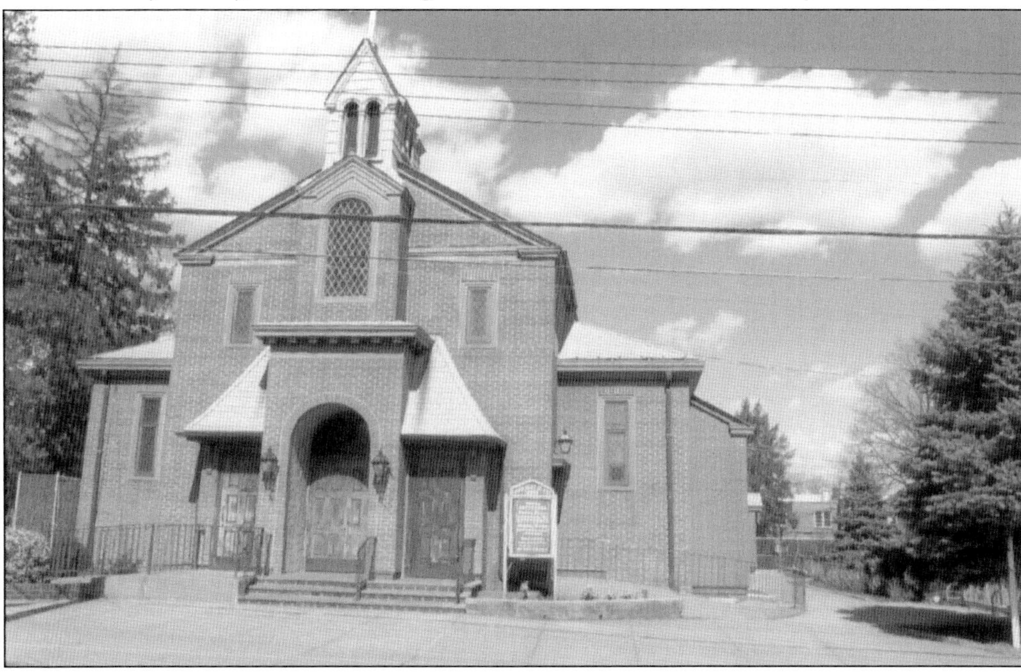

Sacred Heart Roman Catholic Parish was founded in 1929 in a building that had formerly been used as the Emerald Park Dance Hall. The parish grew rapidly, and this new building was dedicated in 1930, with its first mass celebrated on the Feast of the Sacred Heart. A rectory, school, and Dominican convent were added in later years. (Courtesy of the author.)

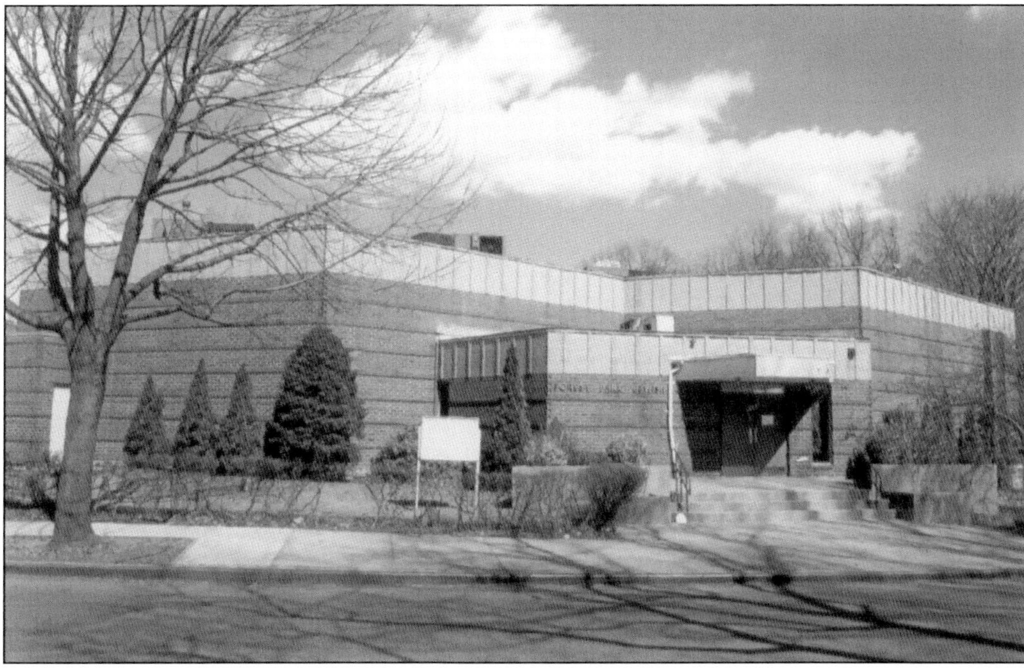

For many years, the Jewish residents of Glendale had to go to nearby Forest Hills or Rego Park to attend services, but in 1956, this facility, located on Myrtle Avenue near Ninetieth Street, was dedicated as the Forest Park Jewish Center. (Courtesy of the author.)

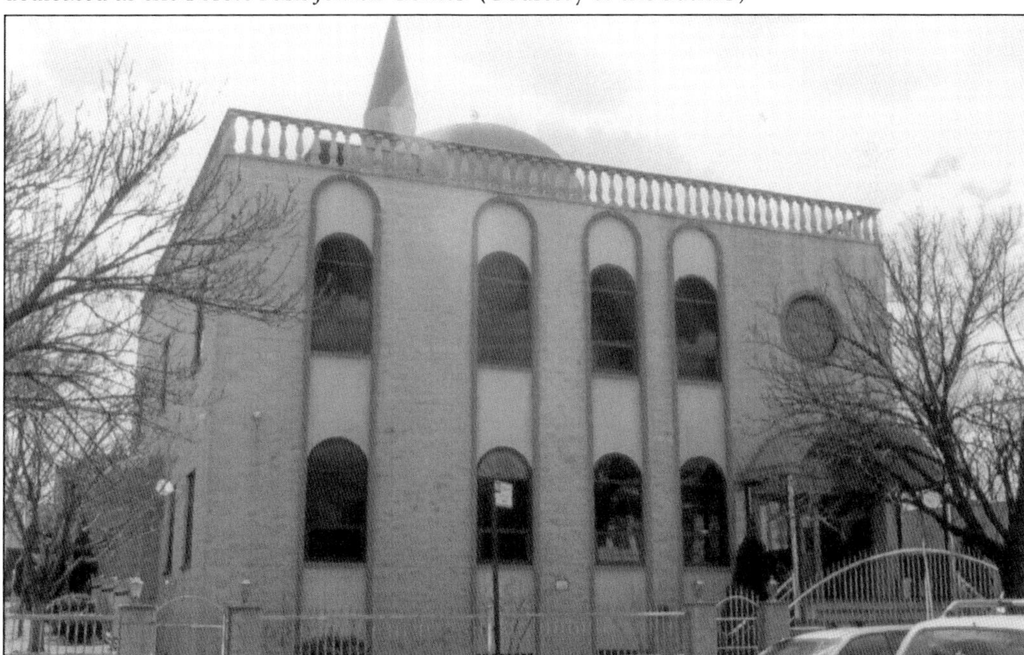

Eastern Europeans of the Muslim faith, as one of the more recent ethnic groups to become a part of the Glendale community, did not have a place to practice their faith until the construction of the Albanian-American Islamic Center in 2002. It is located on Myrtle Avenue near Seventy-second Street and is distinguished by its lovely minaret and dome. (Courtesy of the author.)

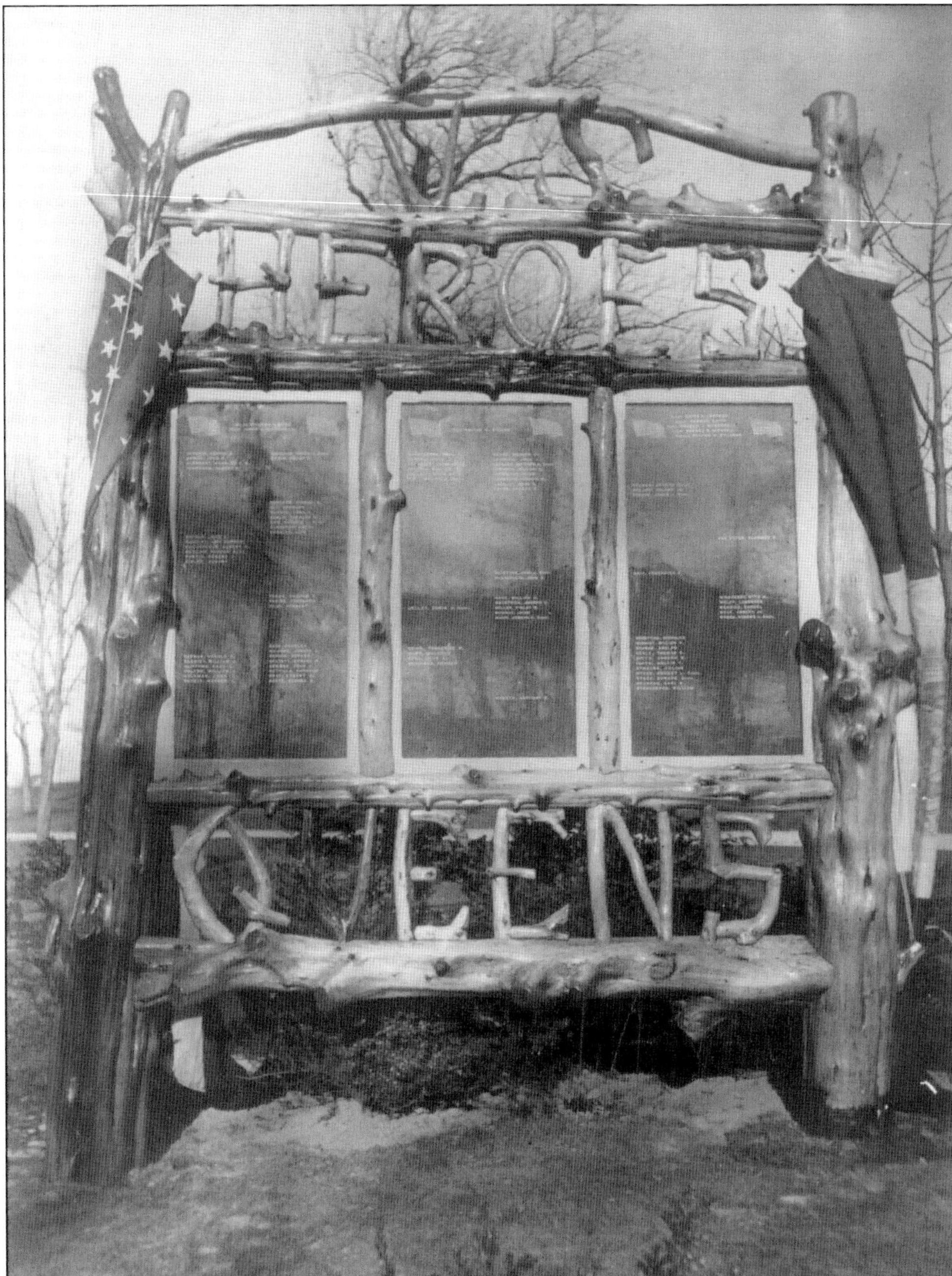

This photograph, taken in 1918, shows a temporary memorial built in Forest Park to honor the area's heroes of World War I. It was simply made of wood and served until more permanent memorials could be erected in Glendale and nearby Richmond Hill. The Glendale memorial commissioned in 1921 is pictured on page 66 and lists the 21 Glendale men who never came home from the war. An additional memorial was built in Richmond Hill in 1925 and features a sculpture of an infantryman, also known as a doughboy, created by sculptor Joseph Pollia. (Courtesy of Queens Borough Public Library.)

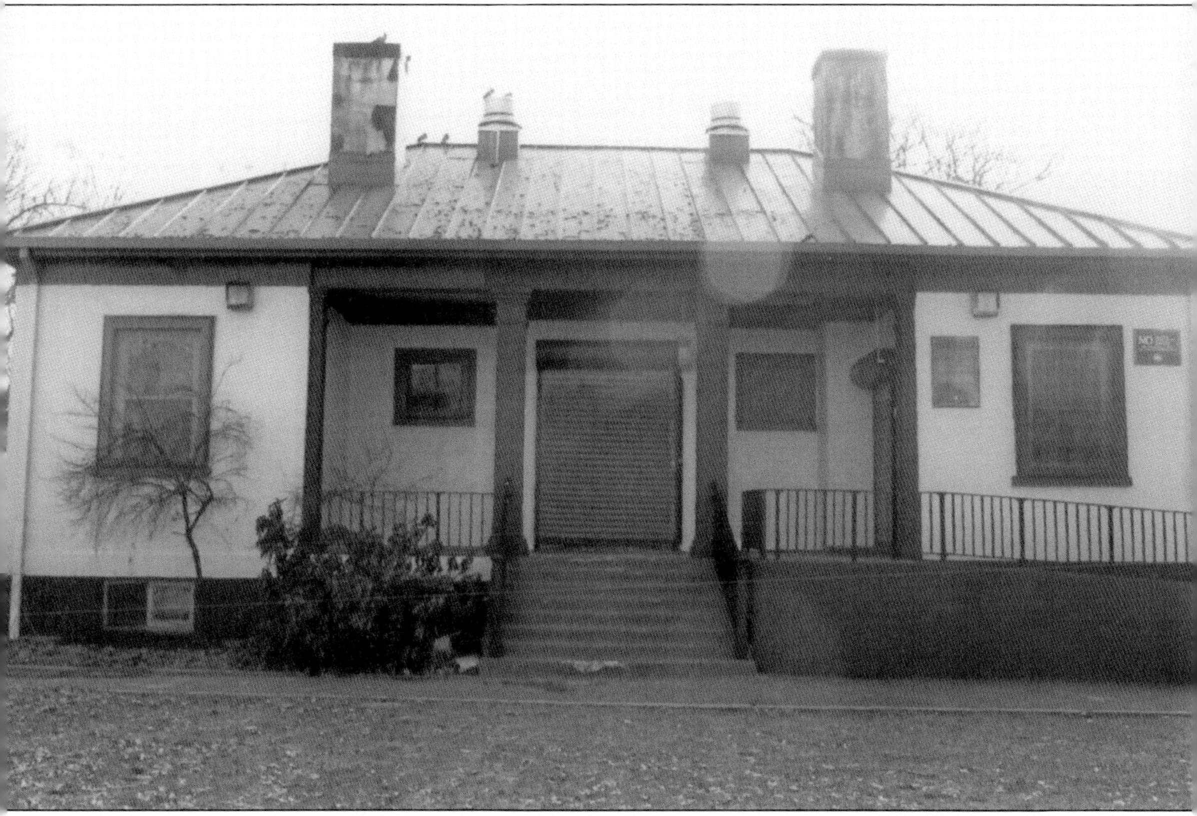

This building, presently used by the New York City Parks Department at the Dry Harbor Playground, is located at Myrtle Avenue and Eightieth Street. The playground name came from one of the original names for the area that would become Glendale. Early settlers in the 1700s, when looking from Cooper Avenue across what was then a valley to Forest Park, would see houses sitting atop the crests of trees and hills, making the view resemble that of a harbor, but with no water. A home built in later years in that area belonged to a French immigrant named Edward Bourcier, who owned 17 acres of wooded land. In 1895, when New York City began to purchase property to create Forest Park, Bourcier sold them 15 acres of his land but kept a two-acre parcel and what was, at that time, a three-story home. The remaining two acres were purchased in 1924, and the original home was reduced to the one-story building that it is today. (Courtesy of the author.)

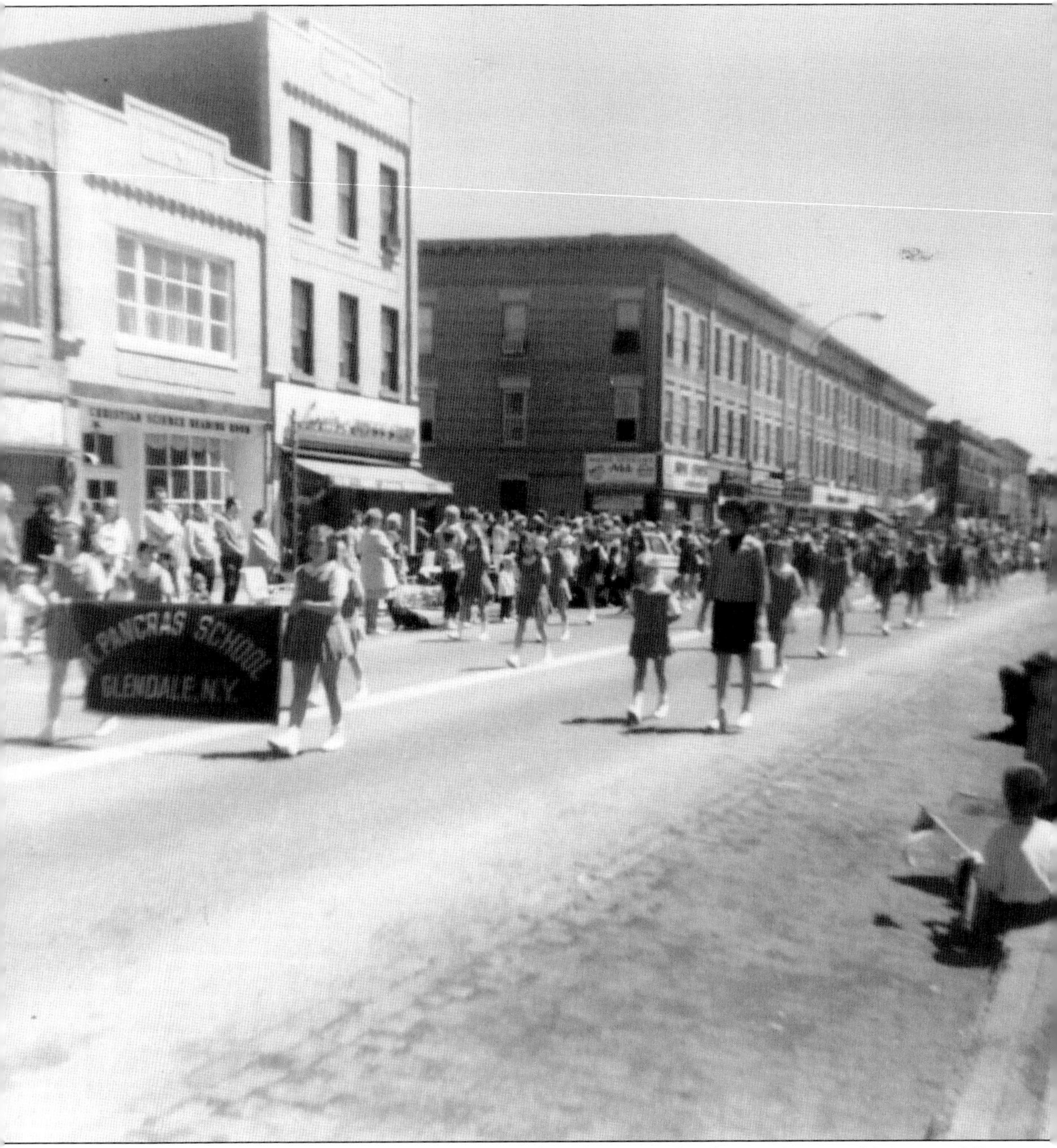

Myrtle Avenue in Glendale has always served as the route for the area's annual Memorial Day parade. At one time, it was also the site of the German-American Steuben Day parade. Pictured here in a 1970s photograph is the St. Pancras brownie troop passing by the Christian Science Reading Room, with the school's marching band in the distance. (Courtesy of Richard and Rose Matzelle.)

Eight

Just for Fun

Summing up the story of Glendale requires touching on a number of different elements in its history that are not related in any way. Many of them are rather lighthearted in nature but support the notion that Glendale was once regarded as a place where people visited just to have fun. The stories of the old picnic parks bear this out, but coupled with this are the stories of the people that lived there and the traditions that they established. One of the best examples of this is an old holiday called Ragamuffins Day that was celebrated on the same day as Thanksgiving. Explaining this practice to anyone who is not from the Greenpoint section of Brooklyn or any of the communities surrounding Glendale, of course, draws incredulous stares.

Glendale has also made its contributions to the entertainment industry, with its own movie studio and places in town that became part of the modern culture because they were featured in television programs and feature films. Over the years, there were roller-skating rinks, bowling alleys, nightclubs, and baseball teams, and at one time, it seemed as though there was a tavern on every corner (even though Glendale never matched Ridgewood in that regard).

Some of this history has been preserved, thanks to the efforts of the historical societies and other civic organizations, but sadly, much of it has been lost. Glendale continues to be a vibrant community, and new chapters in its history are being written every day. The old German restaurants have been replaced by all of the dining options available in the mall at the old Atlas Terminal site. The picnic parks are gone, but Forest Park still offers golf, outdoor concerts, and ample space for picnicking. The diversity continues, as more people of different nationalities move into the area, bringing with them a variety of cultures, so that they can write their own future chapters in the history of this wonderful little town.

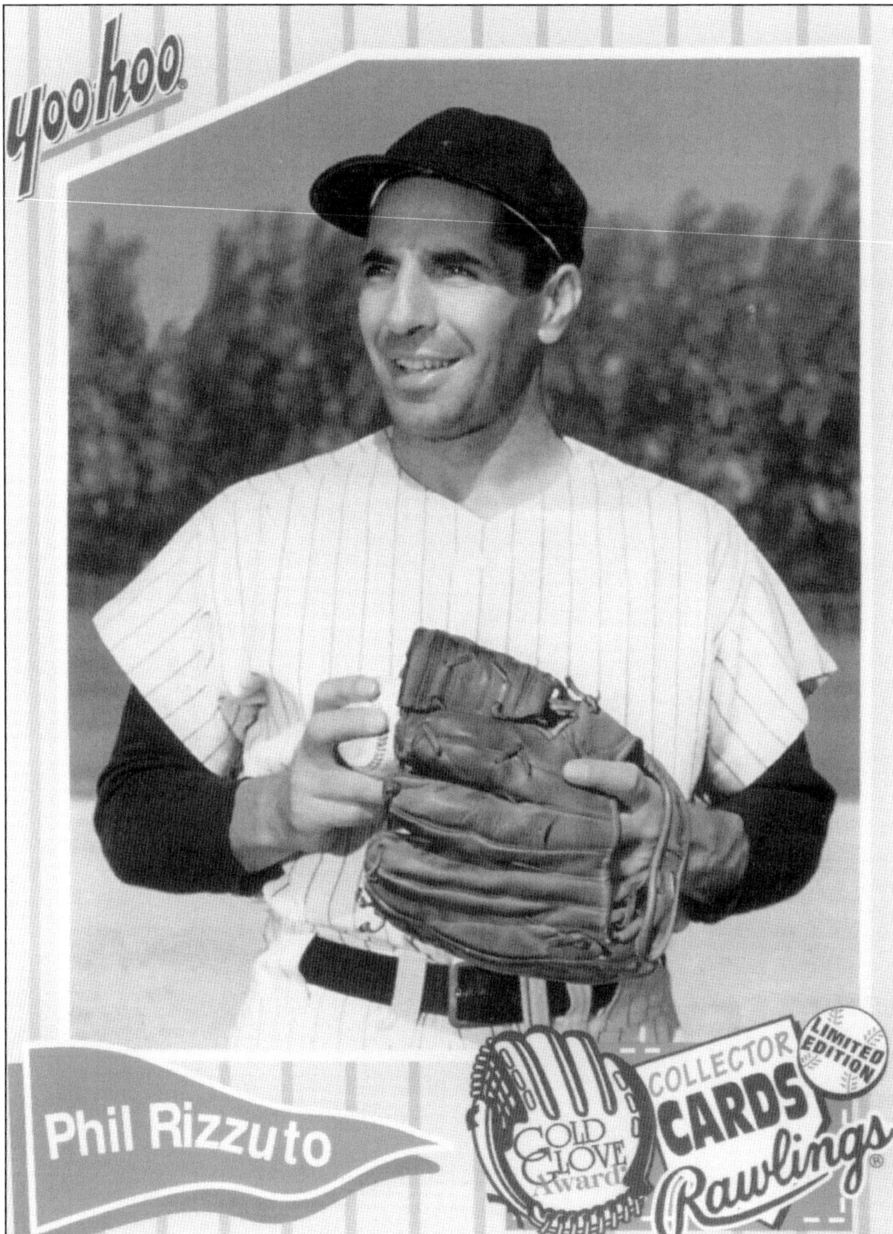

Legendary New York Yankee shortstop Phil Rizzuto grew up in Glendale's Liberty Park section and was a star ballplayer for nearby Richmond Hill High School. He was born in 1917, the son of a trolley car motorman, and lived in Glendale for many years. The Yankees signed him in 1937, and he played for them until 1956. "The Scooter," as he was known, wore no. 10 for the Yankees and played in seven world championship games. He was a five-time all-star and the American League's most valuable player in 1950, and he was voted into the Baseball Hall of Fame in 1994. Rizzuto went on to do play-by-play and sports announcing for the Yankees for an amazing 40 years after his playing career ended. Several generations of Yankee fans watching or listening to games waited for the excitement of the play to reach a high enough level that they heard Phil Rizzuto call out his trademark expression, "Holy Cow!" (Courtesy of GRHS.)

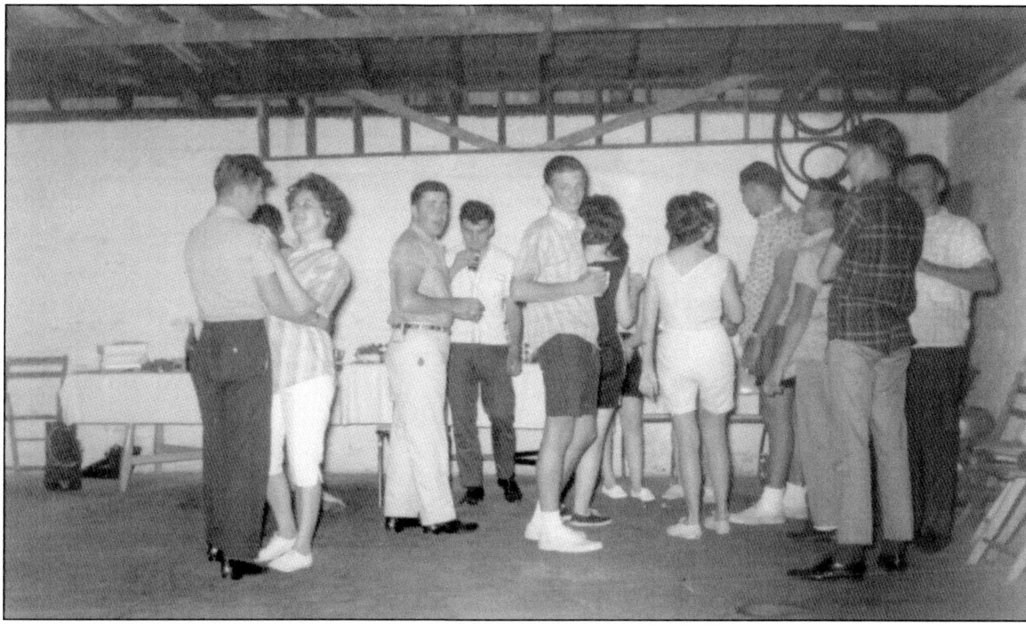

In the 1950s and 1960s in Glendale, young people looking for something to do on lazy summer evenings would sometimes throw impromptu parties. Frequently, the place chosen for the evening would be an oversized garage in someone's backyard. It took some last-minute scrambling, but with everyone doing their share, the cars would be moved out, the floor swept, and some tables and chairs appropriated from several houses. Then, all that was left was to plug in the phonograph. This particular group of friends, some of whom are 18 years old (the legal drinking age at the time), appear to be enjoying a couple of Rheingold or Pabst Blue Ribbon beers, while the ladies on the side wait for someone to ask them to dance. (Both, courtesy of the author.)

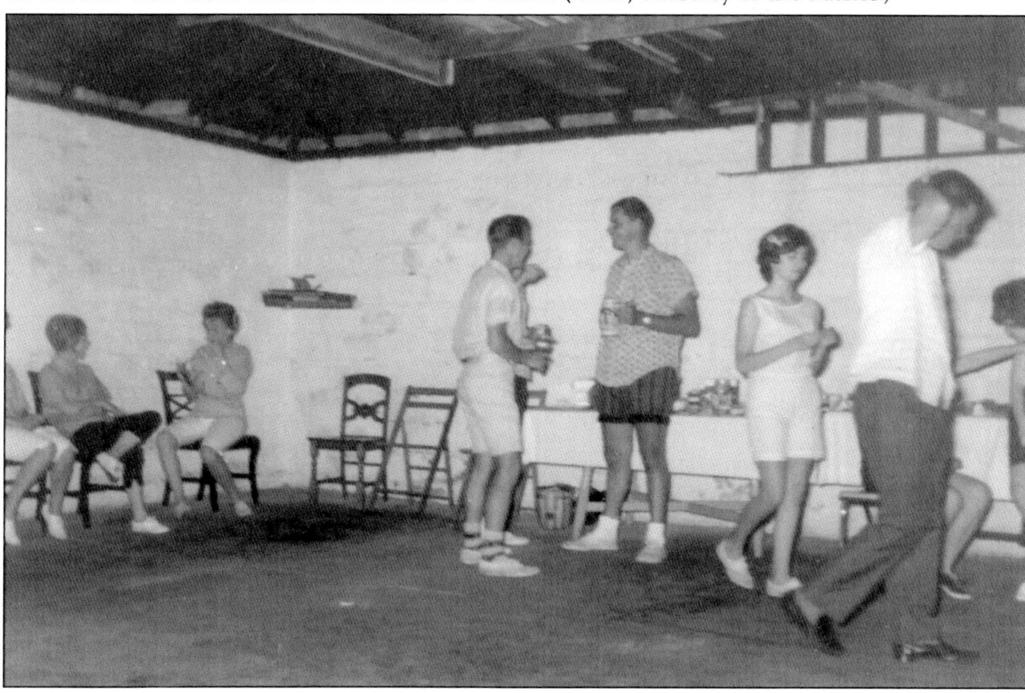

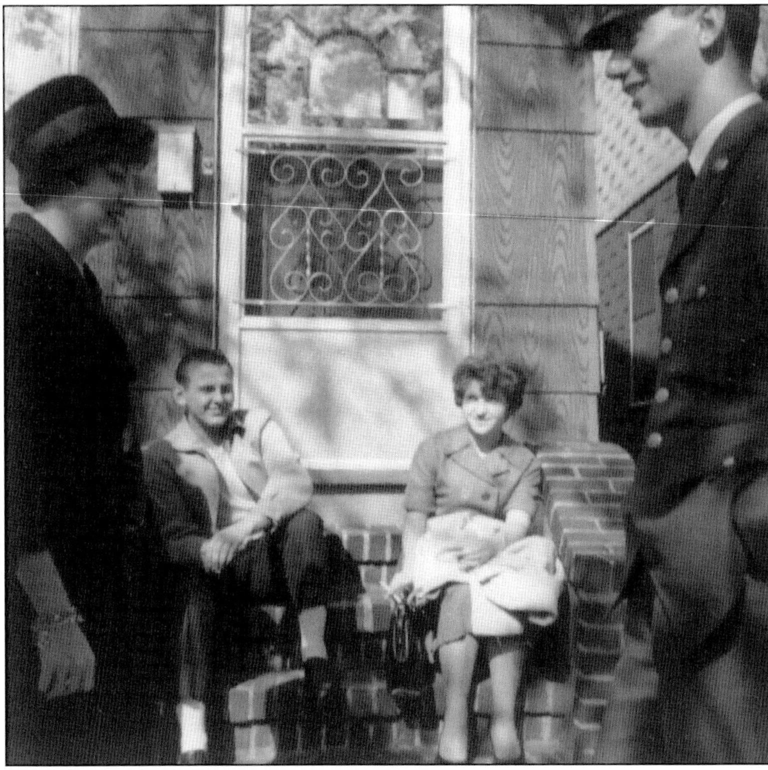

The brick or cement front stoops of many Glendale houses also provided entertainment to young people in the 1950s and 1960s. It could either be a social gathering point to visit with friends and make plans, or a place for a challenging game of "stoop ball," in which a Spaulding rubber ball was thrown against the steps to score a certain number of points. (Courtesy of the author.)

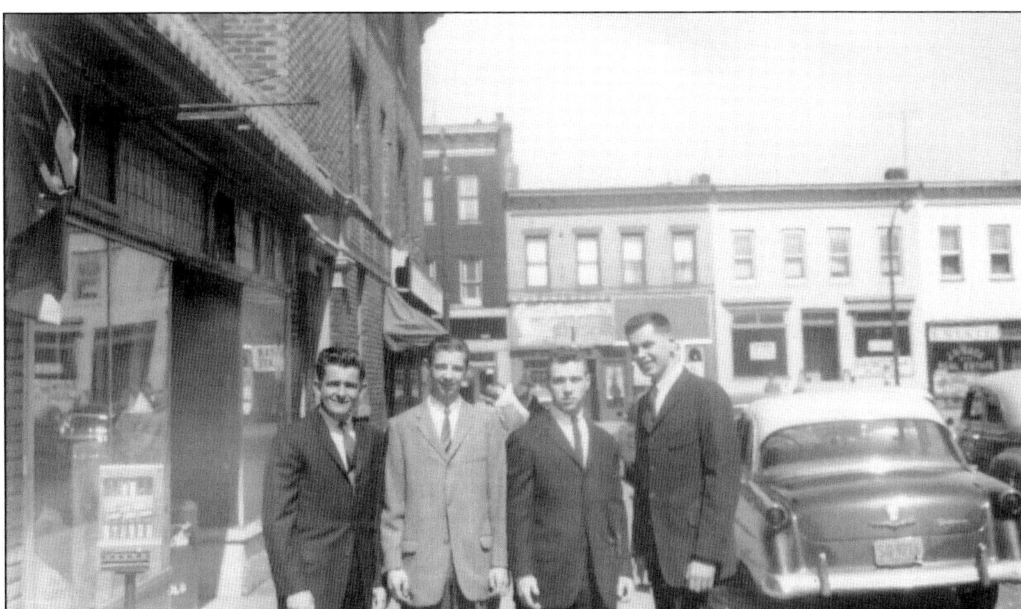

This group of men's fashion trendsetters stands outside of George Eck's candy store sometime in the late 1950s on Sixty-second Street just off Myrtle Avenue. The business behind them on the corner was the Rainbow Pizzeria, and on the far side of the street, above the street level, was a barbershop known as Up the Steps, as well as Smitty's Photograph Shop. (Courtesy of the author.)

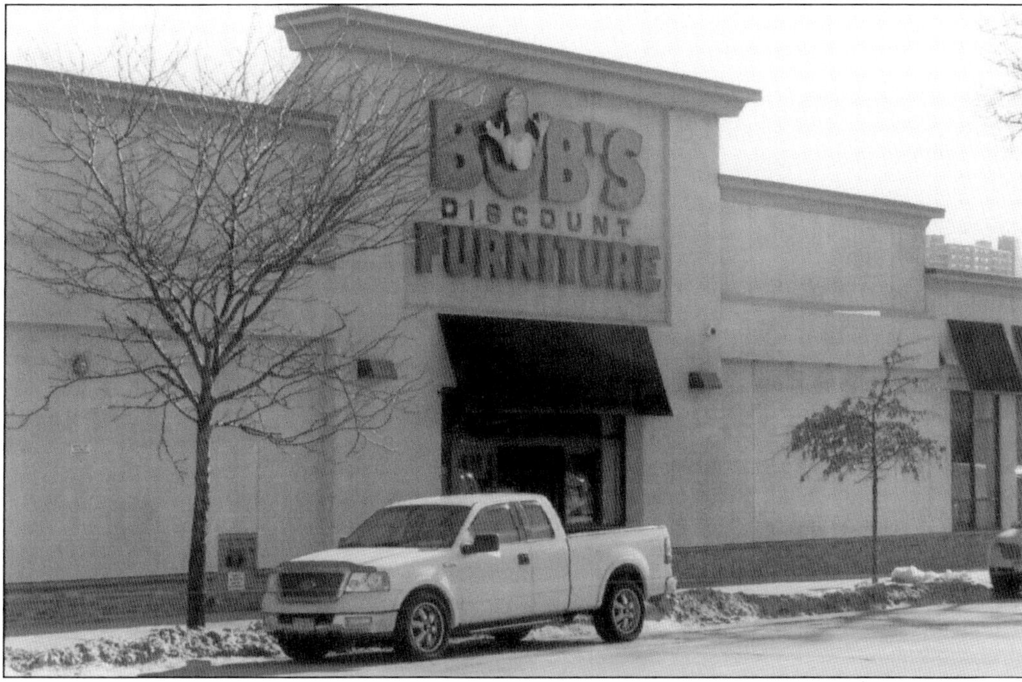

This is not just a plug for Bob's Discount Furniture, as the building holds some historical significance. Located on Woodhaven Boulevard north of Myrtle Avenue for more than 50 years, this building housed the bowling alley Woodhaven Lanes. It was a 60-lane establishment that was a gathering place for Glendale residents and home to many of the bowling leagues that were so popular during that era. The popular television program *Jackpot Bowling*, which used two other venues as well, did live broadcasts of their program from Woodhaven Lanes in 1959 and 1960. Woodhaven Lanes was closed in 2008, and much to the credit of the owner of the Bob's furniture chain, he had the plaque below made to commemorate the history of the building. (Both, courtesy of the author.)

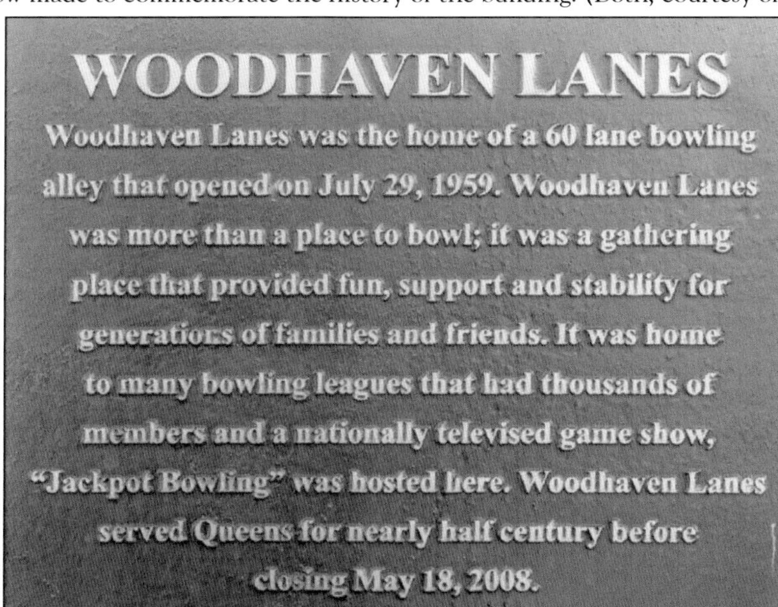

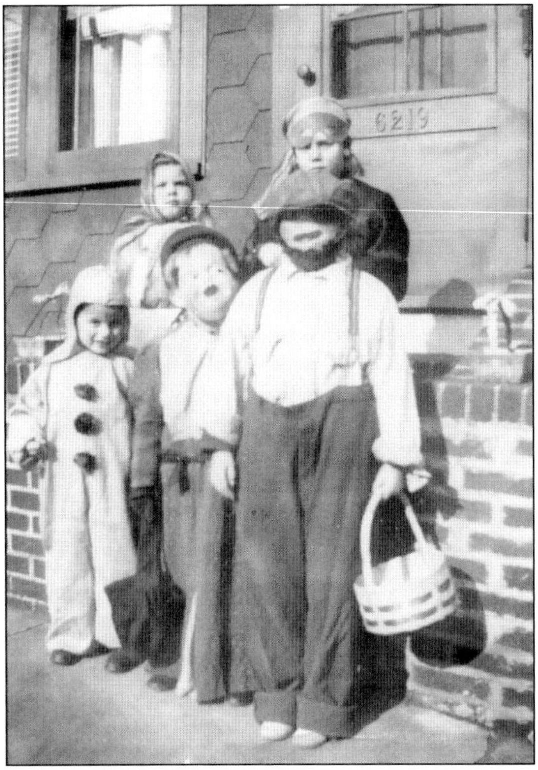

In the 1940s and 1950s, long before the practice of trick-or-treating on Halloween was as popular as it is today, children in Glendale and its surrounding communities spent their mornings on the Thanksgiving holiday going around to their neighbors' homes "begging for Thanksgiving." They would go out dressed in makeshift costumes as hobos, beggars, or circus clowns and hope that their neighbors would favor them with treats or a couple of coins. Most did not even know that the practice they were participating in was originally known as Ragamuffins Day, which dated back to the late 1700s. At that time, homeless men would dress as women and beg for food and money during the holiday season. (Both, courtesy of the author.)

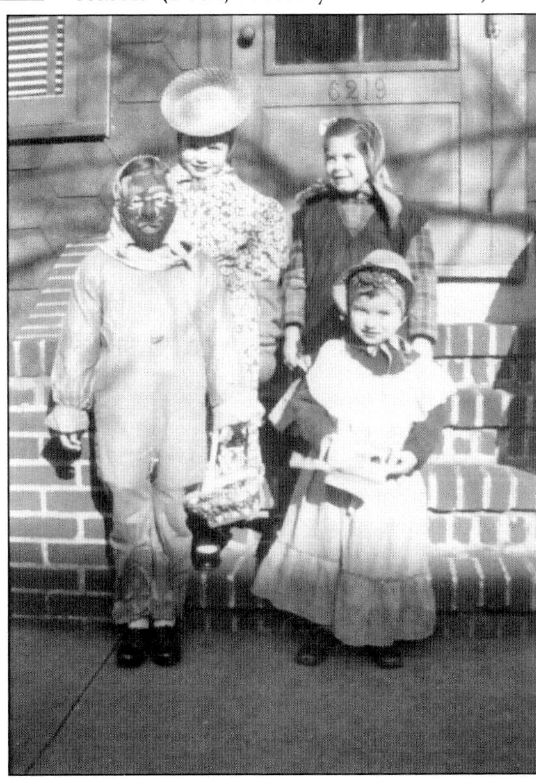

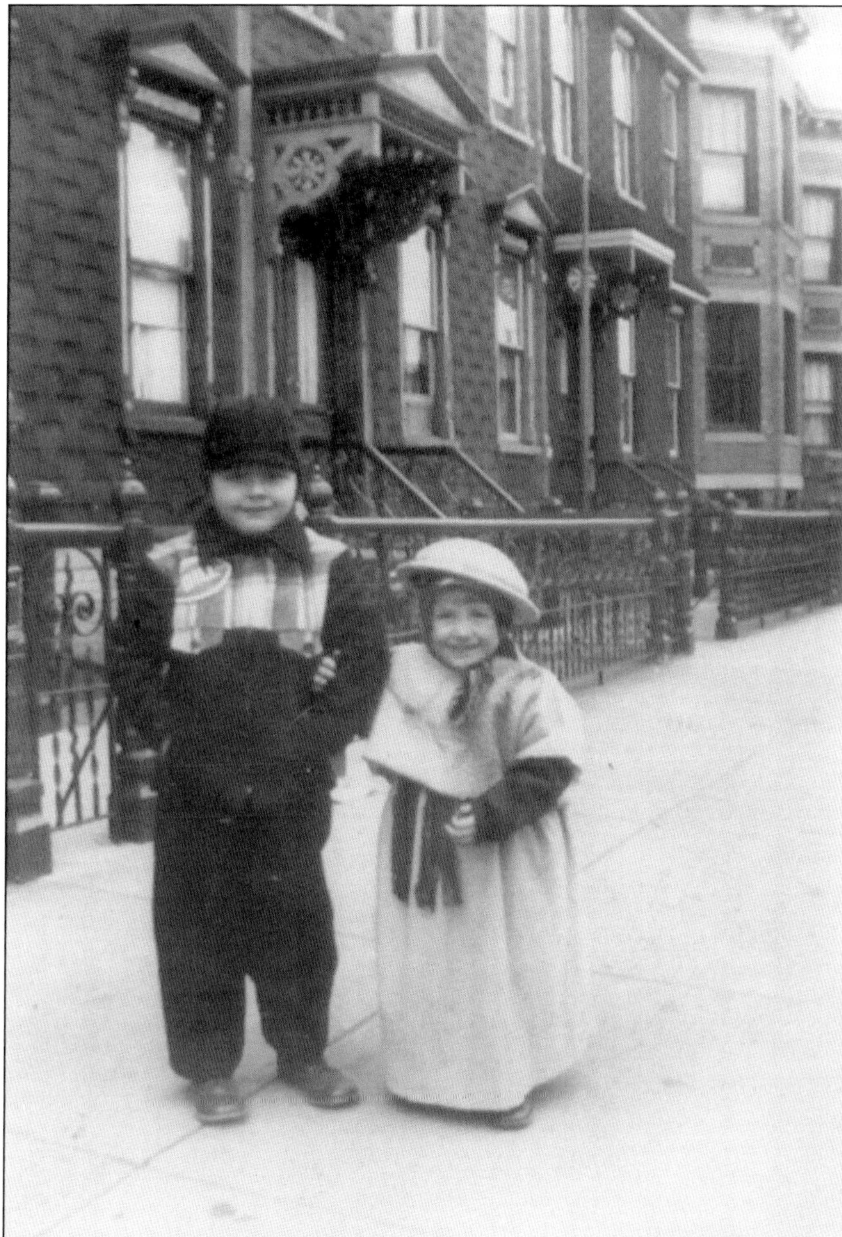

Just as on Halloween today, when someone answers the door and children exclaim, "Trick or treat?," the proper entreaty on Ragamuffins Day was, "Anything for Thanksgiving?" The history of nearby Greenpoint, Brooklyn, states that children would dress in rags or masks and be known as "Thanksgiving maskers," but for these two and other Glendale children, the rules were different. One can only suppose that the little girl here is meant to look like a gypsy, while her very patient older brother decided to forgo the costume part entirely. Ragamuffins Day ended in 1941 when Pres. Franklin Roosevelt established Thanksgiving as a federal holiday, but the traditions lived on for many years in the Glendale area until Halloween overshadowed the Thanksgiving holiday practice and ended the tradition of begging for Thanksgiving. (Courtesy of William and Loretta Stahl.)

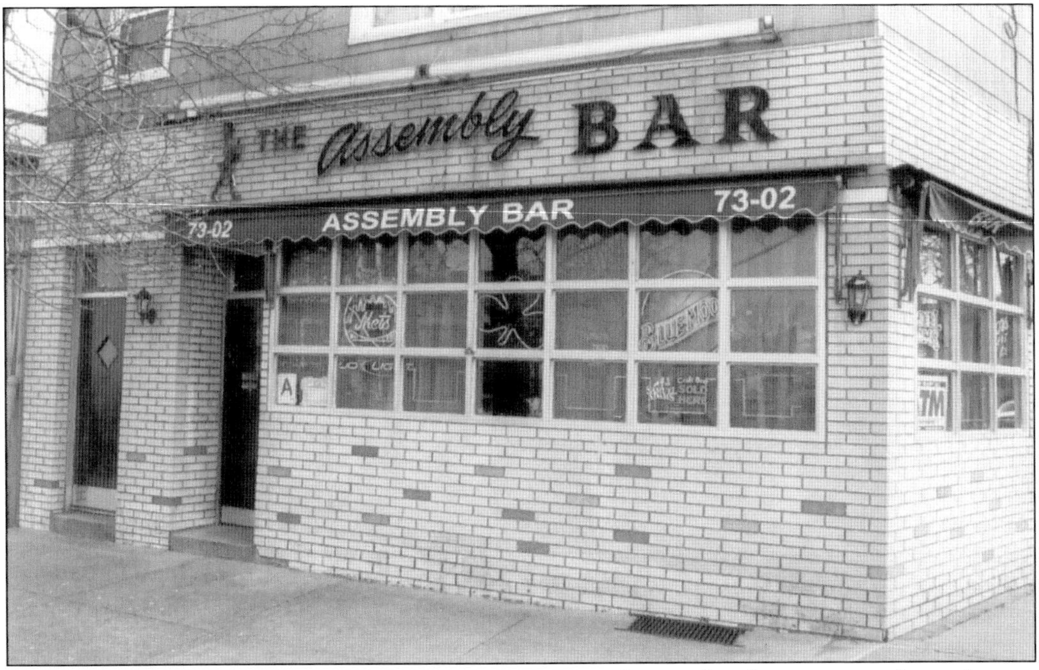

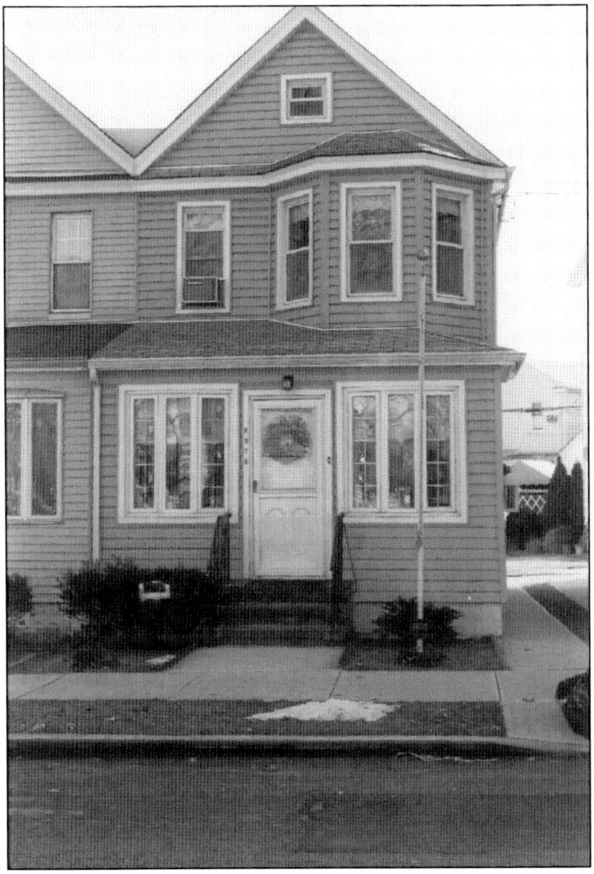

Long after the movie studio and picnic parks were gone, Glendale continued to exert some influence on pop culture. The Assembly Bar and Grill, located on Cooper Avenue, was featured in the 1996 movie *Trees Lounge*, written and directed by Steve Buscemi. It was the set for the fictional bar from which the movie took its title. (Courtesy of the author.)

"Those were the days," or so they said in the theme for the television program *All in the Family*. But it was not Hauser Street, as Archie Bunker used to say, it was actually this house on Cooper Avenue that was used as the home for the Bunkers in this 1971 CBS comedy. There is nothing outside of the house to give a hint about its place in sitcom history. (Courtesy of the author.)

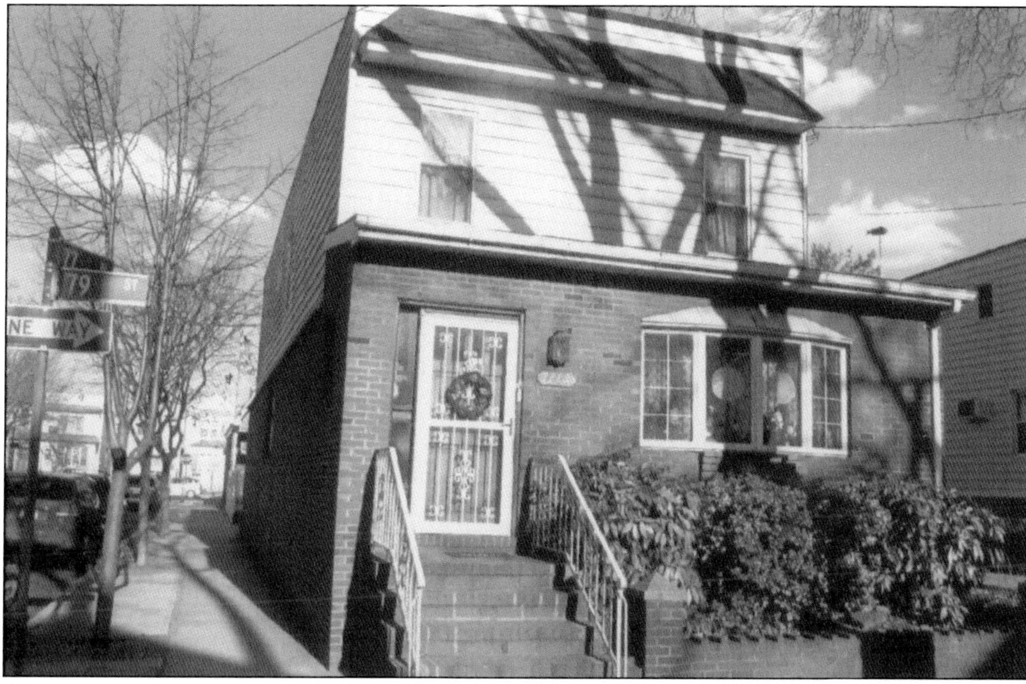

Glendale's architecture and the charm of its neighborhoods continued to appeal to filmmakers and television producers as recently as 2014. This lovely home was used as a setting in the movie *The Cobbler*, starring Dustin Hoffman, Steve Buscemi, and Adam Sandler. (Courtesy of the author.)

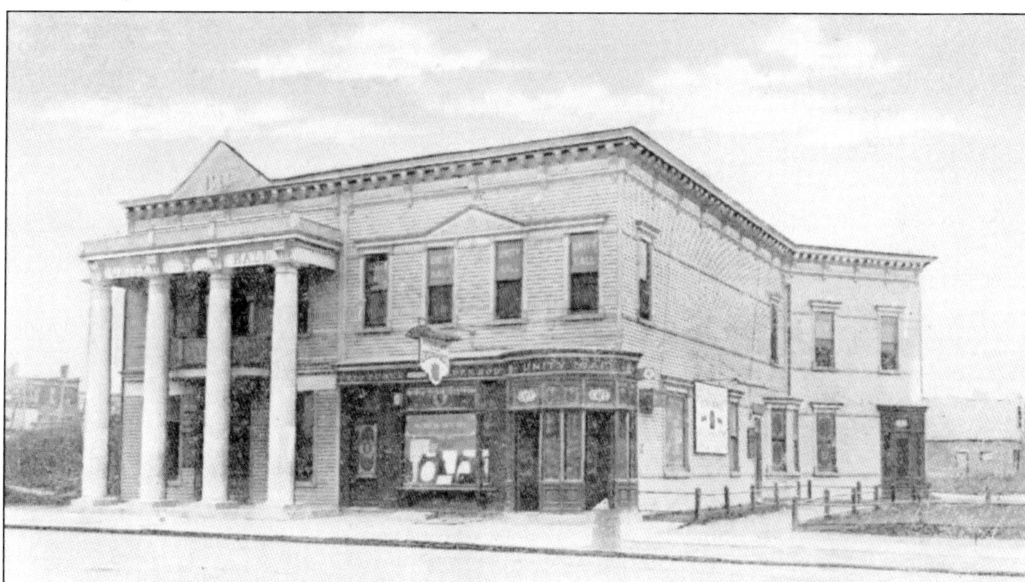

This postcard from 1916 shows the building on Myrtle Avenue that stood adjacent to Gebhardt's Restaurant. At that time, it housed Unity Hall, a social gathering spot that featured a bowling alley in the basement, a saloon on the ground floor, and a second-floor hall that could be rented for meetings. In later years, it served as a courthouse and police precinct, but it has since been torn down. (Courtesy of the author.)

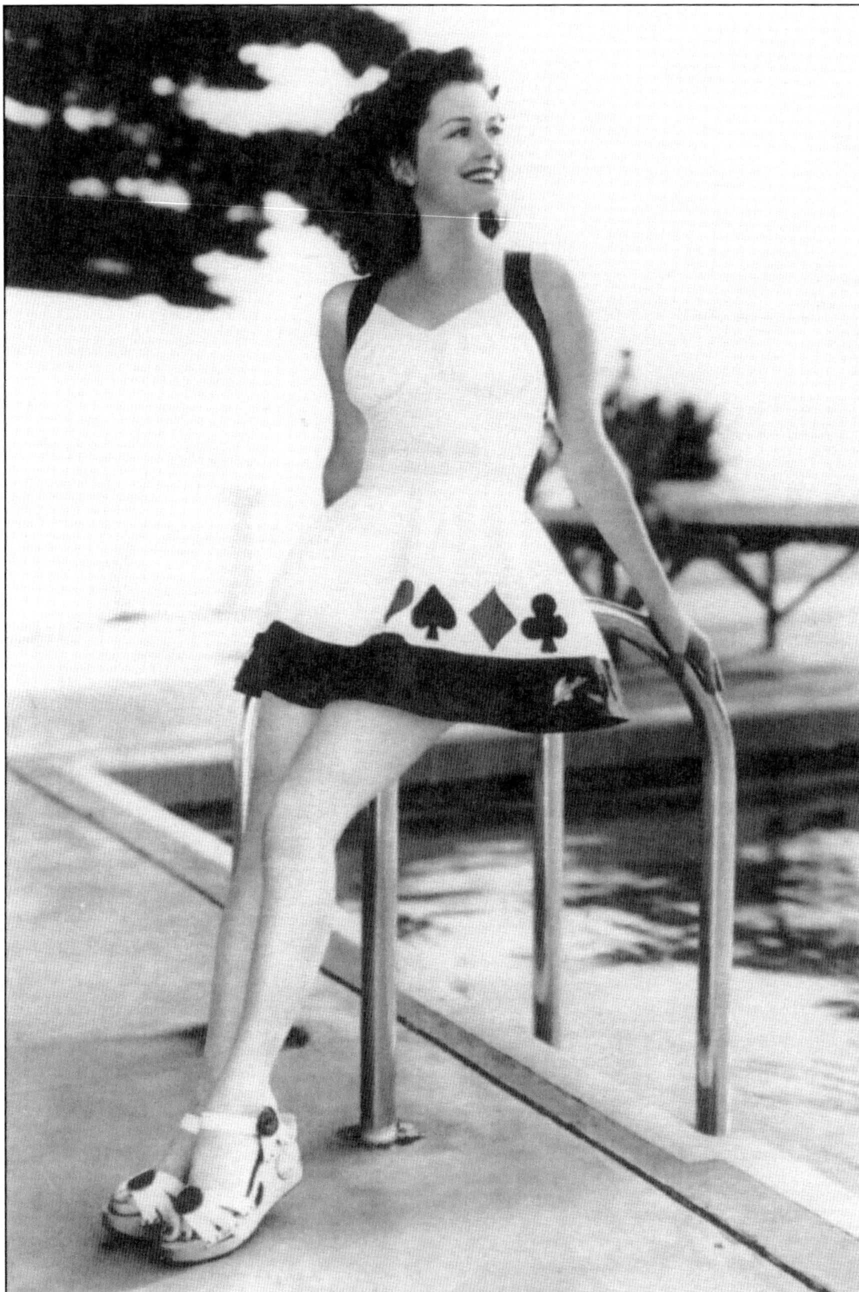

One of Glendale's more glamorous contributions to the entertainment industry was Dorothy Darrell, who lived here in her early years. She was born Dorothy Hallenbeck in 1920 in Greene County, New York, but moved to Glendale and lived with an aunt and uncle on Seventy-fifth Street. In her childhood, she attended Public School No. 119 in Glendale and nurtured dreams of becoming an actress. She adopted the stage name Dorothy Darrell and moved to Hollywood with the hopes of succeeding in the movie industry. Her efforts did earn her some degree of stardom, and she appeared in Abbott & Costello's 1941 comedy *Buck Privates* and was a featured player in *It Started with Eve* and *Hello Sucker.*

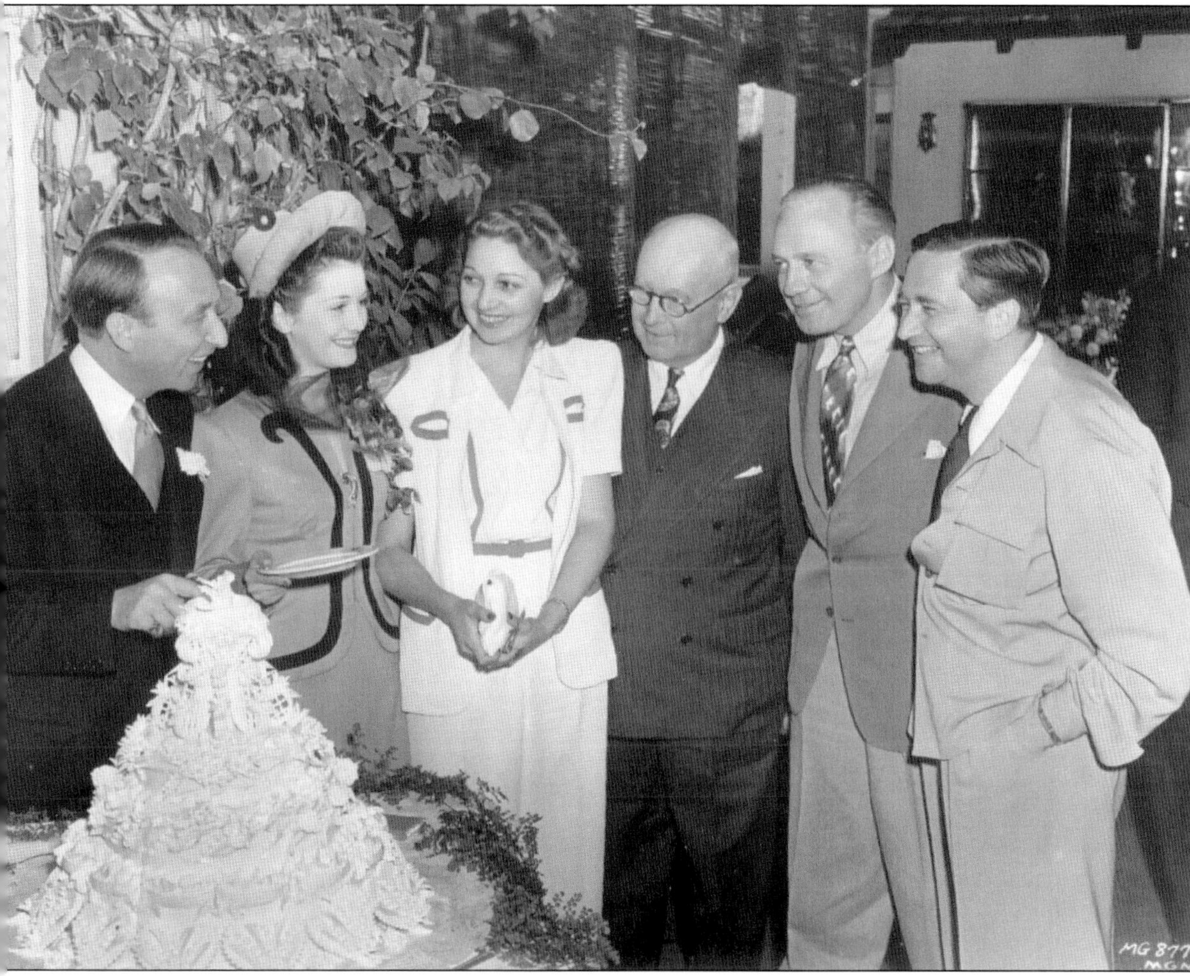

Hollywood success also brought Dorothy Darrell a celebrity wedding. She married Joe Pasternack, the head of Universal Studios in the 1930s, and enjoyed the luxurious lifestyle of people in the movie industry. Dorothy is seen here second from the left in a photograph from her wedding, flanked by her husband, Joe (left) and Mary Livingston (Jack Benny's wife), followed by the unidentified judge who married them, Jack Benny, and film producer Mervyn Leroy. (Courtesy of GRHS.)

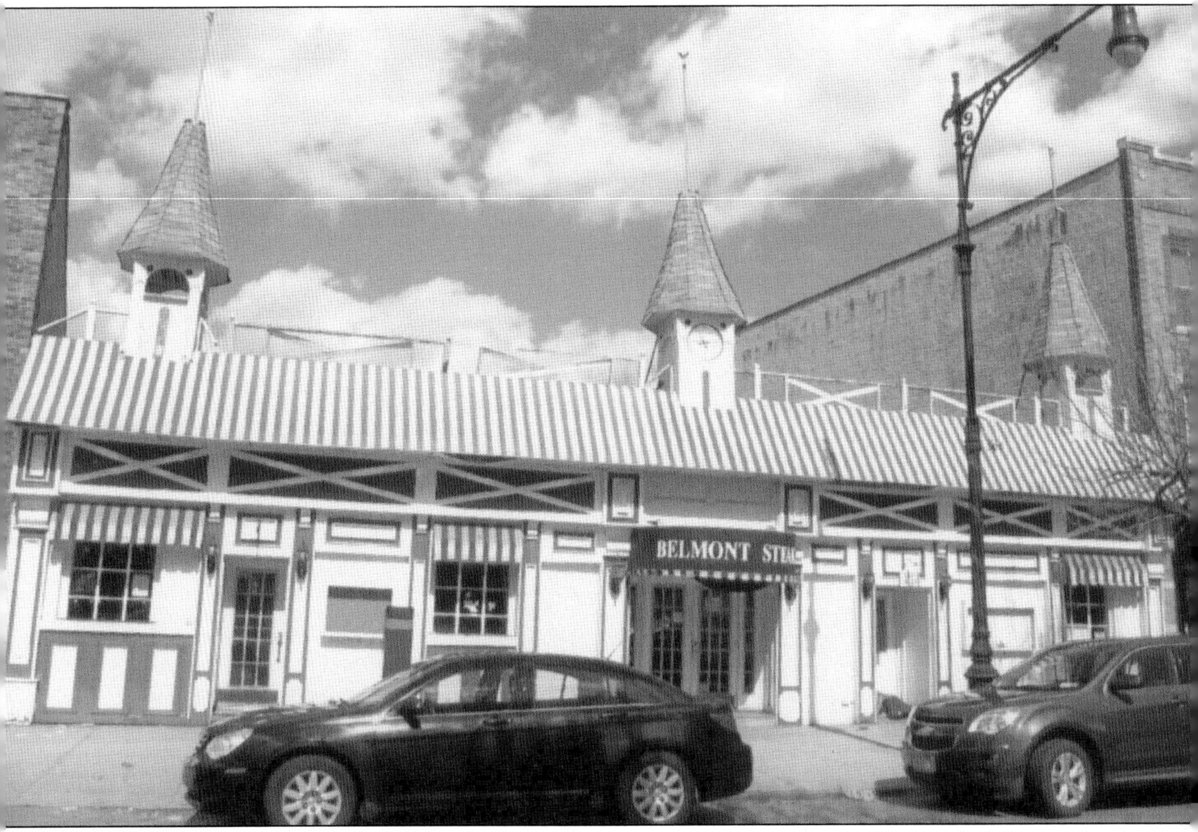

Unfortunately closed just before this book was written, for many years, Glendale's Belmont Steaks restaurant was known throughout the area for its excellent steaks and fine dining. Many of its local patrons were unaware that the restaurant's exterior design was patterned after the clubhouse at the Churchill Downs racetrack in Kentucky, the site of the annual Kentucky Derby. This photograph of the restaurant shows the three towers on the roof, which were built to resemble the towers over the grandstand at the Kentucky racetrack. Hopefully, any new owners of the property will decide to retain the look to preserve this piece of more recent Glendale history. (Courtesy of the author.)

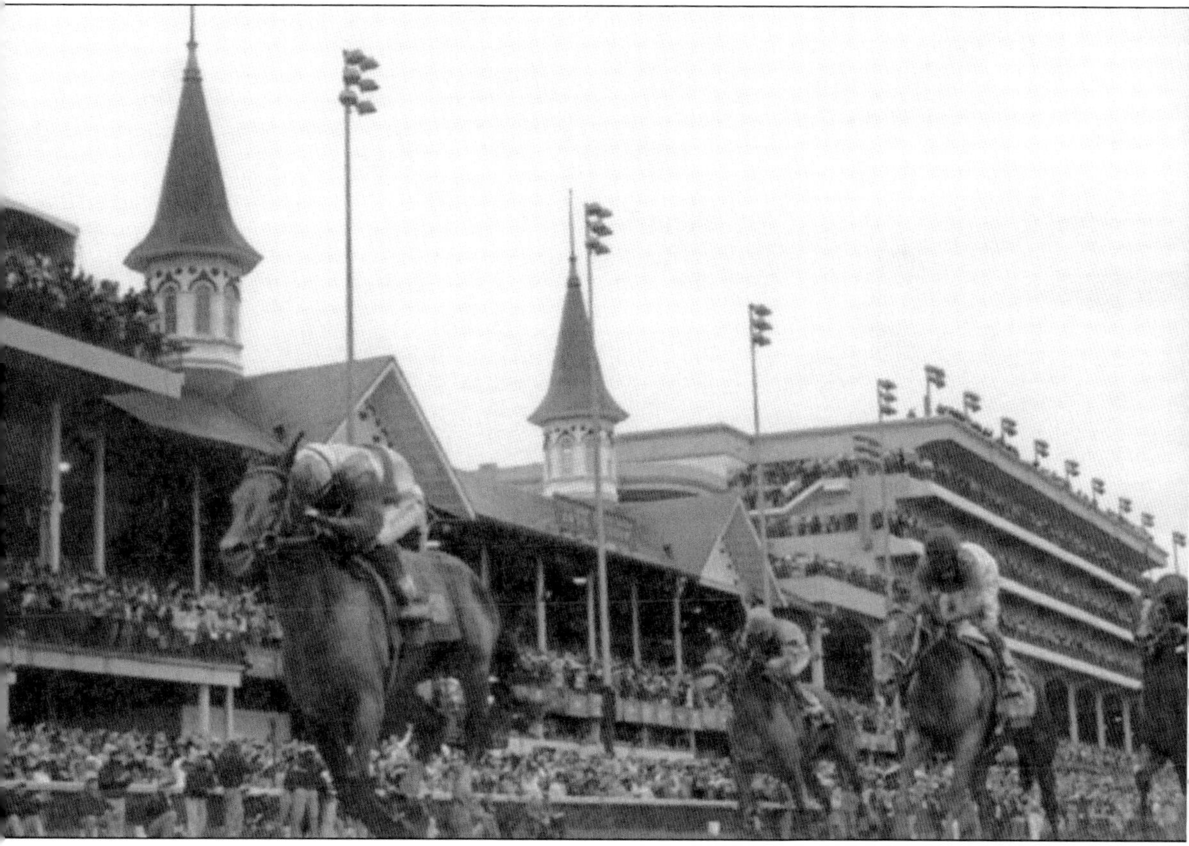

Two of the three towers over the grandstand that were used as models for the roof additions at the Belmont Steaks restaurant are shown here in this exciting race-to-the-finish photograph at Churchill Downs. Note that the grandstands and the field-level spectator locations are completely packed, indicating that this photograph was taken during the annual running of the Kentucky Derby. (Courtesy of www.churchilldowns.com)

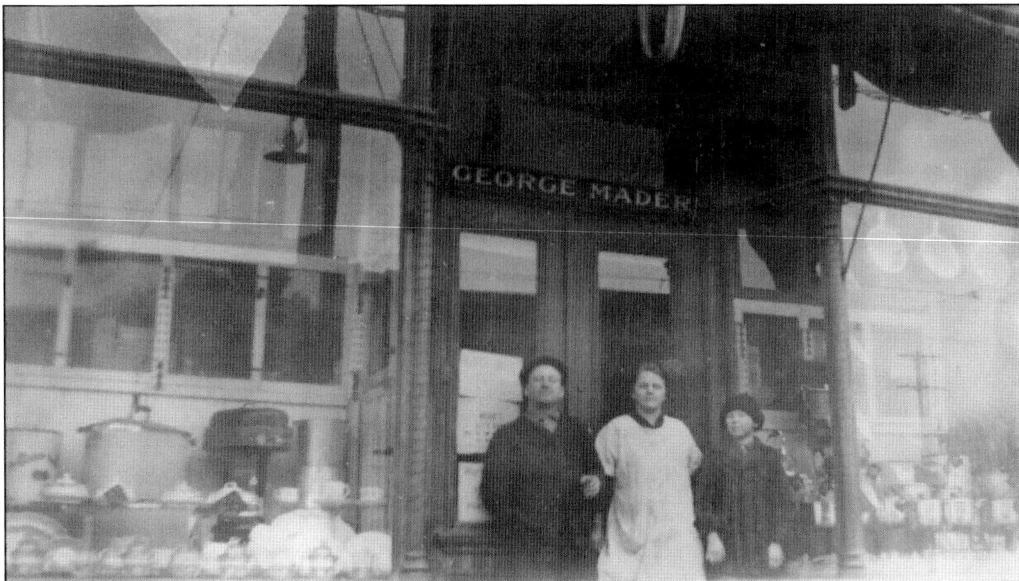

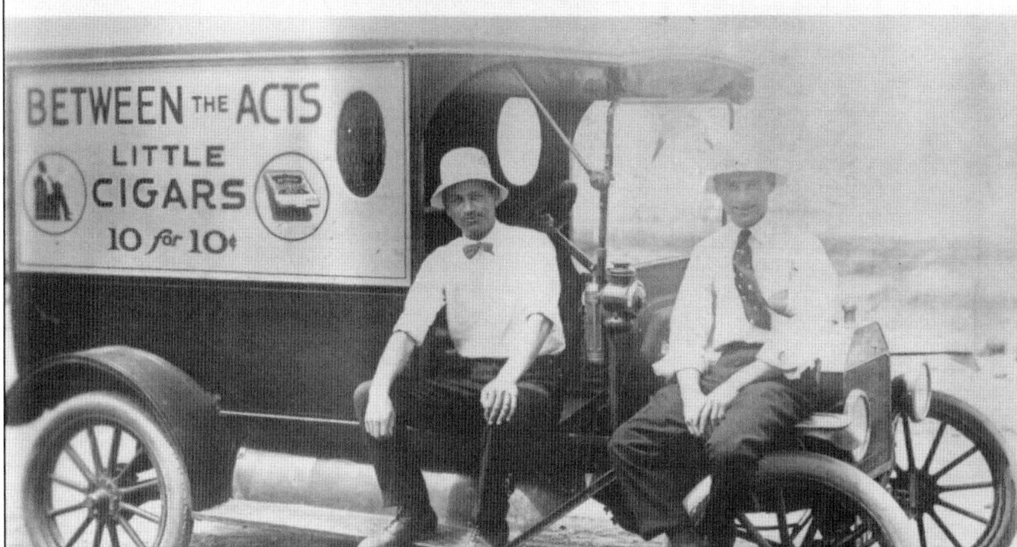

To conclude this journey into Glendale's past on a vintage note, it ends with two split-image photographs from the town's past. This 1912 pair show proprietor George Mader and two employees outside of his home furnishings and hardware store, located on Myrtle Avenue near Sixty-ninth Street. The delivery vehicle in the second photograph has advertising on its side for a brand of cigarette-sized cigars. The practice of selling advertising space on trucks was not that common in 1912, and there is no explanation for the matching white hats that the two men on the truck are sporting. (Courtesy of GRHS.)

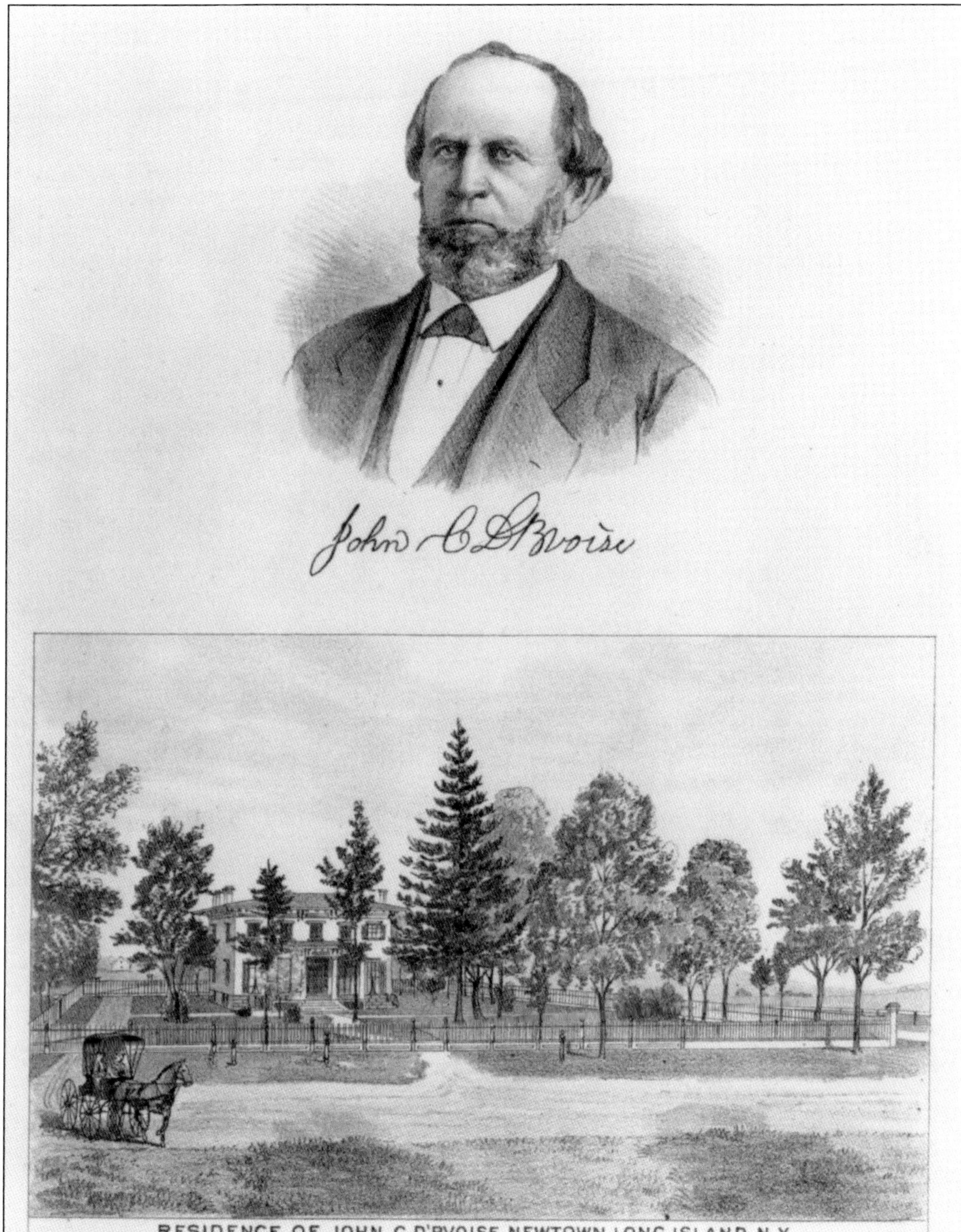

This last image seems to include a sketch of his home superimposed over a drawing of John DeBevoise himself (mentioned on page 26). Apparently his nickname of "Ropewalk" was not something that he wished to include on something as formal as this portrait, but the oddity in this exhibit is that his last name is spelled "D'Bvoise." This conflicts with just about every other record of his history, and lacking the letter "e," would be difficult to pronounce.

Consistent with our mission to preserve history on a local level, this book was printed in South Carolina on American-made paper and manufactured entirely in the United States. Products carrying the accredited Forest Stewardship Council (FSC) label are printed on 100 percent FSC-certified paper.

MADE IN THE USA